DIRTY SECRETS
OUR ASIO FILES

MEREDITH BURGMANN was radicalised at Sydney University by the Vietnam War and was one of the leaders of the anti-apartheid movement, infamously receiving a two-month gaol sentence for disrupting a Springbok rugby match in 1971. She taught industrial relations at Macquarie University for eighteen years and was later a Labor Member of and President of the Legislative Council of New South Wales, retiring in 2007. Until recently she was President of the Australian Council for International Development, the peak body for Australia's NGO aid agencies.

Also by Meredith Burgmann:

Green Bans, Red Union: Environmental activism and the NSW Builders Labourers' Federation (with Verity Burgmann)

The Ernies Book: 1000 terrible things Australian men have said about women (with Yvette Andrews)

DIRTY SECRETS
OUR ASIO FILES

edited by
MEREDITH BURGMANN

NEWSOUTH

This book is for my comrades who were so steadfast through all those years and still are. I especially remember my co-convenors in the Stop the Tours campaign, Denis Freney and Peter McGregor. It is also for Paddy Batchelor, in the hope that the next generation of political activists don't get spied upon.

A NewSouth book

Published by
NewSouth Publishing
University of New South Wales Press Ltd
University of New South Wales
Sydney New South Wales 2052
AUSTRALIA
newsouthpublishing.com

This collection and introduction © Meredith Burgmann 2014
Individual essays © individual contributors 2014
First published 2014

10 9 8 7 6 5 4 3 2 1

This book is copyright. While copyright of the work as a whole is vested in Meredith Burgmann, copyright of individual chapters is retained by the chapter authors. Apart from any fair dealing for the purpose of private study, research, criticism or review, as permitted under the Copyright Act, no part of this book may be reproduced by any process without written permission. Inquiries should be addressed to the publisher.

National Library of Australia
Cataloguing-in-Publication entry
Title: Dirty secrets: our ASIO files / Meredith Burgmann, editor.
ISBN: 9781742231402 (paperback)
    9781742241753 (ePub)
    9781742246819 (ePDF)
Subjects: Australian Security Intelligence Organisation – Archives.
    Australians – Archives.
    Intelligence service – Australia – History.
    Internal security – Australia – History – 20th century.
    Secret service – Australia – History.
    Australia – Politics and government – 1945–
Other Authors/Contributors: Burgmann, Meredith, 1947– editor.
Dewey Number: 327.120994

Design Di Quick
Cover images Mark Aarons, Peter Cundall and Phillip Adams photos: courtesy of ABC; Kevin Cook photo: Penny Tweedie; Peter Murphy photo: Gill Leahy; other photos courtesy of contributors.

All reasonable efforts were taken to obtain permission to use copyright material reproduced in this book, but in some cases copyright could not be traced. The editor welcomes information in this regard.

This project has been assisted by the Australian Government through the Australia Council for the Arts, its arts funding and advisory body.

CONTENTS

INTRODUCTION
by Meredith Burgmann
11

HOW TO READ YOUR ASIO FILE
by David McKnight
21

THE FILES

Michael Kirby 49
THE COMMOS AND ME

Anne Summers 69
NUMBER C/57/61: WHAT ASIO KNEW

Gary Foley 91
ASIO, THE ABORIGINAL MOVEMENT AND ME

David Stratton 113
THE MAN IN THE RED TIE
(IN CONVERSATION WITH MEREDITH BURGMANN)

Joan Bielski 129
FEAR AND LOATHING IN THE FIFTIES

Dennis Altman 147
WHY ME?

Rowan Cahill 159
JOINING THE DOTS: C/58/63

Phillip Adams 171
I WAS A TEENAGE BOLSHEVIK

Jean McLean 181
MY LIFE IN A DISTORTING MIRROR

Jack Waterford 199
SMASHING THE STATE

Frank Hardy 213
THE HARDY WAY (BY ALAN HARDY)

Alan Hardy 235
VERY INTERESTED IN THEATRICS

Lex Watson 241
MY OWN 'PINK FILE'

Wendy and Jim Bacon 249
A BACON FAMILY AFFAIR
(BY WENDY BACON)

Mark Aarons 271
STATE AFFAIRS AND LOVE AFFAIRS

Kevin Cook 291
THEY JUST DIDN'T CARE
(WITH HEATHER GOODALL)

Colin Cooper 303
ASIO AND THE POSTMASTER-GENERAL

Clive Evatt 317
CLIVE RALEIGH EVATT AND ASIO
(BY ELIZABETH EVATT)

Frances Letters 331
TWO CHEERS FOR ASIO!

Verity Burgmann 343
I WAS A TEENAGE TROTSKYIST
(IN CONVERSATION WITH MEREDITH BURGMANN)

Peter Murphy 363
THE NOT-SO-SECRET LIVES OF OTHERS

Tony Reeves 375
MY LACKLUSTRE LIFE ACCORDING TO ASIO

Tim Anderson 391
POSTCARDS FROM THE SECRET POLICE

Penny Lockwood 407
LACK OF EVIDENCE PROVES NOTHING

Peter Cundall 425
THE RED WITH THE GREEN THUMB
(BY HELEN RANDERSON)

Meredith Burgmann 437
THE SECRET LIFE OF B/77/26 (AND FRIENDS)

ACKNOWLEDGMENTS 457

INDEX 459

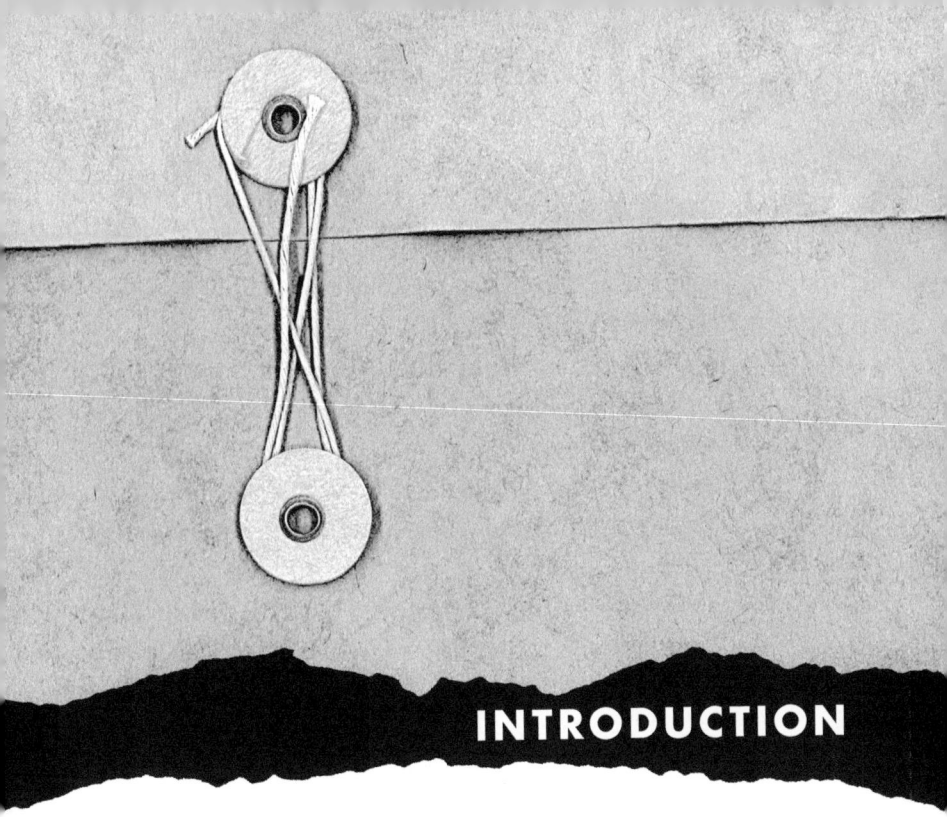

INTRODUCTION

In these days of increased intelligence powers, a ballooning national security budget, a giant new ASIO headquarters in Canberra, and endless discussion about WikiLeaks and the right to know, I wanted to look at the effect of spying on those who have been its targets. David McKnight and others have written extensively about our spy agencies. This book is the stories of those spied upon. There is particular satisfaction in the fact that a group of Australians who have had their lives secretly recorded in detail over many decades are at last getting their own back. *We* are finally writing about *them* instead of *them* writing about *us*.

I became interested in the early ASIO story when doing my Masters thesis on the Chifley Government and Russia. At one stage I interviewed former Immigration Minister Arthur Calwell and Postwar Reconstruction Minister Jack Dedman, who delighted in giving me gory details about atom bomb secrets, the birth of ASIO, the tumultuous incidents surrounding Sir David Rivett and the *Secrecy Act* and so on. To read my own extensive file much later was a fitting bookend to this early interest.

In compiling this book I approached almost a hundred people who I thought were likely to have been ASIO targets, and gave them instructions about how to apply for their files. About half were told they did not have files. In some cases this was simply not believable. Nadia Wheatley was told she did not have a file although her arrest record was similar to mine and she was heavily involved in the targeted areas of Aboriginal rights and anti-Vietnam war activity.

Not everyone was keen to see their files. My sister Verity, a historian and one-time Trotskyist, did not want to look at hers in case she found out that someone she knew and liked was an informant. Academic Ann Curthoys was so reluctant to look at hers that in the end she declined to participate. I found myself strangely unable to open my own large parcel for many months. Some were reduced to tears. The writer Roger Milliss wept as he read about the extensive surveillance his father had endured; including twenty pages of intrusive details about his father's funeral.

During this process I became a bit of an expert on who seemed to attract files and who did not. Being in the Communist Party or a Trotskyist group was an obvious qualification, but some CPA members, strangely, did not have files. Being arrested could trigger a file, but not necessarily. Being involved, however marginally, with Eastern European countries almost always aroused interest, as did having progressive views and being involved with communications systems or scientific research. Any combination of these factors was a likely trigger.

I am indebted to Dr David McKnight who has written the chapter 'How to Read Your ASIO File' for this book. Not only has he set out the meaning of all the various notations and initials scribbled on our files (as the reader will discover, many of us could only guess what the shorthand meant, at the time of writing), but he has reduced his major academic works on ASIO into a useful 'Cook's Tour' of ASIO's history and present context. It was David who pointed out that some of the language in the files, which had seemed so formal and polite to me, was simply 'public service-ese'. The men and women employed by ASIO were public servants – unusual public servants, for sure, but they knew how to file and index and write polite notes to their superiors.

Each of the twenty-six chapters is very different from each other. The life experiences of each ASIO target varied greatly, from Col Cooper, a fifteen-year-old telegram boy at the PMG, to Michael Kirby, a civil liberties solicitor; Frank Hardy, a struggling, mostly penniless writer; Anne Summers, a strident early feminist; Gary Foley, an angry young Aboriginal activist; and Joan Bielski, a newly qualified English teacher.

The contributions encompass five decades of political spying, from the early fifties with Clive Evatt, Frank Hardy, Joan Bielski and Michael Kirby, right through to the 1990s when the NSW Special Branch was closed down by the Carr Labor Government and New South Wales activists were granted access to their files.

The different political beliefs and activities that attracted attention are also diverse. Some, such as Mark Aarons, Penny Lockwood and Alan Hardy, acquired their files as intergenerational gifts from their Communist Party parents. But then we have Verity Burgmann, a devoted Trotskyist; Dennis Altman and Lex Watson, pioneers in the early gay rights campaigns; Gary Foley and Kevin Cook, Aboriginal activists; David Stratton, an apolitical film buff; Peter Cundall, a communist gardener and early environmentalist; Wendy Bacon, an anarchist member of the Push and her brother, Jim Bacon, a student Maoist; Jack Waterford, a radical student prankster; Tony Reeves, a crusading journalist; Peter Murphy, a Catholic ex-seminarian; and Phillip Adams, an outspoken broadcaster. They are all so different.

Each has a different take on ASIO's intrusion into their lives. Some do not believe a secret police force should ever exist, others believe that it should, but not behave in the way ASIO did. Elizabeth Evatt and Jean McLean have views about how ASIO could behave better. Some contributors even admit that ASIO occasionally 'got it right'. All, however, are shocked at the waste of money and resources spent on following them around and recording minute details of their everyday lives. As Michael Kirby comments:

> ... looking back at my story, my little file in ASIO, you can see how futile, how pathetic, how wasteful of resources it was to be following me around and taking solemn notes of what I was saying to the Council for Civil Liberties, or to other bodies.

Being told they did not have a file affected people differently. Some colleagues were absurdly crestfallen when told they did not have a file and most refused to accept it. There does seem to be a hit and miss attitude to the production of files. Both my father, as Chairman of CSIRO, and my grandfather, as a radical bishop, had ASIO file numbers written beside their names in my dossier, but when I applied for their files, they were not forthcoming.

Debate has broken out recently between historians who want ASIO files to be retained and made available to researchers (let's face it, the ASIO targets were often interesting and active members of society) and privacy campaigners who believe that all records should be destroyed. Having recently discovered some excellent ASIO material while researching the Australian anti-apartheid movement, I am now convinced that files should not be destroyed. But I do know that some potential contributors to this book were distressed by what they found in their files. I was not particularly concerned about what was written about me, but friends and acquaintances get caught up in the process. The NAA is dealing with the privacy issues in various ways and some ASIO targets, such as Tom Uren, have chosen to insert rejoinders in their open access files.

Each chapter as it arrived contained something that was able to shock me. My own file had disturbed me in two ways. First it revealed that an agent had stolen my address book and investigated the background of everyone mentioned in it – possibly destroying the career of one friend and seriously compromising another. Second, that the NSW Special Branch still had me under surveillance in the 1990s when I was a Labor MP.

Michael Kirby revealed that he first came to ASIO's notice at the age of twelve when he was taken to the zoo by his communist step-grandfather.

Alan Hardy, Frank's son, revealed that after the jury in the *Power Without Glory* criminal defamation trial returned a not-guilty verdict, ASIO's Director-General called for reports on all the jurors.

David Stratton was considered a bit of a leftie because he wore a red tie to a function at the Polish Embassy on Poland's national day.

Verity Burgmann's file was pretty standard – a description of endless reasonably boring Trotskyist meetings – but her photo file was spectacular. It consisted of ten photos, all of her standing on a beach in a bikini.

Penny Lockwood discovered that a young man with whom she had a relationship was actually an ASIO agent.

Joan Bielski was followed for the rest of her life because, as prim 'Miss Ward', she took a job teaching English to two Soviet diplomats in Canberra in the 1950s, one of whom happened to be Vladimir Petrov.

Some chapters reveal interesting sidelights. Wendy Bacon was amazed to discover the extent of her parents' political activity. Alan Hardy learned a huge amount about his father Frank's changing political beliefs as Stalinism crumbled and Frank's disputes with the CPA leadership escalated. Jean McLean discovered why she was sacked from her banking job. Similarly Col Cooper discovered why he was transferred from working at the Overseas Radio Terminal to a domestic telephone exchange. Anne Summers phoned me late one night affronted at an agent's description of her as 'fashionably but not very well dressed'.

The most astonishing ASIO report I have ever found occurs in early feminist Lucy Woodcock's ASIO file. In November 1950 it records for posterity:

> Mrs Reed very militant, active … Son Johnathon (4 ½ years old) an active school propagandist … Organises groups away from teacher's grasp.

When the secret police are filing reports on four year olds we have serious problems.

During Michael Kirby's research for his chapter, he applied for his NSW Special Branch file. Disturbingly, he was refused access to it in 'the public interest'. He was not even offered heavily redacted pages. He was refused all access. What could possibly be in the file?

There is also some evidence that ASIO embarked on harassment. The strangest example of this is the late night visit Peter Murphy received from an intelligence agent who questioned him for some forty-five minutes.

Most contributors are surprised by the lack of analysis in the reports. There is immense detail about how people looked or who they spoke to but almost nothing about what people thought or believed. Both Rowan Cahill and Peter Murphy bemoan this dehumanisation of the subjects.

ASIO was intensely interested in the tiny political groupings around Australia, particularly the Trotskyists, and often had plants inside these groups. However the agents showed little understanding of what each group believed.

Kevin Cook laments the fact that the agents showed no interest in the final results of the endless planning meetings they attended. They recorded in detail all the preparations for the 1982 Commonwealth Games demonstration but did not report on how well the rally went. Kevin was very disappointed.

Often the agents got things very wrong. Peter Murphy gets confused with another Peter Murphy in student politics and Tim Anderson is believed to be Glen Anderson in another state. A letter claiming Dr Anne Cooper is a shonky psychiatrist is filed in Anne Summers' dossier. In fact Tim Anderson's chapter shows how easily information can be misinterpreted or just plain wrong – and how damaging this can be. In his file, agents taping an informant's interview are duped into believing a simple flag stealing stunt was actually a paramilitary plot.

Mark Aarons and I were both horrified to see how our friends' lives were affected by our own surveillance. Elizabeth Evatt points out the disastrous consequences that can flow from this 'guilt by association'.

Justice Robert Hope conducted two royal commissions into Australia's intelligence services, the first in 1974–77 and the second in 1983–84. In his first report he wrote that he believed there was too much coverage of peaceful, mainstream anti-Vietnam protesters whose meetings were recorded in minute detail:

> … ASIO has pursued radicals beyond what is required to obtain security intelligence relating to subversion … it is hard to escape the conclusion that ASIO accepted the soft options.

Certainly there is plenty of evidence in these chapters to confirm the view that agents were often involved in 'make-work' activity – recording endless number plates, compiling lists of journal subscriptions, noting that David Stratton rented a hire-car, filing copies of the YMCA newsletter Peter Cundall edited, recording who accompanied me to a bottle shop.

Nicola Roxon recalls querying an intercept warrant when she was Attorney-General. When the intelligence officer could not explain the need for the intercept, Roxon refused to sign the warrant without further information. She was told that this had never been done before.

If the nation decides that it needs a secret intelligence organisation, then that organisation should employ clever, skilled and astute agents, and have powerful and well-resourced oversight and an appropriate appeals mechanism. There is much evidence in this book – in some cases up to 1996 – that this has not been the case with ASIO.

In reading these chapters one can see that ASIO's behaviour is at various times improper, incompetent, irrelevant, inappropriate and intrusive. One of the most concerning of these is impropriety. It is clear that Australia's secret police have been used from time to time for party political objectives rather than national security concerns. In some of the chapters in this book there are examples of the conservative political leadership using ASIO as an extension of their own political agenda rather than as a neutral agency. For instance, it is obvious from Jean McLean's chapter that ASIO had tapped the phone line of Jim Cairns when he was a senior Labor MP, and in my file Director-General Spry sends a report on my anti-apartheid activity directly to the prime minister's department during a relevant question time in Parliament. Given this low-level political partisanship, it is not surprising to learn from the recent release of MI5 files that Spry had advised that in the event of Dr Evatt winning the 1954 election the British Government should withhold important secrets from Australia.

That the agency's early brief was to keep tabs on something as vague as 'subversion' was a particular problem. When this was changed, after the second Hope inquiry, to 'politically motivated violence' (PMV), there should have been more rational decisions made about who ASIO targeted. This does not seem to have happened.

ASIO wrote of Anne Summers: 'capacity for violence – nil'. This caused Anne some chagrin but was of course the correct question to have asked. This was the question they should have been asking about all of us. Once answered in the negative, they should have closed the file and moved on.

Because of the thirty-year rule (changing gradually to a twenty-year rule), what we discover may well be regarded as ancient history, but it should shine a light on the nature of our secret police. Can a leopard really change its spots? Given ASIO's long history of incompetence, can we really trust it to protect us today? At a time of considerable expansion of its resources and powers, do we simply ignore the history and cross our fingers about the future? When does dissent become subversion and when is spying on citizens the legitimate role of government?

The young students, Christians, mothers, and unionists of the anti-Vietnam movement, land rights campaigns, gay rights action and so on, were never a danger to the government. We should have been dealt with as a public order issue, not as a threat to the state. On the evidence of these chapters, ASIO has not shown that it is capable of making that distinction.

HOW TO READ YOUR ASIO FILE

David McKnight

For more than twenty years the files of Australia's internal security agency, the Australian Security Intelligence Organisation (ASIO), have slowly been coming to light. Individuals who have been under ASIO surveillance have been able to read what was said about them and historians have been able to piece together ASIO's secret operations during the Cold War. Nearly 10 000 ASIO files are now publicly available at the National Archives of Australia (NAA) in Canberra.

Reading an ASIO file is an unusual experience, as I can personally affirm. The file can evoke anger or amusement. A personal file can reawaken old memories, long forgotten. Most people who were the subject of ASIO's attentions are bemused by the extraordinary effort and expense that led to tiny details being recorded and now revealed in the files. They are often shocked by the intrusiveness of the surveillance, which included placing informers within political groups or the use of telephone taps, as well as more prosaic methods such as copying birth certificates, immigration files or newspaper clippings.

An ASIO file is a window into a previous era, into the passions and prejudices of the Cold War. But the window is invariably narrow, offering a distorted glimpse and depicting twisted images. In this chapter I want to put some of the contributions to this book into context by talking about the nature of ASIO's files, its information gathering methods, structure and ethos.

When it was founded in 1949, ASIO took possession of the files of several older organisations that had conducted political surveillance up to that point. The most significant of these was the Commonwealth Investigation Service (CIS), formed in 1946 and the forerunner of the Commonwealth Police (now known as the Australian Federal Police). The CIS had, in turn, inherited records from the wartime Security Service, which collected information on threats from pro-Japanese and pro-German groups. Another set of files handed over to ASIO in 1949 was from the Directorate of Military Intelligence, which unofficially collected information on a very wide circle of people deemed to be sympathetic to socialism and communism.

So some ASIO files pre-date the organisation's formation in 1949 and are a treasure trove for historians of the twentieth century. The early files of novelist Katharine Susannah Prichard, a well-known radical and feminist who joined the Communist Party in 1920, derive from early police 'special branches' and military intelligence. They contain, for example, a 1912 report kept by the WA Police Special Branch detailing how, in London, 'she busied herself with various reform movements such as Communal Kitchens and Co-operative Housekeeping'. The consequence of these radical activities was that 'she has become notorious for her extreme, almost revolutionary, socialism and communism'.

The files also cover the other end of the twentieth century, notably the rise of the student movement and the New Left in the 1960s and the beginnings of feminist and anti-racist movements and social movements for cultural and political change. These movements posed a problem for ASIO. Its central target was communism and the Communist Party of Australia. This increased scope did not prevent ASIO from spying on a variety of non-party organisations and individuals, but the justification for this was always that these people and groups were 'front organisations' of the CPA, or in some way under the CPA's influence. The movement against the use of the atom bomb in the 1950s and 1960s, even though led by religious figures, was a case in point. Other supposed 'fronts' were the earliest groups fighting for justice for Indigenous Australians. Such movements, in which many CPA members played an active part, were deemed legitimate targets under the ASIO doctrine, which regarded anyone who co-operated with communists as a 'dupe' or worse, a fellow traveller.

Seeing the hand of the CPA in many places was not entirely a misperception. The CPA dominated the organised left in Australia from the 1930s until the late 1960s at least. For a considerable period it was difficult to be active in the Australian left and *not* have some connection with the CPA. The influence of Marxist ideas went well beyond the organisational boundaries of the CPA and the party had a strategy of working broadly with all kinds of people around short-term goals. But the new movements for social change were clearly not front organisations and this posed something of a dilemma for ASIO. It resolved the problem by stretching the definition of subversion (which it was legally tasked to oppose) to include movements such as the Vietnam moratoriums, which were largely against the longstanding Liberal–Country Party government, rather than having any revolutionary potential.

In spite of the CPA's genuine influence in some areas, a study of ASIO's files reveals that it had an exaggerated idea of the political influence the CPA had on people and events. ASIO assumed radical ideas were a contagion that infected anyone who worked with communists. Some historians speak of the 'disease model' used by internal security agencies like ASIO. Other assumptions smacked of the doctrine of Original Sin. Once tainted by contact with the CPA, an otherwise independent individual was considered to have 'fallen', and became a legitimate target worthy of a file and of ongoing attention. Even the most sensible reforms, such as a global ban on nuclear bomb testing, became suspect if the CPA supported them. Most non-communists who co-operated with the CPA did so with their eyes open, even if ASIO tended to assume that non-communists had no minds of their own and were mere putty in the hands of the party.

ASIO files are also windows into the activities and assumptions of the organisation and the people who compiled them. It is important to remember that ASIO files were drawn up as internal working documents. They were never intended to be publicly released. The fact that the information in the files would never be tested in a court case meant that all kinds of suspicions and speculation could be aired. As well, especially with files on people who were not dedicated members of the organised left, it is important not to assume that ASIO was always consciously targeting particular individuals. Sometimes personal files were merely repositories of odd bits of information picked up during surveillance of others.

As unusual as it was, it must be remembered that ASIO was part of the traditional public service. Its internal correspondence is carefully formal, usually dry, and obsessive about detail. It operated according to the public service's bureaucratic routines and its internal hierarchy. But because ASIO officers worked on a certain set of political assumptions, its files are unlike those of other government agencies. They are infused with an air of suspicion and distaste toward anything deemed subversive or 'a threat to security', sometimes a very elastic phrase. The language of ASIO files reflects a military ethos. ASIO officers talked of the strength of the CPA in terms of its 'order of battle'; they planned 'operations' against party members and organisations which were described as 'targets'; they addressed senior ASIO officers as 'sir' and calculated time, as in the Army, by a 24-hour clock. The use of courtesy titles from wartime military service survived much longer in ASIO than elsewhere in the bureaucracy.

Near the start of most personal files appear one or more documents that attempt to establish the identity of the person in question. Very early in its existence, when the Menzies Government was trying to pass the bill to ban the Communist Party, ASIO provided Menzies with the names of people alleged to be CPA members. It turned out that many of those named were not who ASIO claimed them to be, and had never been members. Menzies was embarrassed by this and privately castigated ASIO. From that time on ASIO took unusual care to establish the precise identity of the individuals on whom it opened files.

This was done by obtaining and spelling out the individual's full name, their date of birth and their parents' names. To get this information, field agents usually began with a check with the Registrar of Births, Deaths and Marriages, a check with the electoral roll, and sometimes a check of immigration files, driving licences and telephone subscriptions. Very occasionally there was a physical check on the home address of the individual. In the case of public servants, ASIO received copies of the Personal Particulars form completed by all employees.

Personal files vary. ASIO collected information on some people on an almost daily basis. The leader of the CPA, the late Laurie Aarons, has at least eighty-four volumes in his personal file, stretching back to the 1930s. Other files may consist of a slim single volume that is little more than a passive collection point for documents referring to other individuals or organisations rather than to the subject of the file. These items were placed in an individual's file only when he or she occasionally brushed up against bigger and more active targets. As well, the activities of some individuals on the broad left simply never triggered the creation of an ASIO file, which disappoints and puzzles them when they discover this years later.

THE STRUCTURE OF ASIO

To fully understand the contents of many of the ASIO files that have become public, it is useful to understand ASIO's internal structure. ASIO was modelled on the British Security Service

(MI5) and ASIO's internal structure largely replicated it. Although the names for different parts changed over the years, the basic structure of ASIO during the Cold War consisted of four main branches:

— the Counter Subversion branch (B1 branch)
— the Counter Espionage branch (B2 branch)
— the Protective Security branch (C branch)
— the Operations branch (Q branch, or later, Special Services Section).

The other major division was between headquarters in Melbourne and regional offices, which existed in all states and, until the early 1970s, in Papua New Guinea. Unlike the British Security Service, which tended to use police Special Branch officers for field work such as interviewing the referees for government jobs and handling offers of assistance from the public, ASIO developed its own 'field section'. Related to this was a squad of officers specialising in the physical surveillance of individuals, known by the acronym OBE (Operations Base Establishment).

The main work of OBE was the trailing of suspected KGB officers based in the Soviet Embassy in Canberra and the consulate and trade offices elsewhere. Less often it would follow domestic subversives. Each regional office had a field section which did most of such field work along with physical surveillance.

ASIO's B1 branch was largely devoted to collation and analysis of subversive activity.

Within it were sub-sections dealing with CPA influence

in the trade union movement, the public service, and the supposed 'fronts', such as the peace movement. There was also a sub-branch dealing with 'aliens' (overseas-born non-citizens).

The Counter Espionage branch (B2) was much smaller than B1 and was oriented almost exclusively to the USSR and Eastern European countries. It closely watched diplomats suspected of being intelligence officers, as well as Australians and Eastern Bloc nationals who had contact with them, often through a variety of commercial or cultural activities. B2 was a super-secret section within ASIO. It largely ran its own agents and kept many files within its own registry. Relatively few of these have been requested and deposited in the National Archives and consequently we know little of ASIO's counter-espionage work, other than through high-profile events such as the Petrov Affair and the later expulsion of Soviet diplomat Ivan Skripov. A point of confusion is that the acronyms B1 and B2 are also used as part of a coding system (A to E and 1 to 5) to evaluate the reliability and source of information.

ASIO's biggest branch was C branch (Protective Security), which carried out routine security checking (called 'vetting') of potential public servants, military recruits and migrants. It also checked applications for citizenship, and in the early years even vetted applicants for grants from the Commonwealth Literary Fund. It was largely for the purpose of vetting that the main body of ASIO personal dossiers and files on organisations was most frequently used.

The heart of ASIO's efforts against subversives (and hence

the source of most information recorded within personal files) was a branch known initially as Q branch or Special Services branch and, by the late 1960s, as 'D branch'.

The initial tasks of this branch were to maintain an index of 'current, discarded and blacklisted agents, registered contacts and potentials'; to maintain a 'target index'; to guide the recruitment and running of agents; and to co-ordinate 'milking' operations with 'friendly unofficial intelligence collecting agencies' (largely BA Santamaria's 'Movement'). This branch was the planning and operational centre for collecting information on the Communist Party and other targets. For many years these basic operational activities of ASIO were either illegal, such as burglary and phone tapping, or outside the law, such as electronic bugging.

Limited forms of telephone tapping were legalised and after 1960 ASIO would apply via the Attorney-General for a warrant from a judge for tapping phones under the *Telephonic Communications (Interception) Act*. Material from ASIO's phone taps appears today in archival files, usually flagged with the phrase 'telephone intercept'. Telephone interception was a vast, time-consuming task and took place behind closed doors within ASIO's regional offices. From 1949 to 1960 ASIO tapped 181 phones, which generated 40 000 pages of transcript. The physical limits of tapping and typing up transcripts were real but a single telephone tap (for example, on an active office of the Communist Party) would pick up information from vast numbers of individual party members, sympathetic contacts, members of the public and the families of party employees. Phone taps on prominent individual cultural figures who were communists collected information from a quite different circle of writers, intellectuals, members of parliament, businesspeople, and so on. So the interception of 181 phones would cover the conversations of many thousands of people who in turn would discuss other people, organisations and events.

A file on the interception of the phone of Francis James, a radical and eccentric religious figure, reveals that the Sydney office of ASIO had available a maximum of twenty-four 'channels' for interception, which presumably all functioned simultaneously. Within ASIO, those running phone interceptions would first produce a 'log' – in effect, a running sheet – with the date, time and parties to a call and a brief description, and this would go to the desk officer who would then decide whether to order a full transcription of particular conversations. A shorthand code in files referring to material gathered from phone interception was 'Hawke' (short for 'Operation Hawke') and this was later changed to 'Operation Bugle' in the light of Bob Hawke's growing political prominence in the early 1970s.

The other central task of the Operations branch was agent-running. The results of this are frequently seen in personal files which contain, for example, direct observation accounts of closed meetings. Each agent was assigned to an 'agent-master' (later described as a 'case officer') who would debrief him or her regularly, typing the results up in a 'contact report' or 'agent record sheet', also sometimes called a 'Q report'. These reports frequently feature on their right-hand side two lines, each with a date. The first begins with the letter 'I', denoting Information, and this refers to the original date that the information was obtained by an agent. The second is 'R', denoting 'Recorded', which states the date that the case officer recorded the agent's information. Many files carry a reliability code usually abbreviated as EVAL and CRED. The evaluation is the reliability rating of the source. A very reliable agent would be rated as 'B'. The credibility is a numerical rating with '2' commonly used for something directly heard from a target such as a conversation. Though all kinds of alpha-numeric combinations were possible under this system, the vast majority of files are designated as B2, denoting an evaluation of B and credibility of 2.

Such was the secrecy of agent-running that the name of the agent never appeared on the Q report; instead an alpha-numeric code was used. Effectively this meant that only those who were actually running the agents knew their identities. There were two kinds of agent, X and Y. An 'X' agent was under ASIO's control and a member of a target organisation. A 'Y' agent was not a member of the target organisation but might be an anti-communist union official who fed a case officer information on left-wing activity in the unions. A 'contact' or 'informant' was usually a member of the public who passed on information about a target but was not under ASIO control, such as a next-door neighbour of a CPA member. In the descriptor, a second letter, representing the state was added, F for South Australia, E for New South Wales, A for Victoria, C for Queensland.

Other sources of information were such things as 'Operation Shiver', apparently a physical surveillance operation which attempted to positively identify all visitors to the CPA's headquarters in Sydney. A more prosaic but valuable source of information was the public record, largely derived from newspapers. The newspaper most closely scrutinised was the CPA's own newspaper, *Tribune*, and it was fairly frank about party activities and individuals. Though many people suspected their mail was intercepted, the files reveal that interception of postal mail was rare. All of ASIO's files were kept within its Registry, which was relatively open for routine security checking (vetting), but contained several sections which were closely held, such as those concerning the identity of agents or information from overseas agencies such as the UK Security Service or the CIA. Each file had a 'transit card' on its cover which noted who had borrowed the file, and the transit card stayed within the Registry. A library of surveillance photographs, including cine film, was also set up.

THE ROYAL COMMISSIONS INTO ASIO

ASIO's system of files was heavily criticised by the 1977 Royal Commission on Intelligence and Security (RCIS). The inquiry, which was set up by Prime Minister Gough Whitlam in 1974 and reported in 1977, was the first independent assessment of the secretive internal security body since its foundation in 1949. The head of the RCIS, Justice Robert Hope, was sympathetic to the need for a security organisation, but he was highly critical of ASIO's intelligence gathering methods and the files on which the results were recorded. He and his staff examined hundreds of ASIO files and he said:

> I am bound to record that I found ASIO's files in such disorder that ... I have been quite unable to establish the truth or other-wise of many of the particulars of matters alleged in evidence.

There were 'serious deficiencies both in aspects of the existing records system, and in the control of access to the information which the system holds'.

Hope urged that management of files be far more professionally handled by experienced officers 'whose quality should make it apparent that "Records" is not some Siberia to which less adept officers are exiled'. Hope was also disturbed that 'many ASIO personnel in fact have had access to files, sometimes without adhering to the procedures, and at other times without any or sufficient need to know'.

Hope acknowledged that 'not a few members of the public are concerned that ASIO might have a "file" on them'. But he argued that a large number of ASIO files on individuals were simply the result of the regular process of issuing security clearances (vetting) at the end of which the individual was found to be of no security relevance. He recommended that while such records should not immediately be destroyed, in the longer term records of no potential security relevance should be. Hope was also critical of the quality of the staff who collected information and interpreted it. Intelligence assessment, he said:

> ... is no simple or routine activity but a highly skilled and subtle task. I must report that I saw little evidence in ASIO that the qualities of mind and expertise needed were recognised, or available in any large measure.

Six years later, in 1983, Hope was again commissioned to head a royal commission following the Combe–Ivanov affair. He found that many of his earlier recommendations had been put into operation. ASIO targets and intelligence gathering procedures were now regularly reviewed under new Intelligence Collection Programs. But he also found that the state of ASIO's files 'still leaves a lot to be desired'.

> Too often files appear to be repositories on which information is placed without much (or sometimes any) thought. There is little sign of effort to review files on a regular basis, or to analyse, distil and reduce their contents. A lot of files I have seen are larger than they need to be and reflect little considered review and assessment of the information that they hold.

Hope was hoping that ASIO would regularly weed out its files using 'culling procedures with a view to removing information that has clearly ceased to be relevant or of value'. But he acknowledged that it should also retain some information even though 'its future relevance or value to security may be uncertain'. He found that since his first inquiry 'over 100 000 old Head Office files had been reviewed for relevance… [and that] 5000 had been destroyed and 15 000 committed to microfilm'. It is perhaps a mark of how the times have changed that today we would be very suspicious if told that an ASIO file had been destroyed, rather than regarding it as some sort of triumph for personal privacy.

Hope was also unhappy with ASIO's criteria for initiating files on individuals. As the result of his previous investigation, a guidance document had been created which set out the criteria for opening personal files. The main criterion was that a person was 'a member of an ASIO target organisation'. This might appear somewhat circular since it raises the question of the definition of legitimate targets. Rather, it was 'not an entirely satisfactory document' because it failed to make clear the difference between opening a personal file, recording someone's details on ASIO's personal index (a less significant step) or opening what was called a head office 'testing file'. The latter were meant to be 'temporary' files to be reviewed after ten years, but this was unsatisfactory because it meant that information accumulated on such files 'simply because they are there'.

It also appeared that ASIO's listed criteria for opening files had what Hope called a 'catch-all provision' to allow files to be opened simply for convenience. He also criticised the way in which material was continually added to existing personal files.

> The process of placing a document on a personal file, in particular, should not be regarded as an automatic process, not as one which can be left to registry clerks. It requires the judgment of an intelligence officer ...

He recommended a 'more disciplined and consistent approach to both the opening of files and to the placing of information on them'. The routine copying of reports, such as a report of a meeting of eighteen people being copied and placed on the eighteen personal files of those attending, can be seen today in many files. As well, ASIO files were used to give advice to other government departments and other intelligence agencies such as the Office of National Assessments (ONA).

ASIO has never been happy with its files being released under the *Archives Act*, in spite of provisions that they must be more than thirty years old (now moving to a twenty-year rule under amendments passed in 2010) and that deletions for a broad range of security-related reasons are permitted. During the second Hope Royal Commission which began just after the *Archives Act* had started to compel ASIO to release some files, ASIO submitted to Justice Hope that the *Archives Act* be changed to prevent the release of any ASIO file, except at the discretion of the Director-General of Security. Hope noted that ASIO had neglected to put in a submission 'during the long period in which proposals for the archives legislation were under consideration'. Nevertheless, he recommended that the government amend the *Archives Act* to remove the obligation of ASIO to release any files.

Luckily, Hope's recommendation was rejected by the Hawke Government. Some years later, after a series of legal actions and agitation by researchers and historians who were frustrated by ASIO's slow and miserly release of files, the Parliamentary Joint Committee on ASIO examined the issue. ASIO submitted that the 'closed period' of thirty years be extended to fifty years and that other restrictions be imposed on the release of any ASIO files. Fortunately, these were rejected by the committee in its 1992 report.

THE NATIONAL ARCHIVES AND ASIO

Hundreds of thousands of security files on people and organisations, accumulated over more than sixty years of investigation and surveillance, are still held by ASIO. Of these, a small proportion are publicly available at the National Archives of Australia in Canberra, which holds the records of all federal government agencies. Unlike other federal government agencies, ASIO is not automatically required to deposit its old records with the National Archives.

Files are released on three conditions. First, they must be more than thirty years old (moving slowly to twenty years);

second, they must be formally requested by individuals under the *Archives Act 1983*; and third, they must have been edited (or censored) to omit the disclosure of information deemed to be damaging to security. The formal request for any personal file is made simply by giving the person's full name, date of birth, if possible, and a brief statement on the nature of the political activity in which the person was involved. At present this entails no fee. Once released, the files are available to the public at the NAA offices in Canberra and a photocopy of the file can be ordered. The titles of all available files and sometimes the actual pages of digitised files can be viewed online via the database 'Recordsearch' found on the NAA website: www.naa.gov.au.

Nearly all ASIO files released through National Archives have deletions and sections blacked out. However, generally speaking, the rules have liberalised over the years. The amount of material released has increased since files were first publicly available in the mid-1980s. For many years pages of transcripts of telephone interceptions were totally withheld, but today such transcripts are released most of the time. The material still withheld usually falls into three types: that which could suggest the identity of an agent; identification of an overseas intelligence organisation as a source; or material on ASIO techniques and 'modus operandi'. As well, the names of many (but not all) ASIO officers are withheld as well as medical and psychological details of the subject of a file.

Often the subject of the file or their family requests access to the file, but anyone can request access to any ASIO file; it is not necessary to be a family member. In recent years, under pressure from individuals surprised at the contents of their file, National Archives has allowed a person to place a statement correcting errors or distortions with the Archives' copy of the file.

The National Archives categorises ASIO's files into several 'series'. The largest series is A6119. These are ASIO's personal files, of which more than 6000 have so far been released. These are classified by the name of the individual, for example, Mary Smith, Volume 1; Mary Smith, Volume 2, etc.

The second largest ASIO file series is A6122, of which 2700 files have been released to the public. These are ASIO's subject files, and usually cover organisations, as well as topics such as 'Communist Party Interest in Labor Party'. Not surprisingly, the largest single target is the Communist Party of Australia (CPA), including its local branches, trade unions and other organisations deemed to be under its influence. The latter covers a wide variety of political, cultural, intellectual and activist groups. Typical file titles are: 'CPA: Adelaide University Branch'; 'Realist Film Unit'; 'Yugoslav Community in West Australia'. ASIO's surveillance went wider than the CPA and those it influenced, so there are subject files on unrelated bodies such as 'Ananda Marga' and 'Students for a Democratic Society (SDS)'. A small number of far-right organisations have files, such as the Melbourne-based National Front, the Nazi Party and the anti-Semitic League of Rights.

A small number of ASIO intelligence briefings prepared for the government are the subject of files. Three valuable groups of files in A6122 are those recording ASIO's memos and formal conversations with the Attorney-General, with the Prime Minister, and with other ministers and heads of department. These show the way in which government ministers were advised by ASIO and, more importantly, they show the politicised use of ASIO during twenty-three years of conservative government until 1972.

The A6122 series also contains ASIO's own internally written history, titled 'History of ASIO by Bob Swan'. These fascinating files include key decisions and policy documents covering the period 1949–1970. Another interesting series of files in A6122, though heavily censored, are those covering ASIO's 'spoiling operations'. These were attempts to foster divisions and suspicions within the CPA and to encourage anti-communist activities, sometimes by planting stories in the news media. A number of ASIO's files dealing with the 1954–55 Royal Commission on Espionage (the Petrov Inquiry) are in this series under the code name 'Operation Cabin 12', but the voluminous records of the Royal Commission itself are best researched by looking at the 'fact sheets' on the National Archives website.

One of the remarkable aspects of ASIO's files is how little we know about ASIO's proactive operations. While the purpose of personal files and subject files is to gather useful information about security targets, the actual operations conducted from time to time that involved these targets remain a mystery. Its unravelling awaits a historian with tenacity and a great deal of time. We know these files are highly sensitive because of the extent of deletions.

The most significant series of operations during ASIO's first dozen years centred around identifying the true extent of the leakage of top secret British documents to the Soviet Union. These operations have been described in Desmond Ball and David Horner's book *Breaking the Codes* and in my own book, *Australian Spies and Their Secrets*. An extension of this was 'Operation Boomerang' in 1958, which targeted Alan Dalziel, the private secretary of the Labor Party leader Dr Evatt; two disaffected ex-ASIO officers; and several left-wing individuals who had had contact with KGB agents. This complicated surveillance and intelligence gathering can be viewed online, as this file has been digitised by the National Archives. Aspects of Operation Boomerang are also covered in a recent documentary film *I Spry*, which examines the life of Sir Charles Spry, the first Director-General of ASIO.

Another operation had the unusual name of 'Operation Ginger Ale', which targeted members of the CPA who had resigned or been expelled in unhappy circumstances. Surveillance of the Vietnam moratorium was tagged 'Operation Whip'. Files on a vast number of other operations remain to be unearthed.

Another popular series, A9626, covers ASIO's still photographs. It contains over 600 items, often of individuals entering buildings to go to meetings, standing in the street or taking part in demonstrations. In nearly all cases the photography was done covertly. For many years ASIO had arrangements with the owners of buildings near target organisations to use their premises to take photographs. The funeral parlour opposite the entrance to the Soviet Embassy in Canberra was one, while similar arrangements existed with buildings opposite CPA offices. As with written ASIO records, members of the public can request copies of any photos that ASIO holds.

A related series is A8703, which is largely cine film of people and events of interest to ASIO. It also contains several feature films such as *Legal Resident*, which is a fascinating account of the surveillance and expulsion of a Canberra-based KGB officer, Ivan Skripov, in 1962–63, as well as footage of anti-Vietnam demonstrations, May Day marches and several training films for ASIO officers.

A small set of ASIO files, A12694, contains fascinating files on 'policy and directives', including files about employing homosexuals in the public service and another set on contact between the Soviet Embassy and MPs. A6126 is a smaller set of microfilmed copies of files deemed of little security interest or once due for destruction, but retained.

ACRONYMS AND PHRASES USED IN ASIO FILES

Finally, reading ASIO files is sometimes a guessing game because of the acronyms and shorthand which are routinely used. The following is based on the author's knowledge from reading files and interviewing former ASIO officers.

APS	Australian Public Service
A/RD	Acting Regional Director.
a/r	Adversely recorded.
ASIS	Australian Secret Intelligence Service.
'Austerity'	Telegram or telex address of ASIO office.
Bugle	Indicates information obtained from telephone intercepts ('Operation Bugle').
B1	Counter Subversion branch of ASIO.
B2	Counter Espionage branch of ASIO (note that B2 could also be a routine source reliability code).
By hand	Stipulates that a document be delivered by hand.
COC	Case Officer's Comment.
Contact Report	A report on the temperament of an agent; sometimes simply the report of an agent.
CPA	Communist Party of Australia.
DG	Director-General of Security (head of ASIO).
DOB	Date of birth.
ICP	Intelligence Collection Program.
IR	Information Report (agent debriefing or similar).
FADG	First Assistant Director-General.
Fnu	First (or full) name unknown, as in, 'A man called Smith (fnu)'.
Gratis/non gratis	Gratis is a classification of the information in a file and means it was publicly available; non gratis means that the information was from a sensitive source and its release could identify the source.

Hawke	Operation Hawke, telephone interception.
k.a.	Known as; for example, John Smith k.a. 'Charlie'.
Master Log	Main log of intercepted phone conversations.
Nar	Not adversely recorded.
Nor	Not otherwise recorded (often: (ui/nor)).
nt or N/T	No trace (a trace was a minor reference in an ASIO index).
NSW	Can refer to the New South Wales regional office of ASIO in Sydney.
OBE	Operations Base Establishment. ASIO's squad of physical surveillance officers.
OIC	Officer in Charge.
Ph or Phon	Phonetic.
RD	Regional Director (of ASIO).
RO	Regional Office.
'Scorpion'	The telegraphic and telex name of ASIO Headquarters.
SLO	Security Liaison Officer, usually British Security Service officer based in Canberra. Sometimes the ASIO officer based in London.
SSB	Special Services Branch.
TCO	Travel Control Officer (liaised with airlines and airports).
Telecon	telephone conversation.
Trace	A brief mention of an otherwise unknown person.
TS	Top Secret. This refers to the classification of a file and also to the section of the ASIO Registry which housed Top Secret files.
u/i	Unidentified.
UKSS	British Security Service (MI5).
VPF	Victorian Personal File (a file held at the regional office).
vr	Voice recognition, used in intercepts, for example 'Bill Smith (vr)'.
Watch list	A list of individuals whose travel movements were referred to ASIO.
WPF	West Australian Personal File.

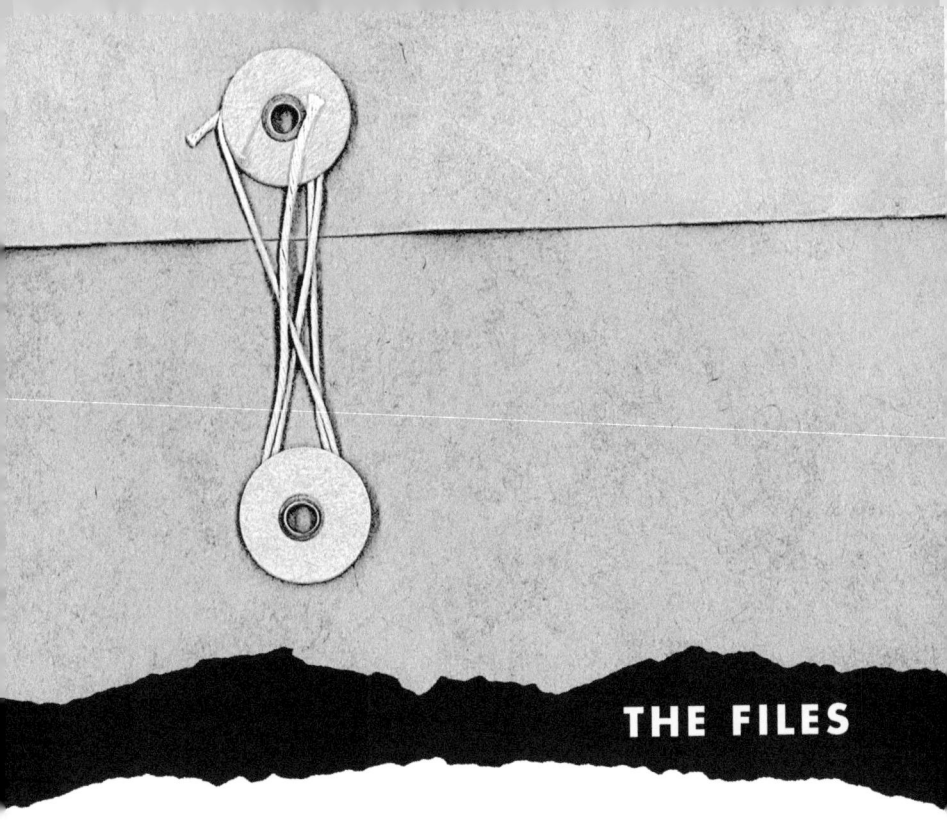

THE FILES

MICHAEL KIRBY

Michael Kirby grew up in Sydney and was educated in the public school system. He attended Fort Street Boys' High School and then the University of Sydney, where he became a 'student trouble maker' and was elected President of the Students' Representative Council. As a young lawyer he undertook pro bono cases for the NSW Council for Civil Liberties, acting on behalf of Aboriginals, conscientious objectors, Vietnam protestors and others. These activities and family connections brought him to the notice of ASIO and the NSW Police Special Branch.

He practised as a solicitor and barrister in the 1960s. In 1975 he was appointed a judge, and chairman of the Australian Law Reform Commission. In 1984 he was appointed the President of the New South Wales Court of Appeal. He later held other high judicial posts, eventually as a Justice of the High Court of Australia from 1996 to 2009.

In addition to his Australian positions, Michael has served in a large number of United Nations agencies, including as UN special representative in Cambodia from 1993 to 1996. Recently he was appointed a member of the new global commission on sustainable health. He has also served as president of the International Commission of Jurists.

He has won many prizes, including, in 2010, the prestigious Gruber Justice Prize, and he has been appointed a Companion of the Order of Australia and a Companion of the Order of St Michael and St George. The University of Sydney conferred on him the honorary degree of Doctor of Laws. Thus, the troublemaker has become respectable. He lives in Sydney with his partner of forty-four years, Johan van Vloten – a man of infinite patience and forgiveness.

With a nice touch of irony, in mid-2013 Michael was appointed to chair a United Nations commission of inquiry on human rights abuses in North Korea: probably the last remaining Stalinist–communist regime. Somewhere in ASIO headquarters, officials must be scratching their heads.

THE COMMOS AND ME

by Michael Kirby

GETTING 'EM WHILE THEY'RE YOUNG

My long association with the Australian Communist Party began when I was but three years of age. Like the Jesuits, the communists believed in getting them while they were young.

My first mention in an ASIO file occurred when I was twelve.

My grandmother, whom I knew as Normie (but who, in the ways of the times, had been christened Alma Caroline), divorced her first husband, Victor Kirby, in the 1930s. A good-looking man, but mismatched, he had been the father of my father, Donald Kirby.

Norma worked as a cashier in the Prince of Wales hotel in what we would now describe as Sydney's Chinatown. She was a reserved, highly intelligent, thoughtful, and very well-read person who, in other times, would have won a scholarship and gone on to university and professional life. But throughout the years of the Great Depression in the 1930s, she was the one member of the family who always had a job. In Australia, hotels

Michael Kirby's grandmother, Norma, with her second husband, Jack Simpson, National Treasurer of the Communist Party. On Norma's knee is Michael's brother David; with Jack is Michael's sister Diana.

never go out of vogue. And the biggest stream through hotels, apart from beer, is cash and people.

Norma's job in the hotel was to count the cash. Invariably she got it right. She was a greatly respected employee. In about 1941, Norma, who had reverted to her maiden name of Gray, met in the hotel many of the leading lights of the Australian

Communist Party. The party headquarters was in a building nearby. Among those leading lights was a man who had been born in New Zealand and named Maurice Flynn but who had later taken the *nom de guerre* of Jack Simpson. It was as Jack Simpson that he became known to our family.

After 1941, Jack courted Norma in the somewhat more leisurely way of those days. Norma was going out at the time with other suitors, some of whom were businessmen and definitely better able to keep her in a style to which she had never been accustomed. Certainly not from the subventions of Victor Kirby. However, as Norma described it to my father, Jack was 'more interesting'. In fact, he was a hero. From New Zealand, Jack had volunteered to fight in the ANZAC Corps at Gallipoli. He did so with courage and, on the withdrawal of the ANZACs from that ill-fated campaign, he was transferred to France where he was gassed and wounded.

During the Depression, Jack Simpson, who had been raised a Roman Catholic, became disillusioned both with his religion and with Australia, to which he had returned from France after the War. So he joined the Australian Communist Party. His intelligence, prudence and reserved demeanour soon led to his assignment to take charge of the Party's finances. Indeed, as Stuart Macintyre points out in his story of the communists, *The Reds*, Jack Simpson was eventually elected the National Treasurer of the Australian Communist Party.

At first, my father did not know of Jack's political background and offices. He was just one of his mother's many suitors. Jack started to turn up at the Kirby family home in Sydney Street, Concord. He came to Christmas dinner in 1942. That is where I first made his acquaintance. Of course, I was too young to remember our first encounter. But I have it on good authority that I enjoyed a good relationship with him, being then but three years of age. He got on well with my mother and my father liked him. Jack tried to reinforce my father's interest in the worldwide struggle of the downtrodden proletariat.

A WARTIME MARRIAGE

My father says that Jack Simpson's relationship with Norma became serious after Christmas 1942. To please his mother (and Jack Simpson), my father would occasionally attend meetings in the Sydney Town Hall called by the Australian Communist Party and its 'fellow travellers' to support the Russian war effort. There he met the leaders of the party, including JB Miles, who looked rather like JB Chifley, right down to the pipe. Other leaders of the party included Lance Sharkey, Laurie Aarons and Jack Simpson himself.

Eventually, Norma and Jack decided to tie the knot. Their wedding took place on 21 April 1943 at the home of Norma's sister Gloria and her Dutch husband, Gerry Boes. This was at 59 Eastern Avenue, Kingsford, which was earlier called 'South Kensington' because it sounded better.

Everyone who was anyone in the Australian Communist Party attended Norma's marriage to Jack Simpson. The celebrant was a Congregational minister named the Reverend Pratt. A distinguished-looking man named Robinson delivered the principal speech. He toasted the bride and groom and, according to my father, spoke very well. Of course, my father attended, and so did my mother, who was expecting another son, later to become Justice David Kirby.

The other members of the family who attended Norma's wedding were my brother Donald (whose twin brother, David

Charles, had died on 9 August 1942 of pneumonia) and myself. Glory was thrilled to have the local Bolshevik aristocracy at her home. As my father recalls it, the event was lavish despite the austerities of the war.

Thereafter, Jack and Norma went to reside in a house at 639 Princes Highway, Tempe. It adjoined a church hall that had been converted to a boot factory. The result was that along the highway trundled the Sydney tram. And next door, a machine was heard at all hours of the day thumping out shoes and boots. When I complained to my father about the noise during overnight stays in Tempe, contrasting this with the blissful silence of Concord, he simply told me to 'shut up' and to stop being difficult. This was advice that many people have tried to give me in life.

When, often with my brother Donald, I would stay at Tempe with Jack and Norma, I would see aspects of life with which I was not familiar. First, they were both smokers. And a glass of beer was never far away. Concord was teetotal.

Secondly, they were avid listeners to radio station 2KY, with its seemingly endless broadcasts of horse and dog races that required occasional visits to the local SP bookie.

Thirdly, they displayed in their home magazines printed on heavy paper titled *Soviet Union*. These journals portrayed the life of bliss and plenty enjoyed by the peasants and workers of the Soviet proletariat. The journal used a photographic technique that seemed quite different from the colour photography with which I was familiar. The apricot toning of the photographs stood out. And all those folk dancers with happy faces seemed determined to show what a workers' paradise existed behind what Churchill was later to call the 'Iron Curtain'.

Fourthly, on the bookshelves in the rather dark lounge room of the Tempe residence were volumes of the collected speeches of VI Lenin and Joseph Stalin. I noted at the time that the books seemed in a pristine state, indeed untouched. No corners were turned down to indicate a well-loved phrase or a point of departure where the reader could go no further. There were no marginal markings to identify precious passages to be learned by heart. Indeed, not to put too fine a point on it, I was not convinced that Jack (or certainly Norma) had ever opened them. But they were on display for all to see.

On the bottom shelf of the bookcase was a large black volume of Boccaccio's *The Decameron*. When I discovered this later, as puberty was descending upon me, I found it infinitely more beguiling than anything that Lenin or Stalin had ever written or said. How sombre and melancholy communism always seemed to me. That was also my father's view. It was all so grim and determinedly optimistic, between gritted teeth, about a folk-dancing future portrayed in apricot tones.

COMMUNIST PARTY DISSOLUTION ACT

The first time I came under ASIO surveillance (so far as I am aware) was in about 1951. At my request, Stuart Macintyre sent me a copy of Jack Simpson's ASIO file, which he had procured under legal FOI rights when writing *The Reds*. In the file, reference was made to an occasion, which I have otherwise forgotten, when I visited Taronga Park Zoo in company with Jack. Other participants in this enterprise were recorded. The three young boys were my brothers Donald and David and me. At twelve, I was the eldest. This was my first mention in an ASIO file.

What the surveillance hoped to discover at the zoo is a puzzle. Perhaps communists were observed 'talking to the animals', even before Rex Harrison did. If ASIO's anxiety was communist corruption of young minds, they need not have bothered. Donald and David shared the scepticism of my mother. I was more like my father. As I came to understand communism, I could see its attractions to those who were disillusioned with the world. But my aversion to apricot and my dislike of endless folklorica put me offside with the messages to which I would otherwise have been susceptible.

Just the same, by 1950–51, I had a child's understanding that something rather serious was affecting 'Uncle Jack'. This was the *Communist Party Dissolution Act 1950*. The Menzies–Fadden Government had been elected in 1949 on a pledge to proscribe communism. I have a dim recollection at the time of lending my considerable support to Mr Menzies because he had promised to provide child endowment benefits to first-born children like me. At that time the Labor government had only rewarded parents who had more than one child. So I did not attract the pretty endowment vouchers which my mother cashed at the local post office for her later children.

Of course, I did not know the details of the anti-communism law. It was enacted early in 1950, high on the new government's agenda. But I did know that it was not a good thing for Jack Simpson or our family. I now know that, as the National Treasurer of the party, he intended to make himself scarce whenever the Act looked likely to come into effect. But that moment was postponed. No sooner was the Act proclaimed, but the Communist Party and a variety of trade unions challenged the statute's constitutional validity in the High Court of Australia.

Dr HV Evatt, by now the parliamentary leader of the Labor Party, took the brief in the High Court for the trade unions. As my father reported it, neither Jack Simpson nor any of the leaders of the Communist Party had the slightest expectation that the High Court would invalidate the legislation. So far as they were concerned, the Justices of the High Court (all of them) were the 'running lapdogs' of the capitalist economy. They were all part of the Establishment, symbolised by the biggest lapdog of all, 'Pig-Iron' Bob Menzies.

At last the day came when the decision of the High Court was to be announced. My father tells me that Jack Simpson went into hiding. Perhaps he had with him on the train, in his modest bags, the accumulated bullion of the Australian communists. However that may be, when the newspapers announced the outcome of the High Court challenge, it emerged that the communists and their trade union allies had won by five justices to one. All I knew was that a tribunal, that I was told was based in Melbourne, had lifted the danger faced by my Uncle Jack. According to my father, astonishment was the only word to describe the reaction of Jack Simpson and his communist friends on learning of Dr Evatt's mighty victory in the High Court.

There followed a referendum throughout Australia in September 1951. Mr Menzies sought to amend the Constitution effectively to overturn the High Court decision. By the narrowest of margins, Mr Menzies failed to secure a majority of the electors. Jack Simpson was to be spared any further legislative harassment by the government.

During the Petrov inquiry that followed, and exploited, the closely divided opinion of the Australian people in the communism referendum, Jack Simpson's name came up. The report of the Royal Commission on Espionage noted:

In the course of [Bruce Millis's] evidence it emerged that in 1943, when the Party was under a ban, he had – jointly with one Simpson (the Treasurer of the Communist Party) – signed a contract to purchase the Newsletter Printery for £14 000. The Printery was bought for the Communist Party purposes and is still used by it. Milliss said he merely lent his name to oblige a friend. We do not believe him.

The fact that Jack Simpson is mentioned only once in this report on the activities of the communists rather suggests that he was not really a major player in the doctrine or 'revolutionary' activities of the party. He was a tried and trusted stalwart who could be allowed the privilege of holding the modest funds of the Communist Party. A glance at his photographs suggests that he was what he appeared to be: a dapper, reliable, prudent keeper of the books. Scarcely a revolutionary, bent on destroying Australia's constitutional fabric.

WORKING-CLASS WARRIOR

I have a distinct recollection, on one occasion, of accompanying Jack Simpson and someone else (possibly Lance Sharkey), around the streets of Tempe near where Jack and Norma lived. The task in hand was to slap paste on electoral posters and to attach them to electric light poles. I think the posters were for the election of Sharkey to the House of Representatives. I dimly recall the red symbol of the hammer and sickle. My job was to carry the glue. Jack and his friend had a small ladder so as to put the signs beyond reach of the Menzies–Fadden opponents. I recall that when I later told my father of this escapade, he was upset because he did not want his children dragged into such communist atrocities. For all I know, there was an ASIO agent peeping behind other lampposts, taking detailed notes of what we were up to.

As I grew up my brothers and I would sometimes debate political issues with Jack Simpson. He was always very patient and tolerant, although I believe he was astonished by the definite views that my brothers had formed about politics at such an early age. At the time, my father would occasionally host meetings in our home at Concord with an interesting crowd of communist sympathisers. He did this to please Norma and Jack. But it greatly displeased my mother. This must have been evident because, rather quickly, the meetings petered out. I fear that my mother was branded an 'Enemy of the People'. My father's reliability would also have been called into vicarious question.

Jack Simpson went up to Queensland in July 1957 to see friends. However, he had some sort of turn. He suffered from emphysema. He was told to return home immediately, but not by plane. This was because, in those days, the cabins on regional flights were not pressurised. Ignoring this advice, he flew home. He died in his sleep that night, on 18 July 1957. He was given a grand funeral by the Australian Communist Party, its remnants then still shaken by the post-Stalin revelations. I remember attending the funeral in company with my father. I was seventeen years of age. By that time, I was in my second year of Arts at Sydney University. I walked solemnly behind the coffin which was draped with the communist flag. At that age, death was so hard to fathom.

In all probability, there were agents of ASIO observing the turnout to farewell this stalwart supporter of the working classes. My recollections of Jack Simpson were of a man who became a little tongue-tied when challenged on his political beliefs. He was no fool. He would not agree if he was agin' it. He was a rational man. There was no way he could have sent critics or opponents to a firing squad. He had seen too much of that kind of conduct in the Great War. For him, communism was simply his new religion. It was his substitute for the Flynn family's Catholicism. In the years that followed, whenever I heard denunciations of communists and communism, I thought of my Uncle Jack. I was then robbed of any fear.

Jack's death did not, however, see the end of my interest to ASIO.

BRAINY BUT REACTIONARY

As chance would have it, in 1996, I was appointed to the High Court of Australia, joining the court that had struck down the legislation that spelt so much civic danger to Jack Simpson and his colleagues. In the course of my service on the High Court, I often referred in speeches to the *Communist Party Case*. Occasionally, in my reasoning in the High Court, I invoked the principles expressed in that case. For me, it was one of the greatest decisions of the court, especially for the libertarian principles that it upheld at a time when that outcome was by no means certain. I would sometimes refer to the decision in the reasoning of my own opinions. In one case, *Thomas v. Mowbray*, a decision concerned with anti-terrorism legislation, I had to introduce a defence of the 1951 decision when one justice (Ian Callinan) doubted the correctness of the *Communist Party Case* decision, and other justices also appeared to cast cold water upon it.

In the last year of my service on the High Court of Australia, those who were undertaking research for the television series *Persons of Interest*, made an application for a copy of my ASIO file.

This was something I had thought about but a sense of propriety, probably excessive, restrained me from requesting a copy of my file whilst I was serving as a justice of the court. I knew that it could not have been too bad because nothing I had ever done had endangered national security. As well, I did not doubt that, for some of my federal appointments over the years, going back to 1974 when I joined the Arbitration Commission, the likelihood was that some form of vetting would have taken place.

In consequence of the researchers' request for my ASIO file, I was alerted that a third party had requested my file. Later, I began to have intensive dealings with the National Archives of Australia (NAA) as I sent off to them truckloads of personal papers that had accumulated during my judicial years. As a kind of reward, the NAA offered me my ASIO file. I accepted. It was presented to me in a beautiful NAA folder on the cover of which, ironically, was the royal seal of Queen Victoria showing the royal coat of arms attached to the Queen's assent to the original Act of the Imperial Parliament that brought the Australian Constitution into effect. It was that Constitution that had struck a mortal blow at Mr Menzies's cherished legislation.

Within this unlikely cover were thirty pages or so of documents from the file that ASIO had opened in my name. Some of the documents are marked 'Secret'. This was astonishing to me when I read the papers concerned. All of them were entirely innocuous. Some of them showed how safely conservative I really was. The period covered by the file is 1964 to 1969. Doubtless there will be other treasures in store as future years' collections are released.

The earliest record, marked intriguingly 'Non Gratis'

(implying perhaps a paid informant) was a note on my Auntie Glory. It records the statement she is said to have made to an ASIO informant sometime in December 1964. It reads,

> GLORIA BOES recently stated that she has a nephew named KIRBY (Michael Kirby NR/NA) who spoke at the Australian Congress for International Co-operation and Disarmament. She said he was very brainy, but was a reactionary.

On this unpromising footing, it seems, my ASIO file was opened and maintained. An entry of about the same time attaches a copy of the text of a speech made by me to the afternoon seminar of 'The Citizens' Conference of the Australian Congress for International Co-operation and Disarmament'. That conference was convened at the unlikely venue of the Trocadero, then Sydney's largest dance hall, in George Street, near St Andrew's Cathedral. It was a place at which I had organised many a popular Law Ball during my time in the Students' Law Society of the University of Sydney.

My speech to the Citizens' Congress was given on 26 October 1964. It is titled 'The Malaysia Issue'. ASIO preserved a copy. Far from being any danger to Australia's security, the speech constituted a rebuttal of the then Indonesian Government's attacks on the creation of the new Federation of Malaysia by the amalgamation of former British colonies in South-East Asia. Solemnly, in the first paragraph, I warn:

> Liberal minded people in Australia and elsewhere should not fall into the dangerous habit of condoning the Indonesian policy because of affection to the Indonesian people or admiration for their successful struggle for independence. To do so would be to

> fall into the same error as prompted some liberals in the 1930s to justify the Stalin Trials in Russia. History has shown only too often the danger of spineless liberalism.

Not too much radical danger there. Even in 1964, I doubt that this constituted the Communist Party line.

In May 1965, a number of pages record my activities in the NSW Council for Civil Liberties (CCL). These were the minutes of that organisation, listing the various participants, a number of whom (Jack Sweeney QC, Marcel Pile QC, RJB St John, Jimmy Staples and myself) went on to state or federal judicial service. In fact, joining the CCL became something of a professional hazard for lawyers. Virtually any lawyer who served on its committee ended up on a bench somewhere. My brother David was recorded in the newsletter of April 1965 as having joined the committee. Obviously, the CCL was under close surveillance. One entry in the file ominously recorded that I had not only given a lecture on the Malaysia issue, but had signed a certificate in support of an application for a passport made by another ASIO suspect, stating that I had known her for two years. Her file number is recorded, as is the fact that she was a CPA member.

Repeatedly during 1965 my name is linked to this same female university student, whom I only just remember. She was married to a singularly handsome young student, Steve Johnson, who took part in the activities of the National Union of Australian University Students (NUAUS). This was the only connection in which I had known her. Yet for my pains, it led to a furious series of records noting the fact that I had given a certificate that I had known her for two years, which, at the time, I undoubtedly had.

Later, for this or some other reason, a 'Secret' entry of October 1969 saw details of the passport issued to me. These details were included, together with a youthful photograph of me which the agent was 'processing'.

Another body with which I was associated, the NUAUS, also brought me under ASIO surveillance. In 1966 or '67, at the Perth Congress of NUAUS, I left that body decorated as an honorary life member. However, seeing that Peter Durack (later Liberal Attorney-General) and Sir Gerard Brennan (later High Court Chief Justice) were similarly honoured, it could not have been too radical an organisation.

The entry of February 1966 recorded that 'Brian' had made a telephone inquiry about a Soviet delegation. It was suspected that 'Brian' was possibly Brian David Aarons, a famous surname in the CPA. Brian was told 'to contact "Richie" (John Richard) Walsh at the Sydney Students' Representative Council (SRC)'. Walsh is recorded as suggesting that the only person who would know about the delegation's movements other than himself would be 'Michael Kirby who had met the delegation at the airport'. My official number in the New South Wales file records of ASIO was given as K/17/82.

In January 1966, presumably on the opening of this file, a record is made of my name and a search of my birth record. My father's name is listed with a description 'possibly K/8/41'. So is my mother's maiden name, but apparently (quite correctly) ASIO had not bothered to open a file on her. She is described as 'N/T', presumably 'not traced'. A later memo of February 1966 instructed the file keeper to delete all earlier descriptions of me and to place them on the New South Wales file K/17/82.

In a record of 1966 from the Deputy Director-General of

ASIO, New South Wales, my name appears under a memorandum headed 'Communist Party of Australia penetration and influence in New South Wales universities'. It is there recorded that I was a 'member of Sydney University' and 'CPA contact'. If 'CPA contact' meant anything but the most tenuous links with the Australian Communist Party, described above, it was completely false. Then the file runs out.

So there it is. A meagre collection of documents that had brought me to the notice of Australia's national security agency. It says much that they came upon me because of their keen interest in university student activities, the Council for Civil Liberties, and a disarmament group which I had lectured on the dangers of the Stalinist trials.

NEED AND BALANCE

In his dissenting reasons in the *Communist Party Case*, Chief Justice Latham justified his opinion, upholding the Menzies' Government communism legislation, on the footing of Oliver Cromwell's dictum during the English Commonwealth. This was that 'being comes before wellbeing'. A threat to the organised polity itself is a danger that must be overcome with priority above the wellbeing of the subjects living in the polity. Doubtless, this was the justification that the ASIO agents, directors-general, informants and others working for ASIO felt in placing me on a security alert.

Every society has people within it who are disaffected with its political system. Even after the law in 1951 delivered to the communists the resounding victory in their litigation in the High Court, there were doubtless party members who truly believed in the 'dictatorship of the proletariat' and the 'revolution of the working masses'. But in Australia, by and large, those believers had been seduced by the warm sunshine into complying overall with our society's way of doing things.

This is not to say that every revolutionary organisation will be so pliant or that the communists were amenable in other countries. The advent of weapons of mass destruction and the capacity to deliver their devastation so as to cause great harm to innocent civilians undoubtedly presented the need to create security agencies like ASIO and agencies for analysis of security related developments, such as the Office of National Assessments (ONA). I do not question the need for such bodies. However, my file shows the critical importance of always rendering security agencies accountable to the civilian government; retaining a measure of scepticism about their occasional over-enthusiasm; and affording remedies to those who are wronged by their collection and use of false or unreliable information.

Any person of common sense who glances at the trivial entries in my ASIO file would have quickly come to the conclusion that I was no threat whatever to the security of Australia. He or she would have ordered the closure of the file and told the agents to get on with snooping that was more likely to be productive. In fact, a particularly attentive reader of my ASIO file would probably have come to the conclusion that my Auntie Glory, life-long feminist and probable CPA fellow traveller, had summed me up pretty accurately in her reported assessment of December 1964. I was, indeed, as she described me, 'very brainy'. But I was also basically (at least from an Australian Communist Party viewpoint) 'a reactionary'. Anyone who has displayed such faith in society as to take part in civic organisations of students, civil libertarians and supporters of nuclear disarmament, can only really be called a 'reactionary'. Dangerous people are much less inclined to talk. Their tactics go beyond words.

If nothing else, my ASIO file of the late 1960s rekindles memories of long forgotten meetings I attended when I should have been out partying. It conjures up images of harmless and often tedious occasions of student affairs. But it also rekindles memories of the fears and obsessions of those times when students and civil libertarians could be seriously perceived as the potential enemies of the people in sunny Australia.

EDITOR'S NOTE

At the time of publication, Michael Kirby is engaged in a lengthy process to secure access, under the *Government Information (Public Access) Act 2009* (NSW) to his file, formerly maintained by the Special Branch of the NSW Police Force (since disbanded). Access to the file was refused by police on statutory 'public interest' grounds. Successive applications to superior police officers did not bear fruit. An application for review by the NSW Information and Privacy Commissioner has so far not produced the goods. The saga continues.

ANNE SUMMERS

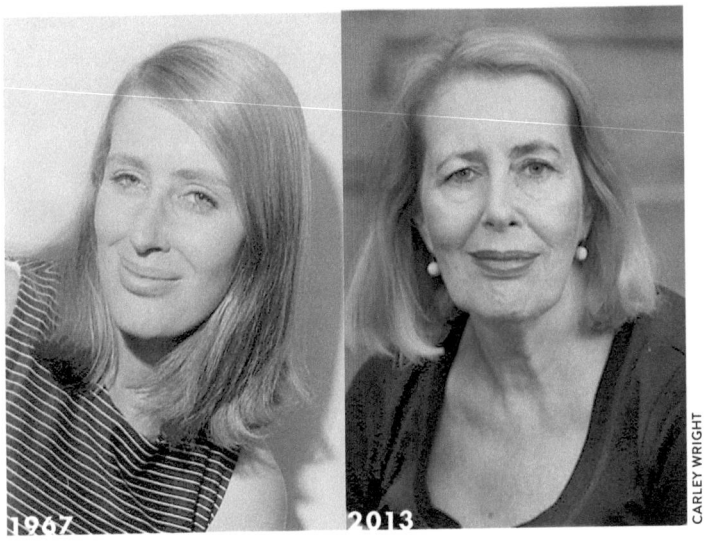

Anne Summers is a bestselling author, journalist and thought-leader with a long career in politics, the media, business and the non-government sector in Australia, Europe and the United States.

She is author of several books, including the classic *Damned Whores and God's Police*, first published in 1975; her autobiography, *Ducks on the Pond*; and *The End of Equality*, *On Luck* and *The Lost Mother*. Her latest book, *The Misogyny Factor*, was published in 2013. She writes on politics and social issues regularly for a number of Australian newspapers, including the *Sydney Morning Herald*, *The Age*, and the *Australian Financial Review*. She is the editor and publisher of the digital magazine *Anne Summers Reports*: <annesummers.com.au/asr>.

She ran the Office of the Status of Women for the Hawke

Government in the early 1980s, and in the early 1990s was an advisor to Prime Minister Paul Keating. In 1987 she became editor-in-chief of *Ms.* magazine in New York, and in 1988, with business partner Sandra Yates, achieved the second only women-led management buyout in US corporate history when they purchased *Ms.* and *Sassy* magazines from Fairfax. After returning to Australia she was editor of *Good Weekend* for five years.

Anne was chair of the board of Greenpeace International for six years from 2000, and a member of the trust of and later deputy president of Sydney's Powerhouse Museum. Apart from the doctorate awarded for her work on *Damned Whores*, she also has two honorary doctorates. In 1989 she was made an Officer of the Order of Australia for her services to journalism and to women.

In 2011 she was honoured along with three other leading feminists by having her image on an Australian stamp.

NUMBER C/57/61: WHAT ASIO KNEW

by Anne Summers

In mid-1969, when I was twenty-four and still a student at the University of Adelaide, I applied to join the Commonwealth public service. My husband, John Summers, had done the same a year earlier. Although we were each just going for entry-level clerical jobs, ASIO was asked to vet us, which, I have to presume, was standard procedure at the time. A report on John, stamped SECRET and dated 9 September 1968, advised, 'very little information is held concerning the vettee [sic] but his wife has come to notice on numerous occasions in connection with Anti-Vietnam activities'. The South Australian Regional Director of ASIO recommended John's favourable assessment the next day. My own clearance was less straightforward.

There was quite some correspondence as the public service and ASIO tried to figure out how much danger to the state I posed. Astonishingly, this application by a young girl in Adelaide to a lowly clerical job attracted the attention of the Melbourne-based Director-General of ASIO. In a letter to the Secretary of the Public Service Board in Canberra dated 14 July

1969 and stamped SECRET, he wrote, 'Mrs Summers has an extensive history of activity in relation to the Vietnam Protest Movement'. While 'this record does not constitute a history of subversive activity …' he continued: 'you may wish to take the information concerning her activities into consideration when deciding her appointment'.

An earlier minute paper dated June 1969 summed up the situation:

> This is one of those cases which could possibly fall into what we have termed 'the grey area' of vetting, i.e. one where the record of the person concerned, though not in itself constituting a history of subversive activity, is sufficiently serious to cast doubt upon the eligibility of the person concerned to impartially serve the interests of the Commonwealth.

In the end, ASIO decided it would not block me from joining the public service, but that it would try to influence what job I was given. In a letter dated 19 August 1969, classified SECRET and copied to the Director-General of ASIO, the Public Service Inspector advised the Public Service Commissioner: 'Clearance has not been withheld (form enclosed) but in view of certain information received, it would be wise to ensure placement in a "safe" department.' I soon found myself working in what was then called the Postmaster-General's Department as a pay clerk. It was a dreary and monotonous job and certainly 'safe'. During my time there the only documents I saw were the time-sheets of the other employees in my section.

After three months, I resigned. This had been my intention all along: to take the public service position as a university vacation job. It was so common for students to do this that if ASIO

ASIO surveillance photo from Anne Summers' file, captioned *Anti Conscription march, Adelaide, 16 April 1966 – 1. Anne COOPER* (Summers). Others in the photo are Peter Duncan, future SA Attorney-General (behind banner); Robyn Layton, future SA Supreme Court Judge (in front of banner); and John Bannon, future SA Premier (on right of police officer).

had been more on the ball, it might have realised and saved the time and effort that was put into vetting me. Had I been intent on a public service career, however, I would probably have never recovered from that initial adverse finding. ASIO's interference would have wrecked my job prospects. What was the 'certain information' that led to this adverse finding? What had I done to merit such a negative judgment? I didn't know then and I still don't know because my ASIO files do not provide this information.

Back in the late 1960s when small groups of us gathered in grungy rooms to plan protest actions, we used to fantasise about being under surveillance. Sometimes we would take semi-serious precautions against 'the pigs' who, we were certain, were watching us. Once we began our street marches, particularly those in support of the National Liberation Front of North Vietnam, (where we would provocatively, and ungrammatically, shout 'Ho Ho Ho Chi Minh, the Viet Cong are going to win'), we used to tell each other confidently that we were being photographed by ASIO. Paranoia was an important component of our radical make-up. And, let's be honest, it made us feel just that little bit more self-important to think our actions were attracting the attention of the state. It was confirmation that our protests were effective, that the authorities were rattled.

As it turns out, we had no idea just how rattled they were.

Now that ASIO's files from those days are available we can retrospectively say that our paranoia was utterly justified. It is clear that we considerably underestimated just how extensively we were being monitored.

I first read my ASIO file in February 2011, on the National Archives of Australia (NAA) website, having earlier paid for the file to be digitised and therefore accessible online. There were 158 pages, starting in 1966 and ending in 1979. The very first item is a letter, stamped SECRET, to the South Australian Commissioner of Police from the Special Branch of the police force advising that 'Contact 349' had provided information about a 'newly formed Committee for Vietnam protest and their intention to conduct a public meeting on the 23rd January, 1966'. The letter also referred to an article, 'Denial of Link with Reds', that had appeared in the *Advertiser* and which quoted me – 'Miss ANNE COOPER' – as stating that the committee was not working under the instruction of any political party. ASIO's principal concern then, and throughout the 1960s and '70s, seemed to be to monitor the extent to which we young anti-

Vietnam radicals (and, later, women's liberation activists) were being influenced by the Communist Party of Australia (CPA).

At first I read the file with a mixture of curiosity and amusement, flicking quickly through the pages, scanning to grasp what was there. The file covered the time of my political awakening as a student at the University of Adelaide in the mid-1960s, prompted mainly by the Vietnam War, through my espousal of radical student politics and women's liberation from 1969, my move to Sydney in 1971 where I engaged mostly in women's politics but also some Resident Action activities and, in addition to studying and writing my first book, began my career as a journalist. As I delved further, though, my mood began to change. I became perplexed at why I was being singled out for so much attention, and then angry when I realised the extent to which ASIO had, for no good reason, significantly interfered with my life.

The information in my file makes it abundantly clear that ASIO *was* there at every planning meeting; ASIO *was* listening in to phone calls; ASIO *was* working closely with the Special Branch of the police, which had its own surveillance capabilities, and ASIO did indeed take photographs of us as we marched along Adelaide streets.

For instance:

— ASIO was present and observing an anti-Vietnam demonstration in Victoria Square, Adelaide on 7 September 1966. Its agent was able to identify approximately eighteen out of the estimated sixty people present. I was one of them. The agent also inserted various comments into his report, noting for instance, after a burning of the US flag: 'The flag was a homemade one and judging by the paint marks on the hands of GILES, it seems probable that he was the person who painted the flag'.

— ASIO was at 34 Le Fevre Terrace, North Adelaide, a sprawling group house occupied mostly by students, on 11 May 1969 at a meeting, attended by just forty people, of the nascent Society for Democratic Action (SDA). ASIO listed the names and Special Branch file numbers of about fifteen of those present, including me, and singled out several others whose names it did not know, including 'Jack from Flinders University' who was described as 'Jewish appearance, black hair and goatee beard', presumably for further investigation. (ASIO would soon discover this was Jack Barbalet, a prominent student and anti-Vietnam War activist.)

— Special Branch was at 130 Rundle Street, Kent Town on 12 March 1970 where fifteen people, representing diverse radical groups and calling themselves 'Moratorium Action', met to plan for a larger meeting later that week that would discuss options for radical actions during the forthcoming moratorium march on 9 May. The report of both meetings was combined in a single document, which found its way to ASIO, and which mentioned, *inter alia*, that at the smaller meeting, 'source claimed there was so much going on that he could not catch all the names mentioned'. He managed to catch mine, however, and the report lists both my Special Branch and ASIO file numbers in the margin next to my name.

— A photograph, taken on 2 August 1969 from the other side of the street, of a motley crowd of anti-conscription protestors walking along the footpath in Adelaide's Victoria Square, with small black numbers hand drawn onto the picture pointing at various individuals. Text reproduced below the photograph in my ASIO file identifies the names of those so numbered.

And many, many more examples.

In March 1971 I left Adelaide and travelled to Sydney. I was leaving behind a marriage and my old life and looking forward to starting a post-graduate degree. I was also going to try to get some work as a journalist. I was both optimistic and apprehensive, as I did not know what the future held. Nor did I know that I was being followed.

According to a one-page document entitled 'Interstate Movements of Persons of Security Interest' dated 12 March 1971, I travelled to Melbourne on 8 March on Ansett Flight 231 and then took Flight 30 to Sydney. The cost of my ticket was $49.50 ('Method of payment not known') and my reason for travel was 'probably for the purpose of study'. There was no return booking. The source of this information was described as an 'Ansett contact'. In the Comments/Remarks section at the bottom of the document were the words: 'Bugle information has revealed SUMMERS's intention to study in Sydney.'

The document cited my file number: SPF.7871. This was a South Australian Police Special Branch file number and was circulated to 'HQ, A.S.I.O. and R/D, N.S.W'. The document noted that the security information of interest was 'Vietnam Protest Movement, Society for Democratic Action, Women's Liberation Movement'.

The 'bugle information' referred to was a telephone intercept. There are numerous copies of reports of my phone conversations in my ASIO file, but this one was *about* me. On 8 March 1971 at 9.23 a.m. – about six hours before I was due to fly off to Sydney – Elizabeth Mary Fisher, who was active in the women's liberation movement (as well being a prominent communist) spoke on the phone to a James Lawrence Moss, and asked if I had 'been in yet'. Jim ran a left-wing bookshop in Adelaide. The message Betty wanted conveyed to me via Jim if I did drop in on my way to the airport was that 'the posting of the contraception pamphlets is all arranged'. I was also to be reminded when I arrived in Sydney 'to ask Mavis (Mavis June Robertson – NSW identity) about the abortion pamphlets'.

Perhaps ASIO thought that 'contraception pamphlets' and 'abortion pamphlets' were code for something subversive. It should have known, since at that point it had been monitoring me for five years, that I was heavily engaged in the newly emerged women's liberation movement and that 'free contraceptives' and 'free abortion on demand' were among our key policy demands. Evidently not, for on 20 April, ASIO's Regional Director in New South Wales wrote to his South Australian counterpart, B Nienaber, asking for information about me. On 28 April, South Australia forwarded my particulars: my full name, including my maiden name of Cooper, and my date of birth. My occupation was given as 'Formerly employed as Clerk in Postmaster-General's Department'. To 'assist further in identification', Nienaber sent two photographs of me to Sydney and, he added, that if it were ascertained that my stay in New South Wales was 'to be of considerable duration', my file would be sent over.

At first ASIO kept tabs on me. On 11 March 1971, just three days after I arrived in Sydney, 'bugle' information revealed that

I had made a phone call from Bob Gould's Third World Bookshop in Goulburn Street to Trevor Kennedy, then editor of the *National Times*. There was no telephone in the flat where I was staying in Glebe and Bob Gould had kindly allowed me to call from his shop. As Gould's phone was tapped this call would have been routinely logged and no doubt alarmed ASIO about the real intent of my move to Sydney.

In 1972 a document in my file had noted that my name was on a list of New South Wales subscribers to the Melbourne-based Marxist journal *Arena*, (along with the solidly conservative Professor Dick Spann who was head of the Department of Government and Public Administration at the University of Sydney). The document had no letterhead but was marked SECRET and NON-GRATIS, meaning the information had been obtained from non-public sources. The document noted that the names and addresses 'are listed in a card index which is normally in the possession of Doug (Douglas Charles) WHITE (VPF 5189)'. Sadly, the Case Officer's notes on how these cards were obtained by ASIO are illegible.

In October the same year, surveillance of the CPA headquarters in Dixon Street had detected me picking up some printed materials. It was letterhead for *Refractory Girl*, a women's studies journal. (The CPA used to allow the women's movement to use its printing facilities at nominal charge.) The agent who wrote this report felt it necessary to comment on my appearance: 'I would describe Anne SUMMERS as about 28 years old, tall and thin,' wrote the spook. 'Has long hair, wears large round metal framed glasses, fashionably but not very well dressed.'

After that ASIO's interest in me was random, to say the least. There are no reports about my women's movement activities. For instance, I am not even mentioned in a lengthy document, classified SECRET, entitled 'Women's Liberation – March Commission of Women' that I found in Wendy Bacon's ASIO files. It is a virtual transcript of the proceedings of a daylong 'speak-out' organised by the women's liberation movement and held at the Teachers' Federation building in Sussex Street on 18 March 1973. I was at that meeting, along with hundreds of other women, but am not among the forty-five who are named. These included Sue Bellamy, Gale Kelly, Pam Stein, Gillian Leahy, Martha Kay, Jill Rowe, Susan Varga, Bessie Guthrie, Sekai Holland and Margaret Greenland as well as CPA members such as Denise Aarons, Mavis Robertson, Aileen Beaver and Joyce Stevens. All these had annotations beside their names and, in some cases, also have agent's comments attached.

ASIO's interest in me did resurface briefly a week later. A newspaper report, which included a photograph, about the short-listed applicants for the job as Prime Minister Whitlam's women's advisor found its way into my ASIO file. The clipping was stuck onto what looked like a standard blank form across the bottom of which had been stamped: 'Please underline names in article requiring copies for personal files'. There were five of us in the photo: Dany Torsh, Eva Cox, Suzanne Baker, me, Elizabeth Reid (who got the job) and Lyndall Ryan. Each of our names was underlined. It seemed that ASIO was going to be sure it kept tabs on whoever advised the Prime Minister on women's affairs.

There is nothing in my file about my involvement in the Resident Action movement or in the illegal squatting in unoccupied houses in Victoria Street, Kings Cross. Neither of my 'resident action' arrests is recorded in my file, although there are press clippings of another, non-political arrest, for 'language' in a street in Balmain in February 1974, and my conviction in

March and subsequent successful appeal in the District Court.

Nor, apart from adding to my file a couple of articles from radical newspapers such as *Nation Review* and *Living Daylights*, did ASIO take much interest in my involvement in Elsie Women's Refuge, which on 16 March 1974 involved the unlawful entry into some vacant houses in Glebe in order to claim squatters' rights.

So why on 22 November 1973, after I had been living in Sydney for two and a half years and doing very little that seemed to be of interest to ASIO, was my file sent over from Adelaide? And not just put in the mail, either. It went by SAFE HAND and had a covering letter marked SECRET. What had I done or, perhaps more to the point, what did ASIO think I was capable of doing to warrant this kind of attention? The answer is not in my file.

I have spent a great deal of time reading various other ASIO files on the NAA website and have been quite taken aback by some of what I have found. To say that all the stereotypes about ASIO in the 1970s were true is an understatement. ASIO was everywhere, observing, reporting, commenting – often in the most personal way. Even at an anarchists 'conference' in Minto, just outside Sydney, in 1971, attended by fewer than forty people. The ASIO agent not only took notes on what was said but made extensive and extremely personal comments about participants, about Paddy McGuinness's drinking, for instance, and his sister's 'illegitimate' child, about the extent of dope-smoking, even about the way Rosemary Pringle walked. ASIO's infiltration of academia and the media is documented, as is its seemingly bizarre pursuit of individuals such as *Age* editor Creighton Burns, University of Sydney economics professor Ted Wheelwright, and Ric Throssell, the son of famous novelist (and CPA member) Katharine Susannah Prichard. Even Gordon Jockel, who was appointed by the Whitlam Government to head the Joint Intelligence Agency, has an ASIO file. Jockel was the subject of surveillance, apparently, because 'subject's mother has Communist views' and because Jockel had been involved in a communist club at university during the 1940s.

ASIO's interest in individuals, including me, was exceeded only by its inability to get – or to get right – personal details. It took ASIO a long time to figure out who my parents were because it could not locate a birth certificate for me (I was born in New South Wales). When ASIO finally worked it out, it did not make the connection that my father actually did part-time surveillance work for them (described in my autobiography). In 1967 ASIO in Adelaide was noting that I had got married in April and was forwarding copies of the marriage certificate to Canberra and to Special Branch but a few years later was perplexed at my move to Sydney and whether or not it involved separating from my husband.

The massive number of ASIO files now available for public scrutiny tell us a great deal but what is still secret are the identities of those who worked for them. Graeme Dunstan, a student activist during the 1960s and organiser of the 1973 Aquarius Festival in Nimbin, recently disclosed he had been recruited by ASIO in 1964 to write reports on student activities at the University of Melbourne. Let's hope others come forward to tell their stories. We might be surprised at who some of them are.

I was amazed to read that ASIO flirted with idea of approaching *me*. The original hand-written request by ASIO for John Summers's security clearance in 1968 had stated:

For assessment, please. (The 'Q' reference need not be mentioned. Apparently Anne COOPER was being considered by 'Q', but no approach was made.)

I was oblivious to these considerations. (As David McKnight points out earlier in this book, 'Q' branch was the Operations branch later to be known as the Special Services Section.)

In late 1975 I joined the *National Times* newspaper as a journalist and ASIO's interest in me appeared to end. Indeed, after the delivery of my file to the Sydney office in November 1973, nothing more was included, beyond a couple of 1974 newspaper reports related to my green ban activities.

It is not until 1978 that further material is added and that involved surveillance of my work as a journalist. 'Unprocessed bugle of 20.1.78 indicates that Ann (probably Ann Fairhurst) Summers (NSW S/42/65) is compiling a story on special branchs [sic] in all states,' reports a telex. The next document is a two-page intercept report, non-gratis and classified Secret, of my telephone interview with Joe Palmada, Joint National Secretary of the CPA, where I questioned him as to whether the CPA had been targeted by Special Branch. These two documents are interesting for a number of reasons. Not only was my name spelt wrongly – Ann, instead of Anne – and ASIO was evidently unaware that I had been working as a journalist for more than two years, but the telex provides the first evidence that I also had a NSW Special Branch file.

ASIO's interest in me during my years as a journalist, first at the *National Times* and, after 1979, at the *Australian Financial Review* where I was Canberra Bureau Chief until late 1983, was mostly confined to noting instances where I was writing articles about security matters. Once, in 1981, a note appeared in my file of a report of an intercepted telephone conversation in which a member of the Socialist Party of Australia referred in passing to an article I had written in that day's *Financial Review*. It is noteworthy that ASIO did not differentiate in its record-keeping between reports of supposed subversive behaviour, such as that which makes up the bulk of the earlier part of my file, and my work as a journalist.

I am also surprised that there is so little commentary in this part of my file. In earlier and subsequent material officers did not hesitate to pass judgment on my activities, my alleged opinions, even – as we have seen – my appearance. But during this time there is no comment. What is especially surprising about this is the fact I had reported in the *Australian Financial Review* on 5 October 1979 that, on a trip back from South Africa where I had interviewed a number of opponents of the apartheid regime, my luggage, containing notebooks of my interviews, had gone missing. I included in my article an account of a phone call I received at my home in Canberra from a person claiming to work for ASIO who told me: 'ASIO has stolen your South African files'. No one except a few colleagues at work knew that my luggage had gone missing so this call was most intriguing. As was the fact that two weeks later the luggage resurfaced in circumstances that were totally perplexing to the airline and which could not be accounted for by the usual ways in which luggage went astray in those days. The contents appeared to have been messed with, but it would not have been possible to prove. As I commented in the article, if indeed ASIO had 'borrowed' my luggage and looked at my notebooks, why had it done so? ASIO is a domestic intelligence organisation and had no brief to monitor the activities of dissidents in other countries. So, I concluded, if ASIO had done this, it must have been to help out the notorious Bureau of State Security (BOSS), the South African domestic agency. In 1973 the newly elected Whitlam Government had ordered ASIO to sever all links with BOSS but, as I wrote in my article, there was scepticism within the government as to whether this order had been obeyed. If ASIO had taken my luggage, it would seem to indicate that it had not.

There are two copies of this newspaper article in my ASIO file but no minute or report or other internal document commenting on the truth or otherwise of my allegations. Back in 1968, when I was a student at the University of Adelaide and also president of the ALP Club on campus, I had claimed in the media that my mail was being interfered with and I said that ASIO was probably to blame. A colleague of mine also told the media that ASIO was attempting to recruit on campus. 'None of the allegations which refer to the University of Adelaide have any truth in them,' stated a letter, dated 6 August 1968 from the Regional Director in South Australia to the Deputy Director (Ops) at ASIO Headquarters. It is interesting that a far more serious allegation eleven years later did not warrant any similar internal discussion.

Yet it seems to have been policy to retain on file every document that mentions a person who had an ASIO file regardless of its relevance or even its accuracy. For instance, the documents released to me include an excerpt from a 1980 handwritten letter seemingly from a member of the public to Justice Edward Woodward, then Director-General of ASIO, that purports to provide information about KGB terrorist activities in Australia. Just one page of this letter is in my file. It describes a 'Dr Anne Cooper (very dangerous), psychiatrist, hypnotist, KGB terrorist'. Someone, presumably from ASIO, with the initials JR has added my ASIO number beside this name, and the date 31.7.80. You would think that after all these years ASIO would have known that I was neither a psychiatrist nor a hypnotist and it ought to have been able to assess that I had nothing to do with the KGB. ASIO should also have known that by the time I got my PhD my last name was Summers. I was not Dr Anne Cooper and never had been. By 1980 ASIO had been keeping tabs on me for fourteen years yet appeared to have learned very little about me.

My experience with ASIO came full circle in late 1983 when I rejoined the Commonwealth public service. This time I was being hired at a very senior level: I had been appointed by the Hawke Government to be head of the Office of the Status of Women (OSW). The Office was located in the department of the Prime Minister and Cabinet (PM&C) and I required a high-level security clearance. As in 1969, the process was far from straightforward – and, again like 1969, all of it is recorded in my file. There is, for instance, a minute recording a telephone conversation on 4 November between Sir Geoffrey Yeend, the Secretary of PM&C, and the DG of ASIO. The minute stated that Sir Geoffrey had said I was about to be appointed to head 'the Women's Affairs Bureau' (there has never been any such organisation) and that it 'would be desirable' for the appointment to take place quickly. Sir Geoffrey is recorded as saying 'he would be grateful for any priority which could be given to the security process'.

Things moved speedily over the next few days, with memos bouncing back and forth between various ASIO offices. The appointment 'will require her to have access to national security information classified top secret', said one telex, dated 8 November. 'Subject is recorded by ASIO as an activist in the women's liberation movement since the 1970s and prior to that was involved in the Committee for Vietnam protest,' the same memo noted.

> While this information has no relevance in the security assessment context, and as such Summers should not be questioned in detail about her activities, she would probably expect us to be aware of them.

The next day, a reworked version of this same memo was sent to the Regional Director of ASIO in Sydney. Infuriatingly, both memos have three lines blacked out. The censored passage comes between the section that lists my previous employment and that which details the organisations of which I had been a member. I had provided all this information on the security questionnaire that I had had to complete as the first stage of the clearance process. It appears that ASIO has blacked out information that I actually gave to it. Why? This second memo also repeated that 'Summers has expressed opinions in several newspaper articles which could be described as anti-ASIO, and as a result the interview may require careful handling'.

On November 9, I went to the eighteenth floor of the building in Chifley Square in Sydney that used to house government agencies. It was only three o'clock in the afternoon but the place had a gloomy air to it as I walked down a long dimly lit corridor, passing empty offices. Waiting for me at the very end was a senior ASIO officer who, I now realise, was most likely the NSW Regional Director. He seemed to be the only person there. My vetting was to be a one-on-one affair. I wish I could remember the conversation but it must have gone smoothly because the next day a hand written ASIO minute/file note addressed to C1B2 said simply 'Please issue a favourable assessment'. It was unsigned. The same day the Director-General formally notified PM&C that I had been cleared.

Five days before my ASIO interview I had attended a reception at the Soviet Embassy in Canberra which, according to an ASIO minute dated 11 November 1983 and headed 'LS Koshlyakov', was 'to celebrate the anniversary of the Great October Socialist Revolution'. The minute reports:

> KOSHLYAKOV was observed to have a lengthy and animated discussion with Dr Anne SUMMERS (formerly of the *Australian Financial Review*).

I have no memory of this function and cannot see why I would have attended as by then I was no longer a journalist. But it was not surprising that ASIO was alert to my interchange with Koshlyakov, who was known to be KGB. He served as press attaché in Canberra from 1974 to 1984. In 1991 he was expelled from Norway for 'undiplomatic activities'. What we discussed in Canberra that night in 1983 is anyone's guess and as far as I recall, that reception was the extent of my dealings with Koshlyakov.

I can't really blame ASIO for monitoring this reception. This was, after all, only a few months since the notorious Combe–Ivanov affair had become public. Combe was an old colleague and friend of mine from Adelaide. After ASIO informed Prime Minister Bob Hawke of Combe's dealings with KGB operative Valery Ivanov, federal Cabinet blacklisted Combe, effectively ending his lobbying business. In June, the Hope Royal Commission into Australia's security agencies was asked by Hawke to report on Combe's relationship with Ivanov and on the government's handling of the whole affair.

Just a few weeks after my chat with Koshlyakov, on 6 December, the Hope Royal Commission's report exonerated the Hawke Government, but found that Combe's dealings with Ivanov had 'serious implications for national security'. By then I was already in my new job in the Prime Minister's department. I was relieved that my long friendship with David Combe had not been judged by ASIO to be an impediment to my getting a clearance.

So much of the contents of my file is puzzling, both what is there and what is not. It is difficult to detect a rationale for a lot of what ASIO deemed to be important but it is very easy to conclude that a huge amount of effort and public money went into keeping tabs on people who were just trying to exercise their democratic rights to express opinions.

GARY FOLEY

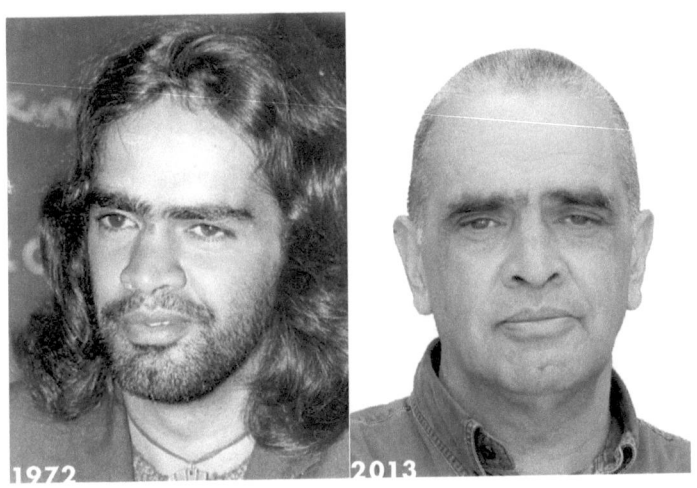

1972 2013

Dr Gary Foley was born in 1950 in Grafton, New South Wales, of Gumbaynggirr descent. He spent most of his youth in Nambucca Heads. Expelled from school at the age of fifteen, Gary went to Sydney as a seventeen-year-old apprentice draughtsperson. Since then he has been at the centre of major political activities including the 1971 Springbok tour demonstrations, the Tent Embassy in Canberra in 1972, the Brisbane Commonwealth Games protest in 1982, and the protests during the 1988 bicentennial celebrations.

Gary was involved in the formation of the Aboriginal Legal Service in Redfern and the Aboriginal Health Service in Melbourne. In 1974 he was part of an Aboriginal delegation that toured China and in 1978 he was part of a group that took films about black Australia to the Cannes Film Festival and then to Germany and other European countries. He returned to England and Europe a year later and set up the first Aboriginal Information Centre in London.

Gary has been a director of the Aboriginal Health Service, and in 1983 became the first Aboriginal Director of the Aboriginal Arts Board of the Australia Council. He was later a consultant to the Royal Commission into Black Deaths in Custody and a board member of the Aboriginal Legal Service. He has also served on the national executive of the National Coalition of Aboriginal Organisations.

His acting career began in 1972 with the revue *Basically Black*. Since then he has appeared in the films *Backroads*, *Going Down*, *Buckeye & Pinto*, *Pandemonium* and *Dogs in Space*, and in the television series *Flying Doctors* and *A Country Practice*.

Gary became a mature-age student at the University of Melbourne and was awarded a BA with first class honours in history in 2002. He was also the Senior Curator for Southeastern Australia at Museum Victoria. Since 2008 he has been a senior lecturer in history at Victoria University and in 2013 he was awarded his doctorate in history from the University of Melbourne.

ASIO, THE ABORIGINAL MOVEMENT AND ME

by Gary Foley

I seem to have first come to the notice of ASIO in March 1970, but I did not realise this until more than three decades later when my ASIO file became available under the thirty-year rule. Thus I first became aware my file was available when in 2002 a French history student from the University of Lyon advised me that he had come across it while doing research with me.

For the ten years since then I have at different times been bemused, excited, angry and appalled by the annual additions to my file that I read each 1 January when they are released by the National Archives. Unlike some whose ASIO files are bulky for a year or two during their days of student activism and then fizzle out as they get older, mine seems to keep growing. So far I have been entertained by the fear and paranoia generated for ASIO in the 1970s by me and my friends in the Black Power movement and I am at present reading about my antics against Malcolm Fraser in the demonstrations at the 1982 Commonwealth Games. At times all this makes for jolly reading and at other times induces both sadness and anger as one figures out who those were who dobbed us in or asked for ASIO investigations into us.

There is not just my file. My name appears in the files of many other individuals, organisations and events. For example, ASIO maintained a voluminous file on the Aboriginal Embassy and kept files on numerous Aboriginal organisations. So keeping up with ASIO's monitoring of my friends and me has become a serious field of study for me. In fact, significant parts of this chapter were originally part of my doctoral thesis on the Black Power movement and the Aboriginal Embassy.

So this chapter looks not only at ASIO's surveillance of me personally, but also the broader context of ASIO's interest in, and surveillance of, the Aboriginal political movement generally. This will provide a better understanding of ASIO's specific obsessive preoccupation with possible communist infiltration or manipulation of the Aboriginal rights movement from 1951 till the end of the Cold War.

ASIO AND THE ABORIGINAL RIGHTS MOVEMENT

In a letter written by Sir Charles Spry in 1962 to the Minister for Territories, Paul Hasluck, the ASIO chief spelt out his organisation's concerns about 'communist penetration' of Aboriginal groups. The letter pointed out to Hasluck that ASIO regarded communist activity among Aboriginal peoples as being directly related to the 1928 World Congress of the Comintern, which had detailed the 'fundamental tasks of the proletarian dictatorship'. These 'tasks' included:

> The recognition and right of all nations irrespective of race to complete self-determination, that is self-determination inclusive of the right to state separation.

And:

> Every assistance ... of the formerly oppressed territories, dominions and colonies, with the object of transferring them to socialist lines, so that a durable basis may be laid for complete national equality.

Spry pointed out that an edition of the CPA newspaper in 1931 had contained an article titled 'Communist Party of Australia Fight for Aborigines: Draft Programme of Struggle Against Slavery'. The article set forth fourteen demands and Spry's letter quoted Demand 14 in full:

> The handing over to the Aborigines of large tracts of watered and fertile country, with towns, seaports, railways, roads, etc., to become one or more independent aboriginal states or republics. The handing back to the aborigines all central, northern and north-west Australia to enable the aborigines to develop their native pursuits. These aboriginal republics to be independent of Australia or other foreign powers. To have the rights to make treaties with foreign powers, including Australia, establish their own army, Governments, industries and in every way be independent of imperialism.

Reading this one can imagine the fear Australian governments had that *their* Aborigines might be exposed to such subversive notions as these. Nevertheless, Spry continues by asserting that when the Communist Party in the Soviet Union had, at its 22nd Congress in 1961, declared its support for 'all peoples who are fighting for the complete abolition of the colonial system', the Australian communists had begun referring to Aborigines as a 'national minority' and had begun attacking the Australian Government's policy of assimilation.

Spry, in his capacity as Director-General of ASIO, had thereby concluded that the 'CPA now regards the aborigines and their problems as an issue to be developed and used by the Party for political purposes, for the furtherance of its own programme for political power in Australia'.

Here then was the prism through which Australian governments and their security agencies viewed Aboriginal dissent from the 1950s until very recently. All Aboriginal protest was interpreted in the context of the international struggle against communism, which as it happened was a convenient way to ignore the legitimate claims of the Aboriginal peoples themselves.

Aboriginal activists came under notice of ASIO as a result of the organisation's preoccupation with the perceived communist threat in the early 1950s. Melbourne activist Bill Onus, along with New South Wales based Ray Peckham and Faith Bandler, were the first black political activists to gain the dubious distinction of having ASIO files opened on them. In the case of Onus, who had married an avowed Scottish communist, it was a negative report against him by ASIO that led to the US Government refusing him a visa to visit the US in 1952. Onus had been invited to America by no less than Walt Disney himself, but even that was insufficient to surmount the obstacle of an ASIO assessment that alleged Onus was a 'fellow-traveller' of communists.

Ray Peckham and Faith Bandler came to the attention of ASIO when both attended a 'Berlin Youth Festival' in the then communist East Germany in 1951. Peckham went on to become a trade unionist and one of the few Aboriginal activists ever to become a member of the Communist Party of Australia (CPA). Consequently his is one of the largest files so far assembled by ASIO on Aboriginal activists. In an ASIO letter in 1965, from no less an official than Director-General Charles Spry, Peckham is said to have 'first come to notice' when he represented the Aboriginal Rights Council at the Berlin Youth Festival; at the time he was an employee of the Communist Party of Australia. According to Spry, ASIO's interest in Peckham stemmed from his having undertaken 'political training' in Moscow at the Institute of Social Sciences, which ASIO regarded as 'a political training school' for 'overseas Communist party members'.

Faith Bandler, who in the 1960s became one of Australia's most famous agitators for Aboriginal rights during the campaign for the 1967 referendum, was also accused by ASIO of being a CPA member. Even if Bandler was a party member for a short period in the 1950s, the more important question should be why ASIO was so concerned about communist influence on the Aboriginal resistance.

During the 1950s the Australian Government was distributing material through its overseas embassies that painted a carefully contrived but false image of its policies on Aboriginal people. This propaganda portrayed Australia as a racially harmonious society where Aboriginal people were being gently 'assimilated' into the broader Australian community.

This was during a period in history when the world was still coming to terms with the genocidal policies of Nazi Germany just a decade or so earlier. Furthermore, it was an era when many former colonial powers were divesting (and being divested of) their former colonies.

These factors no doubt were part of the Australian Government's determination that no news of Aboriginal political activity should be allowed to disrupt their carefully controlled international campaign. As well, in the context of those times, the great fear that communist agitation *might make the natives restless*, was the apparent explanation of ASIO's interest in Aboriginal activists who had any form of communist associations.

There is little evidence that the Australian Government was aware of the inherent contradictions in their reasoning. If the Aboriginal people were perfectly happy to comply with the imposed process of assimilation as the government propaganda suggested, then how could they be susceptible to external communist agitation? Nevertheless, ASIO's interest in possible communist influences in the domestic Aboriginal political movements continued for at least the next thirty years.

But despite the intensification of ASIO's interest during the 1950s and 1960s, especially with the advent of the first national Aboriginal political organisation, the Federal Council for Aboriginal Affairs, the security agency found remarkably little hard evidence of communist infiltration, manipulation or influence in the local Aboriginal networks. This did not prevent frequent allegations and assertions by some connected with the intelligence community that eminent Aboriginal leaders such as Pastor Doug Nicholls, poet Kath Walker and Charles Perkins were either communist-influenced or communist dupes.

In 1958 an ASIO report titled 'Communist Party of Australia Interest in the Federal Council for Aboriginal Advancement', the security agency effectively declared the Council a communist front organisation before it had even become operational. The report's opening paragraph reads:

It is expected that the formation of a Federal Council for Aboriginal Advancement at a conference in Adelaide ... will provide the Communist Party of Australia with a further important target for penetration and control.

This report concludes by asserting that the early part of the campaign that led to the 1967 referendum was communist inspired and directed, as were protests against mining on Aboriginal land and the call for Aboriginal people to be eligible for child welfare payments and the old age pension.

Today these ideas seem bizarre, especially given that most of the founders of FCAA were conservative Christians such as Presbyterian Church Moderator Dr Charles Duguid and Pastor Doug Nicholls. But ASIO had actually regarded Nicholls as a suspected dupe of communists anyway, such was the strange world that they lived in. ASIO was so preoccupied with its obsessive quest to uncover imagined communist subversion that they clearly denied any ability of Aboriginal people to think for themselves. This was a recurring theme with almost all Australian government agencies throughout the 1950s and 1960s.

The Aboriginal Embassy protest action first came under the notice of Australia's security agencies within hours of it being established on the lawns of Parliament House in the darkness of 26 January 1972. At eight minutes past six on the morning of 27 January, ASIO headquarters received a telex message from its Canberra office advising that the protest had been set up and seeking urgent information on the four young black men present on the lawns.

Although Aboriginal organisations, especially the Redfern Black Power group, had triggered ASIO and NSW Special Branch attention earlier, after the setting up of the Tent

ASIO surveillance photo from Gary Foley's file, captioned *Gary Foley outside CPA HQ Sydney 4/11/71.*

Embassy, surveillance increased. One of those investigations was triggered in June 1972 when a report appeared in a Sydney newspaper claiming that the organising committee for the forthcoming 14 July Black Moratorium demonstration (dominated by the Redfern Black Power group) had invited famous American Black Power activist Angela Davis to visit Australia.

In Melbourne *The Age* newspaper had reported that not only had Angela Davis been invited, but also two of the founders of the US Black Panther Party, Huey P Newton and Bobby Seale. This was not the first time that Australian government officials and security agencies had been confronted with this sort of situation. On two separate occasions the previous year similar scenarios had created concern in government circles.

The first occasion had been on 24 March 1971 when the Brisbane *Courier-Mail* reported that a 'group of fifteen men and women', described as 'Black Power workers', were due to arrive in Queensland to visit Aboriginal communities for the purpose of 'fact-finding' and 'explaining how black militancy works'. This report prompted an outraged letter from Neville Bonner to Prime Minister McMahon, who in turn asked his department to advise him what his response might be. The department firstly sent an urgent 'confidential' communiqué on 30 April to the Australian Embassy in Washington to find out if any radical black Americans had applied for Australian visas, and if any had, their applications should be 'withheld pending clearance' from Canberra.

At the same time the Department of Prime Minister and Cabinet sought advice from the recently formed federal government agency, the Council for Aboriginal Affairs (CAA). The CAA Secretary, Barrie Dexter, responded with a letter outlining his understanding of the newly emerging Black Power movement in which he speculated that if a visit was impending, then it must have something to do with Aboriginal activist Bruce McGuinness, whom he described as 'an extremist'. Dexter concluded that whilst it was 'difficult to gauge the degree of support ... among Aboriginals' for Black Power, in his opinion the concept 'had not yet impinged to any great extent on the great bulk of Aborigines'.

Ultimately someone in the Australian Government must have discovered the innocuous nature of the visitors, because Prime Minister McMahon was able to write to Neville Bonner reassuring him that in fact this was a group of Christian workers.

The group would consist of 'an American group of multi-racial Christian youth' and the trip was being arranged jointly by the Australian Council of Churches and the United Presbyterian Church of the USA. The group was coming to Australia to discuss race relations with 'young Australians in a Christian perspective'.

They were hardly a bunch of terrorists, but the uninformed reaction to word of their visit illustrates the occasionally irrational response of Australians to non-white people who might in some way be 'political'. Not unlike certain aspects of Australia today.

Another significant investigation at that time had been requested by the Council for Aboriginal Affairs. Today Mr Dexter presents a more benign image of the CAA in his memoirs, but it is apparent from correspondence in 1972 between Dexter and the Regional Director of ASIO in Canberra that the CAA was very concerned about alleged connections between the Communist Party and the Redfern Black Power group.

On 3 November 1972, some six months after the removal of the Aboriginal Embassy from the lawns of Parliament House, Dexter, as Director of the Office of Aboriginal Affairs, wrote an extraordinary letter to Colin Brown, the Regional Director of ASIO in Canberra. The fact that Dexter addresses Brown as 'Colin' indicates a level of familiarity that is unusual in ASIO correspondence files. Given Dexter's previous career as a diplomat and Australian ambassador, one can believe that he was very comfortable in his relations with members of the security and intelligence fraternity.

In the letter, Mr Dexter states that the 'core' of the former Tent Embassy had continued to operate as an 'informal grouping' functioning under the name of the 'Black Caucus'. Dexter advised that the Black Caucus 'seem to be the most cohesive grouping of urbanised Aborigines' and said that members included Bobbi Sykes, Paul Coe, myself, Gary Williams and Billy Craigie of Sydney. Associates of the group included Denis Walker and Len Watson of Brisbane and Pat Eatock of Canberra.

Dexter then got to the point by saying that he had 'recently heard' that the Black Caucus might be 'under the domination' of the BWIU, by which he presumably meant the NSW Builders Labourers' Federation, then under the leadership of Jack Mundey, Bob Pringle and Joe Owens. Mr Dexter pointed out he had 'no evidence of this' but nevertheless:

> I wonder if your people have any information on this. I would not ask them to undertake investigations to prove or disprove it if they do not have the information readily at hand.

This is an unusual request in that Dexter does not seem to be seeking a formal investigation but is rather informally asking an apparently close friend to check on a rumour. But because Dexter makes no real mention in his memoirs of his relationship with certain officers of ASIO, we can only speculate as to the nature of any such associations. What is clear, however, is that the three men who comprised the Council of Aboriginal Affairs remained cautious about their dealings with members of the Black Power collectives, and were much more comfortable dealing with those they considered to be the 'real Aborigines' in the Northern Territory. The ASIO files merely confirm that this was the case.

Examining the ASIO files released since 1998, it is very apparent that the key people in the Aboriginal movement who were regarded as most dangerous by police and security agencies were Paul Coe, Denis Walker and myself. My own file is largely uninteresting because it consists mostly of newspaper clippings, idle gossip, and inane conversations recorded on other people's telephones. The surveillance photographs are furtive but flattering if one appreciates daggy fashion. Several of those photographs are of me entering and leaving a doorway, and as I tell my students, anyone can be made to look suspicious if you photograph them with a telephoto lens as they enter or leave a doorway. But to the mind of a surveillance-oriented person they would have been very exciting.

But ASIO got it very wrong if they thought these photographs of me were evidence of a Black Power–communist plot. These photographs were taken of me entering and leaving the Dixon Street HQ of the CPA in Sydney in late 1971. One of the photographs shows me carrying what ASIO probably considered 'subversive' material, but the truth was much more mundane.

What was actually happening was that I had asked Noel Hazard, photographer with the CPA newspaper *Tribune*, to teach me how to develop photographs and he had kindly assented and told me to come into the *Tribune* office where he had a darkroom. Thus, rather than attending the CPA headquarters for my political instructions (which is what ASIO assumed) I was simply learning a handy new skill from Noel Hazard, who was a close friend of many Aboriginal activists at the time. Indeed, it was Noel Hazard who drove the four Aboriginal men to Canberra on the night of 26 January 1972 when they established the legendary Aboriginal Embassy.

Therein resides the basic mistake that ASIO made in their interpretation of the Black Power movement and our relationship with other external political activists, especially those associated with the CPA. While ASIO chose to interpret our association as evidence of CPA manipulation of the Black movement, they failed to realise that most of the close association was due to pure and simple friendship. As we Redfern activists developed political links with external groups we came to know and respect many of these white activists who then became our close friends. We admired the leaders of the NSW Builders Labourers' Federation and became good friends with Bob Pringle and Joe Owens in particular. We did not judge our white friends on whether they were communists or not, but rather on the quality of their personal character. Thus there was never any question of them (communist or otherwise) trying to influence or manipulate us because our relationships were based on mutual respect. This was a difficult notion for ASIO agents to grasp because like most of Australia they had come to believe the tabloid inspired idea that because we were Black Power we were therefore black racists who hated white people and therefore could never form friendships with white people. The lunacy of their logic was that, despite thinking we were black racists, they still believed that we were taking orders from white communists.

Another contradiction I noticed when perusing my ASIO file was the level of incompetence and amateurism on the one hand, yet on the other the sheer beauty at times in the recording and revelation of details. I now know the names of all the people who attended hundreds of meetings I was at from 1970 through till 1973, and I know in detail what was on the agenda at all those meetings, happily, thanks to a dedicated band of stenographer/agents who dutifully recorded all this information and made sure it was there for me to discover some thirty years later.

Now having said that ASIO was basically incompetent, I will provide an example of an occasion they got it right.

In 1972 in the lead up to the Black Moratorium demonstration to be held in July, ASIO had maintained its covert surveillance of the embassy tents and certain people associated with the protest. The main concern of government appeared to be monitoring evidence of communist involvement and/or manipulation, and trying to contain or counter negative media coverage internationally. These seem to be among the primary concerns expressed in a secret ASIO report on the embassy dated 22 June.

The report summarised the protest to date, noting that the tents had been of particular embarrassment during February when they had been in sight of two visiting dignitaries, President Suharto of Indonesia and US Chief of Armed Forces General William Westmoreland. It also noted that both Soviet and Chinese communist media were reporting on the embassy in Moscow and Peking, and that Russian diplomats from the Russian Embassy in Canberra had visited the Tent Embassy. But in its conclusion the ASIO report not only clears the embassy protest of communist manipulation, but also makes a reasonably accurate summary of the protest so far, and is worth quoting in full:

> The initiative and basic support for the 'Embassy' appears to have arisen from the efforts of young New South Wales Aborigines. Although it is apparent that they have had support from other Aboriginal groups and white organisations, some of security interest, the 'Embassy' would appear to be fundamentally an Aboriginal-directed protest measure which aims to obtain publicity and recognition for the *alleged* [my italics] injustices Aborigines are subjected to under existing conditions especially in the Land Rights issue.

Thus despite the bad grammar and minor qualifications, the ASIO report essentially acknowledges that this was an entirely Aboriginal conceived, controlled and directed political action, free of any external manipulation from communists or anyone else. This would not be the first or last time that ASIO reports would try to spell out to government officials that the Black Power and land rights movements were genuine Aboriginal community-grown and sustained political movements.

My own file reveals the remarkable amount of political activity that my friends and I in the Redfern Black Caucus were engaged in, despite our growing commitment to running the community organisations that we were establishing throughout this period. The files show that we Aboriginal activists were involved in political activities across a diverse range of issues from anti-Vietnam War demonstrations, through to a key role in the anti-apartheid movement and speaking out in the campaign against foreign (US) bases in Australia. All this was in addition to the major land rights rallies we organised nationally and which rattled the McMahon Government. Later in the 1980s the files reveal the paranoia of security agencies regarding the activities of myself and Bruce McGuinness when we managed to breach the tight security surrounding the 1981 CHOGM in Melbourne, as well as close monitoring of me and Queensland activist Denis Walker during the 1982 Commonwealth Games demonstrations in Brisbane.

And that is not even taking into account the time spent partying and drinking for which the Black Power activists were also quietly renowned. It seems most of our most outrageous acts of minor vandalism (throwing black paint over statues of Captain Cook) and campaigns of terror (nocturnally spraying land rights graffiti in public places) went almost entirely unnoticed by ASIO. Yet our appearance at anti-war or anti-apartheid rallies would generate a flurry of paperwork as agents telexed in their reports (note for young people: different sort of text messages in those days). Versions of these reports would be sent to regional and national offices of ASIO and copies would be placed in the files of the people named. Thus providing me with interesting information about the wide range of activities in which we in the Black Caucus were involved.

Despite the fact that my file contains many pages where names of agents and informers have been blacked out, it is often not too difficult to figure out who some of the informants were. Some were a surprise, like a former father-in-law, and others were not unexpected. A few who dobbed us in were acting out of malice, and often they were reporting out of concern for our welfare. So there is no point in bearing any grudges, not least because most of those who dobbed are now dead. If I was a religious person I would probably think that was divine retribution.

I want to conclude by examining two of the more ridiculous aspects of surveillance by Australian security agencies. The first involves the nature of the files that are ultimately released to public scrutiny after thirty years has elapsed. In all of the files I have examined, including my own, it is obvious there are large gaps in the information contained within them. In some instances this is because all files released to the National Archives of Australia (NAA) have a list of 'exemptions' included at the beginning. In the first volume of my ASIO file is a notice saying that under Section 33 (1) (a) of the *Archives Act 1983* certain documents have been withheld on the grounds that they contain 'information or matters the disclosure of which could reasonably be expected to cause damage to the security, defence or international relations of the Commonwealth'.

Now while I find it strangely flattering to think that some minor political escapade of mine committed forty years ago might still be considered a potential danger to the Commonwealth of Australia, I nevertheless am perplexed by the possibility. This further attests to the bizarre nature of security organisations that seem to be capable of sensing dangers that sometimes don't exist. Another aspect of the files provided to the archives is that many have large areas blacked out, presumably to hide the identity of agents and informers. The fact that most of these former agents and informers are probably long dead does not seem to deter the censors with the black pen. But sometimes they take that to an even more ridiculous level, such as a document that appears in my file with almost the entire page blacked out apart from the heading 'Communist Party of Australia' and eleven words saying I was due to arrive in Brisbane. It prompts one to ask, 'Why bother to include it in the file if it is all blacked out?'

Another aspect that both amused and irritated me was that I noticed in my file (as well as in the files of most of my Aboriginal associates) that ASIO had great difficulty in obtaining first-hand information about our little Black Power collective in Redfern. Indeed, in one report where ASIO was asked to investigate possible communist infiltration of our group, their final report stated that the 'Redfern Black Caucus' had such tight security measures that not even ASIO could penetrate it, let alone any communists. On the other hand, it irked me to discover thirty years later that most of the information gained by ASIO about me was gathered in surveillance and phone taps of loose-lipped white political associates of ours who seemed too frequently to shoot their mouths off. This makes some of the transcripts of telephone taps on some of the myriad white Trotskyist groups of that era very interesting reading indeed. Among other things it reveals how amateurish some groups were when it came to security at a time when it was blatantly obvious that they could expect to be under ASIO surveillance.

The final tale probably sums up my low opinion of the perspicacity of the agents who were assigned to shadow us. Reading through my ASIO file I came across a page that was a report of a telephone 'intercept' (wiretap) that said that a certain woman from Brisbane had called a number in Sydney looking for me. The following page was a report that this woman had now spoken to me and that I had told her I was coming to Brisbane and then going to Gympie. According to the report I had asked this woman if she was interested in coming to Gympie. The details contained in the report make it clear it was a full transcript of a taped intercept, and the woman and I ended up agreeing to meet in Brisbane and then go to Gympie for three days.

Unbeknown to me, this woman in Brisbane was a member of the Communist Party and someone in ASIO decided that this was an interesting possible political connection between the CPA and the Black Power movement. Over the next week there were a series of telexes and reports advising of the details of my flight arrangements and speculation on the purpose of my trip. Then there is a report advising of my impending arrival and the fact that I would be met by the woman in question. That report states that if this woman and I have enough money we will leave for Gympie immediately, and then enigmatically it says, 'Reason for the Gympie trip is not known at this stage.' The final communiqué reports my departure from Brisbane after leaving the house of Denis Walker, a 'known residence of a number of coloured militants'.

When I had first read this series of documents in my ASIO file I was quite perplexed. I remembered this woman and I remembered the nature and purpose of our trip to Gympie, and it was certainly had nothing to do with politics as ASIO had imagined. This had been a romantic liaison and nothing else, yet ASIO agents had convinced themselves of some ulterior political motive. This illustrated to me yet again the incompetence and apparent stupidity of people who are tapping phones and actually hearing the conversation but are still incapable of realising that the conversation is about sex, not politics.

Mercifully, in those days we were probably more of a danger to ourselves than in any real danger from ASIO.

DAVID STRATTON

Born in England, David emigrated to Australia as a 'ten pound pom' in 1963, intending to stay only two years. However, always passionate about the cinema, he became the director of the Sydney Film Festival and for the next seventeen years travelled the world to bring the best international films to Australian audiences.

David's best-known role has been as the co-host, with Margaret Pomeranz, of *The Movie Show* on SBS and, more recently, *At the Movies* on ABC1. Since 1986 the duo has entertained Australia with their honest and often controversial reviews and interviews. David was the film consultant to SBS from its inception, and then presenter of both the *Movie of the Week* and *Cinema Classics* for over twenty-two years. He is a former film critic for the international film industry magazine *Variety*, and is currently film critic for *The Australian*.

David is a recipient of the Australian Film Institute's Raymond Longford Award, and has also served as President of the International Critics Jury for the Cannes and Venice film festivals. He has authored two books, including his intriguingly titled memoir, *I Peed on Fellini*, and is currently lecturing in film history as part of the continuing education program at the University of Sydney. He is also a past president of the Film Critics Circle of Australia.

David's long list of awards include: the 60th Anniversary Medal awarded by the Festival du Film de Cannes, the Chauvel Award by the Brisbane International Film Festival, and a Commander of the Order of Arts and Letters by the French Government in 2000.

THE MAN IN THE RED TIE

*David Stratton in conversation
with Meredith Burgmann*

David James Stratton. File number S/37/79. David's file consists of two folios containing ninety-nine pages. They are wholly concerned with the activities of the Sydney Film Festival. The file begins in July 1960 and ends in July 1981, although it may continue past this date.

MB: During your time involved with the film festival, did you at any time think you were being monitored by ASIO?

DS: No. It never occurred to me at all. I was probably pretty naïve in those days. I was raised in England as a good conservative … I used to attend fundraising functions for Harold Macmillan and things like that. So it never occurred to me that, because we were screening films from around the world, including communist countries, I would attract any kind of attention from ASIO.

MB: Did it ever occur to you when you were in Czechoslovakia or Russia, that you might have been of interest?

DS: No, especially the first time I went to those countries, Czechoslovakia, Hungary, Poland and Russia in 1966, quite the reverse really. I thought that if anything was going to happen (I'd seen enough spy movies), it might be the Russians or the Poles or the Hungarians tapping my phone.

MB: Well, there's that amazing bit in the file where the agents wonder whether they should warn you about honey traps.

DS: No such luck, I'm afraid.

MB: How do you feel about the fact that they were obviously quite interested in you?

DS: Well, I just feel a bit amazed. As I say it would not have occurred to me. I don't feel particularly angry about it, only in the sense that I feel what a waste of time and resources and money. Surely they could have seen from the most cursory examination that I wasn't any kind of threat to anybody except perhaps myself, so I don't get it at all.

MB: It's interesting how many people I've interviewed where that's their exact response, how insignificant everything they did was, and why was ASIO even interested.

DS: Yes.

MB: When you got the file and read it, how did it make you feel? Did it make you feel creepy?

DS: Honestly it didn't because it was so long ago and some of the details were so weird, like the colour of the tie I was wearing. I'm described at one stage as having well-known left-wing ideas, which was news to me because, like I said, I think I voted Liberal for quite a long time.

MB: So why do you think you were being followed?

DS: I guess it was the censorship issue ... I was coming out very strongly against government policy in terms of censorship, but that was not political, at least I didn't think it was political. I suppose it was, but not in the sense of 'Cold War political', but maybe it had something to do with that.

MB: Were there any particular surprises or inaccuracies in the file?

DS: There were. They refer at one stage to my secretary at the time and they get the name wrong.

MB: Well, they call you 'David Strutton'.

DS: Yes, they get my name wrong too. I mean that's the other surprising thing, too, it's not always very accurate but *what a boring job.*

MB: It's the recording of every detail.

DS: It must have been incredibly tedious to sit outside ... if what they were doing was sitting outside the Russian Embassy. Didn't they know that in order to go to Russia in those days you had to get a visa? I hated going to the Russian Embassy and the reason I had to go was to get a visa.

MB: They also have details of you hiring a hire car.

DS: To get around Canberra.

MB: There is some evidence that there was someone inside the Sydney Film Festival who was giving information. Since getting your file have you talked to others in the film festival, has there been any speculation as to whom it might have been?

DS: I only talked to one person and anyone who was giving them information is now dead, because we're talking about a long time ago. I can think of a couple of people it could have been and both of them are dead now.

MB: So you prefer not to speculate?

DS: Yes, what does it matter in the scheme of things? They thought they were doing the right thing and no real harm was done.

MB: That's interesting that you think that, because other people are quite angry about what happened because they could see that harm had been done. For instance in my case a friend of mine was denied a job he desperately wanted simply because he was in my address book and I still feel angry about that. You don't feel you were ever denied access to something?

DS: No, on the contrary, I was always very lucky. The only reason I left the Sydney Film Festival after eighteen years was because SBS had started and Bruce Gyngell asked me to come and program films for SBS and so on. I would be horrified to think that any of my friends or colleagues were in any way affected, but I'm sure they weren't. I'm trying to think of the people who were even tangentially mentioned there and they've all gone on to success, but I would certainly be furious if I knew of anything like that. That would be iniquitous.

MB: It's quite clear that whenever they rang you or you rang them that various Eastern European consulates were tapped, and also on one occasion it's quite clear that the Third World Bookshop was subject to interception. Do you think that there was any other tapping? Do you think that the actual festival itself was tapped?

DS: I'd be surprised, I really don't think ... well nothing would surprise me really but I can't see the point of that. They seem to be interested as far as I could tell whenever I was in direct contact with an Eastern European embassy or whenever we were wanting to invite a guest from an Eastern European country.

MB: Here's an interesting entry in the file. In 1964 they list the executive of the Sydney Film Festival.

DS: That was before my day.

MB: But it's quite clear that they all had ASIO files. Their file numbers are listed beside their names ... Allan Ashbolt, Hans Bandler, Professor Stout.

DS: Just old lefties.

MB: But very mainstream respectable lefties ... so you were destined to get a file.

DS: As soon as you became involved with this organisation.

MB: There is this continued reference to 'the source', who is obviously the informant inside the festival.

DS: It would be intriguing to know.

MB: This entry is a description of a function at the Polish Consulate General in Point Piper on 22 July 1968:

> Two guests recognised were Mr Ferguson Labor MLA for Fairfield (TS) F/1/7 and David J Strutton [sic] the director of the Sydney Film Festival 3/2/1059. The latter celebrated the occasion by wearing a red tie and pocket handkerchief. Kowalski said that some two years ago he had been advised that Strutton [sic] was distinctly left wing in his views.

This last phrase is underlined by hand. The report continues:

> Since Kowalski is very interested in the Film Festival of documentary and other type [*sic*] of films, he has frequently been coming in contact with Strutton and until seen last night he had never noted any evidence of communist sympathies ...

So obviously just wearing the red tie was enough ...

DS: Or attending the Polish Consulate. I think it was Polish National Day.

MB: And even conservative politicians wear red on suitable days.

DS: I remember that tie. It was a very smart tie, I was very proud of it.

ASIO surveillance photo from David Stratton's file: David Stratton outside the Soviet Embassy, Canberra, 7 May 1969.

MB: So you didn't see it as anything more than a bit of sartorial elegance and an 'homage' to the occasion.

DS: No, in 1968 I'd been directing the festival then for two years. I'd been to Poland once already and I think I was only too pleased to get an invitation to a few free drinks to be honest.

MB: And go and see the consulate … check it out.

DS: The drinks would have probably been the appeal, because we were working on the smell of an oily rag then and they had vodka … I just think I was probably a fairly well brought up young man who was invited to Poland's National Day and I thought, 'I'll wear a red tie because it's Poland's National day and the Polish colours are red and white … long before communism'.

MB: And here you are being reported in August 1969 as visiting the Soviet Embassy. You're 'an unidentified male stranger' and four photographs were taken of this male 'who is possibly identical with David Stratton. This male left the area at 15.25 hours and walked towards Manuka … ' Now I'm quoting from 1 July 1966 …

DS: That was my first year as director of the festival.

MB: Here is a report from the Deputy Director-General of NSW Operations. It says:

> David Stratton, the above named, the director of the Sydney Film Festival is not adversely recorded at Headquarters. He is mentioned in your contact report … dated 10 June 1966 … It seems possible that (DS) met Volkov …

Who's Volkov?

DS: I think Volkov was in charge of consular affairs at the Russian Embassy in Canberra, so if you wanted to get a visa you had to go to Volkov and it was Volkov we had to correspond with. We sent him copies of the letters we were sending to Moscow to invite films to the Festival.

MB: This is fascinating. It says: 'It seems possible that having met Volkov he may be studied by the RIS' (presumably the Russian Intelligence Service) 'for use as an agent of influence. It seems that this could be used as a pretext to have a friendly chat with him with a view to assessing his Aztec potentials.'

DS: Whatever Aztec means.

MB: It continues:

> Of course it would be preferable to see him before he proceeds overseas so as to warn him of RIS techniques particularly in regard to compromise operations and provocations in respect of black marketeering … it may now be too late in which case he should be seen after his return … would you consider obtaining a personality study of Stratton from [blanked out]…

And of course later we get a personality study of you. So you had no idea any of this was going on?

DS: No, and I'm sure nobody contacted me on my return. I know 1966 is a long time ago but I'm pretty sure that I left before 1 July because I went to America, that other terrible place, in the summer of 1966.

MB: It's quite a big file and whenever your name comes up it's mainly about you contacting the embassy or the consulate about visas for the visiting film directors.

DS: That's interesting because we were also inviting French directors and Italian directors. If they just looked at the overall picture they would surely see that it was a very even pattern. I was going to Paris every year as well as going to Prague and Stockholm every year.

MB: They were obviously obsessive. Here's a conversation:

> From the Third World Bookshop on Wednesday 24.6.70. Jim (James Malcolm PERCY v.r.) contacted David STRATTON at the Sydney Film Festival office and asked if STRATTON had heard anything from Mr de Antonio (ph) regarding the film 'Year of the Pig'. STRATTON replied in the negative.

And there's another conversation later where this is raised.

DS: What that's all about is Emile de Antonio, [who] was a very political American documentary film maker who made a film called *In the Year of the Pig*, which was about the American involvement in Vietnam. It was a very detailed documentary attacking America's involvement in the war and quite inflammatory, I suppose, but a very, very good documentary and I had seen the film somewhere and invited the film, and probably at that stage I was still waiting confirmation that it would be shown in the festival. We did show it in the festival and we also showed a later Emile de Antonio film about Richard Nixon. I can't remember why the Third World Bookshop should ring me ...

MB: I think they wanted to use it for a fundraiser.

DS: Obviously they were being tapped ... and if they wanted to use the film, I couldn't allow it to be used for any other purposes.

MB: I think this page might be the personality profile they talked about when they were so worried about you wearing a red tie:

> Agent comment: I believe David James STRATTEN [*sic*] to be the type of person who expects something from anybody he befriends. He puts a value upon his friendship, and I suggest that he may be in receipt of some form of compensation from the Soviets if he actively promotes their films.

[David laughs.]

> His appreciation of films would be mainly concerned with the message or story they portray, rather than the techniques involved in their making. If he enjoys a film, it would be because of his personal conviction that the film was worthy of his patronage, rather than that he was being pressured into pushing a particular film that he may not like personally.

It's a pretty opinionated piece.

DS: Yeah.

MB: It reminds me of the personality profiles ASIO did of the actors at the New Theatre and I suspect the same guy did the profiles of the actors because he goes into a lot of pseudo-psychological stuff. He said Roger Milliss would make a good low-level tax inspector in the Soviet bureaucracy.

DS: Yes.

MB: Do you get offended by that profile?

DS: I can't say I really get offended, I mean it's not true. I've never expected anything from anybody.

MB: It says here, 'He is a bright individual, who expresses his aesthetic likes and dislikes in a manner which gives him a degree of authority.'

DS: Well, there you go.

MB: Well, doing that has been your life.

DS: [Quoting the file] 'He lives and breathes film.' This has obviously been written by someone who's talked to me about these things. Why he should think I expect something from somebody ... I don't know. Certainly if I like a film I want other people to see it. I want to share my liking with other people ... It's not that I'm giving the film my patronage, that's a strange way of putting it.

MB: Why I think this is interesting is that the people at the New Theatre believe that the stuff that was written about them was by a bloke who wrote detective stories under another name. It's the same sort of pseudo-psychological stuff.

DS: I wonder if that was written by the person who was probably still then on the festival committee? I'm trying to think who it was.

MB: It's someone who sees themselves as an outsider. It's not someone who knows you well.

DS: I would be fairly sure. I could tell you off the record who it might have been. I think it was ...

[David names the person and the organisation he was identified with].

MB: Ah yes, he's mentioned very early on.

DS: He's there very early on. I had cause to criticise him more than once. He was a conservative ... and in my uppity way, before I became Director of the film festival, I criticised the [named organisation] for its conservatism in comparison with organisations from overseas and I think he never liked me very much. So that's who I think it was but I wouldn't like to say, it's pure speculation.

MB: This page is headed the 'USSR Consulate 3 June 1977'. This is about Alexander Mitta.

DS: Mitta was a guest of the festival. We wanted to get as many guests as possible and it wasn't easy in those days. We didn't have much money. We only had a certain amount of money to invite people every year. The only country that paid for their people to come was the Soviet Union and usually they sent us interesting people and Mitta was an interesting film maker. They sent a guy called Abuladse once. They were always interesting but if we wanted to get someone from, say, Czechoslovakia, we had to pay because they didn't have enough money to pay.

MB: This page says on the top, 'Scorpion'. That's the telegraphic name for ASIO headquarters in Melbourne.

DS: What they wouldn't say, what they probably don't even know, was that in 1968, the same year that I went to the Polish National Day on 21 August, I went and protested outside the Polish Consulate at the invasion of Czechoslovakia.

MB: Well, funnily enough they report that in my ASIO file, the fact that I demonstrated in Martin Place on the day of the invasion and they report that as if it's just another anti-Vietnam demo. They don't even see the significance of it. They just report I was at it.

DS: I do remember [Paul] Hasluck saying something like 'they're all communists' or something like that 'and it's not very important'.

MB: But that was the importance, the fact that communists were demonstrating against communists.

DS: And having been to Prague and discovering ... That was what opened my eyes, going to places like Prague and Warsaw and Budapest and meeting just ordinary people. Well, maybe filmmakers are not ordinary people but I discovered that really the Russians were more like the Americans than anything else. They were imposing ...

MB: It was cultural imperialism.

DS: Yes. I even made a speech which my translator wouldn't translate at a university in Sofia in Bulgaria in 1979. I was asked to talk to film students and I said something about Mosfilm (the big studio in Moscow) being on the same level as Twentieth Century Fox, as imperialistic ... They're both as bad as each other and the interpreter said 'I can't translate that' but there were people who obviously understood and they laughed ...

MB: Was there a change in your views? You said you were really quite conservative yet they were still following you around in 1981.

DS: Well, I was less conservative by then. I think Whitlam did it for me. Or maybe it was Billy McMahon.

MB: And Vietnam.

DS: ... And Vietnam, but it was also Prague, because the Czechs were such wonderful people, so Prague for me was a big thing. It was all that ... and Quebec as well, remember what happened in Quebec, that whole state of emergency in Canada ... because I was there too. I guess it was all of that. So, yes, I changed.

JOAN BIELSKI

1958 **2012**

Joan Ward was born in Narrabri in 1923 and was educated in the Catholic school system in Armidale and Gunnedah. She left school before her Leaving Certificate and worked in a newsprint factory before joining the RAAF, where she served as a telegraphist from 1942 to 1945. Assisted by the ex-servicemen's rehabilitation scheme, she did her matriculation at Sydney Technical College and eventually earned a BA and DipEd from Sydney University and the New England University College. She taught briefly in Canberra, which is how she managed to attract lifelong ASIO attention.

In 1953 Joan married Jerzy Bielski, a Polish socialist who had survived Auschwitz. She became an advocate for migrant welfare and joined the Immigration Reform Group. Joan taught in high schools for twenty-three years and was an active member of the Teachers' Federation. She spent the 1950s and 1960s involved with research and advocacy about women's education and workplace participation. She was a founding member of the Council for Civil Liberties and worked with Resident Action in the early 1970s. She was a founding member of the Women's Electoral Lobby (WEL) in 1972.

In 1974 Joan became the principal research officer with the Royal Commission on Human Relationships. Her contribution to the final report was mainly about adoption and equality for women. From 1977 to 1984 Joan headed the social development unit in the New South Wales Ministry of Education.

Joan was also involved with the Women in Education group for almost twenty years and in 1992 formed the non-party-political Women into Politics organisation. Her focus in WEL was women's education, employment and anti-discrimination law and in 1988 she published the book *Women Engineers* because she saw such little progress towards equality in the workforce.

Her continuing activism and good humour earned her the Grand Stirrer trophy at the 1999 Edna Ryan Awards. Joan died in August 2012, shortly after finishing this chapter.

FEAR AND LOATHING IN THE FIFTIES

by Joan Bielski

In February 1951 I arrived in Canberra a recently graduated teacher, unmarried and using my family name of Ward. I had spent some years in the WAAAF (Women's Auxiliary Australian Air Force), and after the war ended I went to university. I was employed by the NSW Department of Education and sent to Canberra as a teacher. I spent 1951 becoming accustomed to what proved to be both a mentally exciting but physically exhausting job.

My political beliefs were and are left of centre. I would describe myself as a democrat and a socialist. At university, attempts to recruit me into the Communist Party by fellow students, mainly self-proclaimed communists from Hunter Valley mining towns, were met with 'I grew up Catholic and I am not about to adopt another orthodoxy' or 'I did not escape one dictatorship to enter another'.

Canberra in the 1950s was like a quiet country town with a population of about 18 000, mainly public servants but also including construction workers building post-war Canberra.

Many of the latter were migrants, with a high proportion from the Baltic States and Eastern European countries. Ben Chifley, Prime Minister in the last days of World War II and by then Leader of the Opposition, walked to work daily about 9 a.m., without any security, from his hotel to his office in the old Parliament House. When the school buses passed him on the way, the kids leaned out of the windows and yelled 'Hello Chif … Good day Chif.' He would respond with a wave, his habitual pipe in hand.

However, beneath Canberra's benign surface the Cold War had already begun. ASIO was in its infancy, learning to get its flat foot in the door. Its activities were already affecting Australian political life and the lives of some hapless citizens. I was about to play a bit part, a somewhat farcical part, in one of the defining episodes of Australian political life in the twentieth century.

I applied for my ASIO file in early 2011. The file is a disorderly collection of facts, misinformation and misinterpretation, so that much of it is nonsense and is a reflection of the hysteria of the early Cold War era. The folios are haphazard, numbers not in numerical sequence, suggesting some ASIO scribes could not count or the removal of some folios. Some folios are cover notes without the supporting memo, some are in indecipherable handwriting. As an ex bureaucrat, I am surprised that such sloppy record keeping was tolerated, especially in an organisation dealing with people's lives and destinies. The file does not lend itself to a coherent chronological story.

BECOMING A PERSON OF INTEREST

Evening English classes for migrants were the norm in 1950s Canberra, and teachers were pressed into service. I resisted becoming a teacher in the classes because the winter evenings were extremely cold and the transport poor. Early in 1952 a colleague who was transferring out of Canberra asked me if I would take over a job she had been doing teaching English at the Russian Embassy. As the lessons were in the late afternoon and the Russian Embassy just a walk across the park from the school where I worked, I agreed.

My pupil turned out to be Vladimir Petrov, Third Secretary at the Russian Embassy and, as later revealed, a Russian intelligence officer and famous defector. Sometimes another embassy officer, Demetri Pavlov, also took lessons.

My ASIO file begins in February 1952 with the twenty or more phone calls made that year between Petrov and myself confirming or cancelling appointments. Petrov seemed to travel a lot, so the lessons were somewhat irregular. Many of the phone calls, twenty-five pages, were verbatim records of our short conversations. They do not make for entertaining reading.

My recollections of Petrov after fifty-odd years is that he was fairly humourless, dedicated to his job and to spreading the Soviet message. This was demonstrated by his plying me with magazines and pamphlets about Russia, most of which remained unread. The fact that he was already middle-aged and had a very heavy accent meant that while his understanding of English and his vocabulary might improve, he was unlikely to become a fluent English speaker. He used to write his speeches and read them out to me to ensure that his pronunciation was correct and that he was using the right word or phrase to ensure his meaning clear to English speakers. Like many Eastern Europeans he could not easily pronounce words including the 'th' sound, so sometimes I was able to suggest suitable less challenging synonyms for him to use.

The phone-call records in my file demonstrate that the embassy was at all times under surveillance, their phones were tapped and even the most mundane matters were recorded.

The file is then silent until October 1952. On Wednesday 22 October an ASIO field officer (name deleted) reported that he/she searched my room at the hostel where I lived. The report reads:

> ...
>
> 2. Whilst there I saw and made notes of the following publications:
> Peekskill USA, by Howard Fast,
> Crisis in Egypt by Rupert Lockwood and
> Literature and Reality by Howard Fast
>
> ...
>
> 3. Also in Ms Ward's room were the following publications which were printed in the USSR:
> (1) 'We have learned the truth about the Soviet Union'
> (2) 'A Quarter of a Century of the Open Heart Furnace'
> (3) 'American workers look to the Soviet Union'
> (4) 'Education in the USSR by A Quarter of a Century of the Open Heart Furnace'
>
> ...
>
> (3) 'American Workers look to the Soviet Union'
> (4) 'Education in the USSR by Yevengy Medyesky'
> (5) 'Soviet Land and People'
> (6) 'J. V. Stalin 'Concerning Marxism in Linguistics.
>
> ...
>
> 4. Also noticed was a blank application form issued by the Department of Territories for a position in the Territory of Papua and New Guinea
>
> ...
>
> 5. Nothing of further interest was noted [Dated 31 October 1952].

He/she was very lavish with the inverted commas.

Rupert Lockwood and Howard Fast are names known to me. I may have been curious to read more about the great controversies of the era but I cannot recall acquiring or reading the books. I assume the other materials listed were gifts from Petrov. The magazines and pamphlets were unlikely to have been available from any other source because as the report says, they were printed in the USSR. The application form for a job in the Department of Territories is a mystery to me, too. I cannot recall ever considering working in New Guinea.

On 5 November 1952, the file shows the Attorney-General's Department in Canberra enquiring of the AG's New South Wales office what, if anything, was known about me. The AG New South Wales branch replied on 8 December 1952 that 'various papers held by the Department of Education have been perused'. Then followed a three-page list of my various addresses, the names and addresses of my father and mother, my uncles and their employment, information about my university degree, how I was accepted for teaching and so on. Amongst the trivia was one pleasant remark: an Education Department inspector had assessed me on 21 January 1949 as 'of superior intelligence, with clear, free, intelligent conversation'. It concludes with the statement that 'Special Branch has no record of the subject.'

Another report dated 14 December 1952 suggests that someone was considering interviewing me about the Soviet Embassy. The report concludes with the statement that 'Miss Ward is known to have in her own personal library several communist publications and books' and that she 'is not a suitable person to interview in connection with the Soviet Embassy'.

Reference to the reading list occurs again from time to time in the file as a reason for being wary of me.

The file shows that on 16 December 1952, a field officer reported that I had been observed three times visiting the flat in Ainslie occupied by Bruce Yuill, then President of the ACT Trades and Labour Council and a member of the ALP, and Fergan O'Sullivan, Dr Evatt's Press Officer. A university friend of mine was then Bruce's girlfriend. The flatmates had good parties and I was often invited. The file says that I was known to have visited 'on at least three occasions … that an informant had said that Ward and Yuill do not recognise each other when they meet in public'. My female university friend never got a mention. Yuill and O'Sullivan were left of centre. Both were later to suffer much career devastation because of their views and activities and by the hares set running by ASIO.

On 22 July 1958, a folio quaintly headed 'Mrs Jerzy Bielski' reports a conversation with me and a source not named, saying that I had seen Bruce Yuill, and that he had said he was 'very disheartened and downcast on the score that because of his previous political background he could not obtain suitable employment'. He died in his mid-forties. Fergan O'Sullivan was investigated as a Soviet contact before the Petrov Royal Commission. His subsequent career is unknown to me but he seems to have vanished from politics and journalism.

The records of my visits to the embassy to teach English were surely enough evidence to demonstrate their purpose, but not so. The secret searching of my room and the list of publications found during the search continued to be a cause of my remaining a 'person of interest'. The secret searching of my room was a gross unprovoked invasion of my privacy and the 'reading list' became the cause of ongoing interest in me.

This interest in me later caused the investigation of my husband when he was seeking naturalisation. Making enquiries of my employer without reason could have had career consequences for me but appears not have done so.

The entry concerning Bruce Yuill shows that not only were private citizens, pursuing their interests through reform and advocacy, being followed, but also that friends of people associated with the Labor Opposition, not just communists, were already under surveillance.

MEETING THE CANBERRA ELITE

Towards the end of 1952 Petrov invited me to the Embassy National Day Reception on 7 November, which, out of curiosity, I accepted. My file (page 24) records a list of those attending and those who declined. The list of those attending included Prime Minister Menzies, Mrs Menzies, Miss Heather Menzies, various ambassadors, high commissioners and foreign embassy officials, some Australian government ministers, a few members of parliament, senior public servants such as Mr Arthur Tange and Harold White, the National Librarian, and luminaries like Professor Marcus Oliphant from ANU. Neither the list of those attending nor those who declined included any Labor Party MPs or anyone known to me then or since as an ALP member. I was in very respectable company. I met the Canberra elite and had my first experience of vodka.

I left Canberra in May 1953, taking up a teaching position in Sydney. This was duly recorded by ASIO. I only ever met Vladimir Petrov once more – in Sydney's Kings Cross sometime late in 1953, when my future husband and I ran into him in the street near the Polish restaurant Adria. He was standing as though he was waiting for someone and seemed uneasy. I assumed that he did not want to renew the acquaintance, so we exchanged a few pleasantries and then went on our way.

One morning in April 1954, I was astonished to read in my morning newspaper that Vladimir Petrov had defected. Later, during the Royal Commission on Espionage, it became public that the Adria was where he had been wined and dined and suborned by his ASIO contacts such as Dr Bialoguski. I then understood his unease.

AFTER CANBERRA

In December 1953 I married Jerzy (George) Stephen Bielski, previously a member of the Polish Socialist Party, a World War II political prisoner, survivor of Auschwitz, and a witness at the Nuremberg trials. He realised after the Yalta Agreement that as a socialist, he would never return to Poland, where he had been keen on a literary career. He was refused entry to the US because of his political affiliation. He then applied to come to Australia because it then had a Labor government. Ironically the Chifley Government fell when he was on the boat off Perth in December 1949. On the recommendation of the International Federation of Free Trade Unions, he was recruited by the Australian Workers Union (AWU) as a union organiser to assist the union to recruit the numerous immigrant construction workers on sites like the Snowy Mountains project. His job was to explain Australian industrial law to them through articles in various languages in the union journal, to translate their qualifications and work documents, to interpret on site, and to integrate them into the union.

My husband applied for naturalisation in late 1954. With his history one could have expected him to breeze through the naturalisation process, but not so. Those of us who lived through this period and who met many of the post-war migrants will be aware that they were often traumatised by their wartime experiences. Some felt declassed because their education and qualifications were not recognised. Many were paranoid about communism and could not distinguish between communism and socialism. Some spread rumours about their fellow immigrants and took their stories to ASIO.

On 4 July 1954, in a folio titled 'George Bielski — Alleged Communist', a field officer reports on information received from a 'Mrs [deleted]' asking for an appointment for another woman [deleted]. An interview occurred in July 1955, when the contact, who said she was an ex-member of the WAAAF, reported her conversations with another woman, 'Mrs [deleted]', who said that she was reporting her conversation about Bielski with the friend's approval. She 'wished to bring to our [ASIO's] notice information about a man Georgius [*sic* – George's Polish name was 'Jerzy'] Bielski given to her by the woman friend who is in close touch with Bielski and his wife'. However she did not say who the friend was. But the information about George suggests that it had its origins in the Polish community.

The report reads as a garbled version of our lives from someone who knew someone who knew someone else who disliked us, and had made it their business to find out something about us. It contained inaccuracies, gave wrong addresses, misinterpreted events and included what can only be called fabrications. The informant is quoted as saying about George:

> From his conversations and statements, there is no doubt he is a Communist. He regards Socialist Revolution in Australia will take place not in the distant future but that which is near at hand.

Damning stuff, is it not? Yet George had migrated to evade returning to a communist Poland and was employed by a union which bruited its anti-communist agenda. Another memo, dated 11 March 1955, regurgitates my history as a factor in questioning his credentials for naturalisation.

The anonymous friend of a friend also reported that until my 'association with Bielski, she was a strict Catholic ... she now shares her husband's political outlook. She has now renounced her religion.' That I could be so influenced will no doubt surprise many of my feminist friends.

The file recording the anonymous friend of a friend shows ASIO giving credence to, and accepting and filing, information which was second-hand, inaccurate, and malicious in tone and perhaps made up by the informant. My husband was eventually interviewed by ASIO. Others, probably officers of the AWU, spoke on his behalf and he was eventually naturalised. Had this not occurred, the consequences would have created some difficulties for him as he would have become stateless.

The political intrigues of 1954 and 1955 coincided with the very public drama of the Petrov defection and the royal commission that followed. The file note of 15 May 1955 concludes by quoting Vladimir Petrov, at his debriefing after his defection, saying that neither I nor any of the other teachers of English at the embassy were seen by the Russians as communist sympathisers.

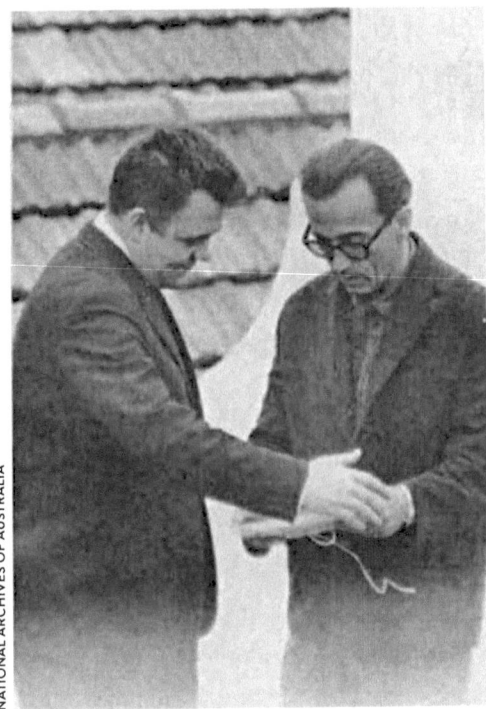

ASIO surveillance photo from Joan Bielski's file, captioned *Persons Entering and leaving Polish Consulate, Sydney 10 August 1966. 1. Bohdan PIASKOSKI 2. Jerzy BIELSKI [HG1482 – 4/1]*.

In 1956 I transferred to the Sydney office of the Commonwealth Office of Education, administering the Colombo Plan scholarships. The ASIO file shows that I was again investigated. A memo dated 29 August 1956 from the Attorney-General's New South Wales branch states:

> Jerzy (George) Bielski has been interviewed in connection with his application for naturalisation for which he has been cleared ... In view of this there would not appear to be any objection to Mrs Bielski's application, and a clearance is recommended.

DISREGARD FOR THE RIGHT TO FREEDOM OF ASSOCIATION

Freedom of association with fellow citizens to organise and advocate for reform is a basic human right. ASIO seems to have thought otherwise. What is interesting to me is that ASIO appeared to have informants inside these organisations. In a long life I have been a member of many such organisations so my name came up again from time to time.

A folio dated 29 November 1963, 'New South Wales Humanist Society' begins, 'Attached is a copy of a printed list of the members of the NSW Humanist Society as at 31 July 1963.' The list has 'three hundred and twenty two (322) names of whom eighty-seven have previously come under notice'. A shorter list for 1964 had 'only 103 persons under notice'.

Then follows a long list of people who have, over the years, been advocates for many progressive causes and reforms; persons who later became acknowledged public achievers in politics, the professions and NGOs and people who have been the engineers of social progress in this society. Included in the list are reminders of friends, some long forgotten, some deceased. As a 'person of interest' my membership was underlined among those who had 'previously come under notice'.

The Humanist Society was an advocate of many issues which were opposed by organised religion and which had nothing to do with national security or public order. The society's members were expressing their right not to believe in a religion. They were non-violent and went about their work in a peaceful manner. None of those persons that I knew on the list were, to my knowledge, members of the Communist Party. Perhaps there were 'Reds under the beds' after all.

The Women's Electoral Lobby (WEL), formed in 1972, was next. The folio, dated 3 July 1973, reads:

> Attached for HQ and New South Wales Secretariat is a copy of a letter and programme sent to members of the Women's Liberation Movement (WLM) by the WEL. The letter invites WLM members to attend the WEL New South Wales State Conference on 14 July 1973 at Macquarie University, North Ryde.

It goes on to say 'People who are mentioned in the letter and program who are of interest are ... Joan (possibly Joan Marie) Bielski, Brigid Gilling and Judy (Judith) Malcolm'. Both Brigid and Judy were activists in Women's Liberation and the pro-abortion issue. I recall I gave a paper 'Women in the Workforce: The State as an Employer'.

This episode confirms what many in the women's movement believed: that the women's liberation movement, Women's Electoral Lobby and the pro-abortion lobby were under surveillance. Members of WEL were known to speculate among themselves from time to time whether WEL was under surveillance. We used to wonder whether the conservative Festival of Light had a plant among our members because so often our deliberations appeared to be in their possession.

A lengthy clipping from the *Australian Financial Review*, dated 15 November 1972, headlined 'PM's Royal Commission Switch Sparks Scepticism' reports an interview with some public feminists, including myself as WEL spokesperson, and representatives of traditional women's organisations, commenting on the Whitlam Government's public undertaking to establish 'a royal commission into improving the status of women in Australia'. Despite the headline, the comments were on the whole tempered and reasonable. It appears that WEL was an organisation under scrutiny and I was still a person whose opinions were being filed by ASIO.

A folio dated 21 February 1974 is fun. This was a year when the green bans and the Resident Action Movement were highly successful in opposing the demolition of the terrace houses in Victoria Street, Kings Cross and in opposing the excesses of the development lobby. I was President of the Resident Action Movement from about May 1974 until December 1974. The folio, headed 'Australian Spartacists League', consists of the league's mailing list, which the file says is self-explanatory. It goes on to list Joan Bielski (name underlined), John Ducker, Pat Clancy, Clyde Cameron MHR, Norm Gallagher, Adrian Hannah, Peter Thomas, Joe Owens, Jack Munday (sic) and Sir Robert Askin. It goes on to quote the paper's 'revolutionary Marxism' masthead. I did not enjoy being on a list with Sir Robin Askin, the developers' friend.

Jack Mundey, Joe Owens and their associates in the Builders Labourers' Federation, through their green bans on controversial and anti-social development projects, saved many Sydney neighbourhoods from the very powerful development lobby of the Askin era. I was again in suspect company by ASIO standards but I am proud to be in their company.

In 1978 there is a press clipping included in my file from *News Weekly*, a conservative Melbourne-based paper established by Bob Santamaria. It proclaims, 'Left-wing takes over the NSW Family Planning Association'. The article begins thus: 'Women's Liberationists, radical feminists, homosexuals and a communist last week staged a successful coup in the NSW Family Planning Association.'

The background to this surprising news story was that feminists, many of whom were members of the Family Planning Association, had long been concerned at the restrictive services delivered by the organisation, especially that young single adults were denied services and information on sexual health. Feminists encouraged others to become members with a view to changing the association's policies but to no avail. Consequently at the Annual General Meeting of 1978, feminists successfully nominated people they saw as a more enlightened for election to the board. These were people such as Allison Ziller and myself (name underlined again) from WEL and Professor Charles Kerr, then Professor of Preventive and Social Medicine and (I quote) 'an anti-uranium member of the Ranger Inquiry'.

ASIO went on spending money, time and effort on keeping tabs on me, a confirmed 'reformist' – the latter a dirty word in some left circles, but I am happy that many of the causes and reforms I espoused got results.

ASIO's interest in me, based on so little, blundered on through the 1950s to the late 1970s until, under the thirty-year embargo, no further information is available.

IT SEEMS THAT ASIO DID NOT ACCEPT THE WORD OF THEIR PRIZE DEFECTOR

Vladimir Petrov's signed statement at his debriefing on 7 March 1955 confirms my story. It reads in part:

> Miss Ward commenced teaching at the Embassy after her predecessor left ... Miss Ward also taught Mr Pavlov but no one else, not even my wife. I have no knowledge of her political views and we never discussed Communism or

any politics. I do not know if she was connected with the Communist Party … Miss Ward was invited to Embassy functions as all teachers were invited. I believe she attended one of the 7th December functions. I think, with a girl friend. She never mentioned Bruce Yuill. The fact that Miss Ward was an English tutor to Pavlov and me is not an indication that she was accepted at the Embassy as being pro-Communist. *In fact, all teachers were considered to be Security Agents and we were cautious in our conversation with them.* [My emphasis.]

As taxpayers, Australians have a right to expect a more sophisticated, politically astute security service, one that understands politics, one that respects human rights; that respects the right to differ and to advocate for a cause or an idea; one that is careful not to clumsily damage people's reputations and lives. Recent cases made public suggest that ASIO is not such an organisation.

DENNIS ALTMAN

Dennis Altman is the son of Jewish refugees, and a writer and academic. He first came to attention with the publication of his book *Homosexual: Oppression and Liberation* in 1972. This book, which has often been compared to Germaine Greer's *The Female Eunuch* and Peter Singer's *Animal Liberation*, was the first serious analysis to emerge from the gay liberation movement, and was published in seven countries. In 2010 it was published in Japan, and in 2012 a fortieth anniversary edition was produced, leading to an anthology about the book called *After Homosexual: The legacies of gay liberation*.

Dennis has written thirteen books, exploring sexuality, politics and their inter-relationship in Australia, the United States and now globally. These include *The Homosexualisation of America*, *AIDS and the New Puritans* and *Rehearsals for Change*; a novel called *The*

Comfort of Men, and the memoir *Defying Gravity*. His book *Global Sex* has been translated into five languages, including Spanish, Turkish and Japanese. Most recently he published *The End of the Homosexual?*

Dennis is Professor of Politics and Director of the Institute for Human Security at LaTrobe University in Melbourne. He was President of the AIDS Society of Asia and the Pacific between 2001 and 2005, and since 2004 has been a member of the governing council of the International AIDS Society. In 2005 he was Visiting Professor of Australian Studies at Harvard, and has been a board member of Oxfam Australia. In July 2006 he was listed by the *Bulletin* as one of the one hundred most influential Australians ever, and in June 2008 was made a Member of the Order of Australia.

WHY ME?

by Dennis Altman

Even for someone as self-centred as myself, a typical Leo as we might have observed back in the 1970s, reading one's ASIO file is deeply disappointing. The great bulk of the materials released are interviews with or articles by me, some of which I had lost or forgotten, plus accounts of my movements in and out of Australia. I learnt that I was 'a self-admitted homosexual', and a 'frequent speaker at meetings staged by organisations of interest to ASIO'. In the 1970s ASIO took a commendably wide interest in many meetings, and their officers were clearly well informed about leftist minutiae. As for the self-admitted homosexuality that, after all, took most of the fun away – no need to follow me to places of dubious assignations if I was likely to write about them in *Nation Review*.

I first came to ASIO's attention in 1962, when I was a baby student politician on the Student's Representative Council (SRC) at the University of Tasmania, which was apparently of interest after the SRC protested against the refusal of an entry visa to a Mr Brenner. (Brenner was an Israeli economist, but I am unable to find any reasons why even our most zealous immigration officials felt he might endanger Australian security, nor do I recall why the issue came before the SRC.)

There is a brief note that the then President of the National Union of Australian University Students, John Ridley (later a figure in the Liberal Party), informed ASIO that I would travel to Leningrad in August 1966 to attend a student meeting, but ASIO made no attempt to debrief me. Perhaps that was a pity: I was appalled by the behaviour of the Russian 'student leaders' (all at least a decade older than the rest of us), and the Orwellian nature of the conference. If ASIO had offered I might have been tempted to become a double agent.

That trip had a deep impact on me: ten years later I received an ARC grant to look at international student politics, then divided between Soviet and US-based organisations. That grant in turn led me into the internal debates about Israel and Palestine, which split the national students' union, and revealed a nasty strain of anti-Semitism among a few leftists, in particular Bill Hartley, one of Whitlam's opponents in the unreconstructed Victorian ALP. ASIO seems to have missed out on all of this, although one feels it might have been somewhat more relevant than worrying about my views on the counter-culture.

Their interest in me flagged somewhat until the development of the anti-Vietnam movement, and that, along with my role in gay liberation, allowed unnamed officers to occupy considerable time at the xerox machines. I suspect some of my writings were read more assiduously in Canberra than by the people for whom I thought I was writing. The editing and censoring of the documents available (twenty-five out of 160 files have been so edited) means that there is no record of what anyone in ASIO thought of the information so diligently collected. This is unfortunate, as the interesting questions go unanswered ... were there people in ASIO arguing that support of apartheid and the escalating war in Vietnam actually strengthened the alleged democratic values of 'the west'? Did someone in the bowels of ASIO think that gay liberation was part of the greater Soviet plan to undermine western societies?

Little that is sinister emerges from these files, though I was tantalised by mention of 'Operation Whip', of which, unfortunately, no details are revealed. Given my squeamishness around sado-masochism of any sort I suspect the operation was not sexual in nature. But ASIO itself recognised my failure as a real subversive, reporting that my paper to the 1970 Socialist Scholars Conference 'seemed superficial'. The ASIO contact found most interesting the 'venomous attacks' by the activists, including Albert Langer and Bob Gould, 'against the pacifist attitudes of the theoreticians', which I think included me, and presumably saw me as a wimp but not a danger to the state.

In this ASIO was of course correct: I never shared the romantic delusion of some of my comrades at the time that the revolution was around the corner, or indeed even on the distant horizon. In 1970 I would have called myself a social democrat, a term I would still use today, which at least reveals a boring consistency. Of course gay liberation, particularly in the United States, flirted with more radical parts of the movement, such as the Black Panthers, but only some of them flirted back. (I discussed some of these links in my first book, *Homosexual: Oppression and Liberation*, and there is a rather different take in Tom Wolfe's famous *Radical Chic and Mau-Mauing the Flak Catchers*, which is scathing about Leonard Bernstein's support for black militants.)

Dennis Altman at a gay lib demonstration outside Liberal Party Headquarters. Left to right: Dennis Altman, Reinhard Hassert, John Ware, Warren Osmond, Sydney, 1971.

ASIO diligently compiled large amounts of material dating from the early days of gay liberation, though, oddly, they seemed not to have read *Homosexual*, which gave me a platform via several ABC television programs to say what was then quite radical, namely that the legal and social persecution of people because of their sexuality was deeply illiberal and indefensible. It's hard to remember that at that stage the debate was around the criminalisation of consensual adult sex, and there were still people prepared to argue for this publicly. When I appeared on the program *Monday Conference*, a television interview show hosted by the late Robert Moore, a defence of the current laws was mounted by Peter Coleman, who prided himself on being a genuine conservative, but based most of his argument on the vague sort of prejudice that has resurfaced in some of the rhetoric of Family First.

During the early 1970s I was briefly one of the best-known 'out' homosexuals in Australia – the competition was far less than now, when 'coming out' has become a career move in some areas. I rarely encountered hostility, certainly none as dramatic as the abuse that followed my colleague and fellow activist Lex Watson when he spoke on television in Mt Isa (one wonders whether a young Bob Katter was there that evening). In many ways homophobia collapsed as soon as it was confronted, which is why coming out publicly was so effective a strategy.

There is, by the way, no evidence that ASIO was interested in tracking down homosexuals, quite unlike the FBI, but then there is also no evidence that ASIO ever had a counterpart to J Edgar Hoover who persecuted homosexuals with a zeal born of self-loathing. It is possible that all sorts of revealing photographs and assignations have been removed from the files, and if so, I trust an officer, somewhere, has derived some pleasure from them.

What is so much more interesting is what is *not* in the papers I've been able to access, although such material may well be in files ASIO has refused to release. It is surprising that my several very friendly encounters with Gough Whitlam are not recorded, as one would think a future prime minister's contacts would be carefully tracked. Gough was fun to flirt with, but after all, a vigilant ASIO agent might have been able to find sinister sharing of state secrets in our lunch together.

Reading Mark Aarons's *Family File*, which is based upon the largest set of ASIO files kept on any one family, I discovered to my surprise that I had been the object of some interest to several communists in the dying days of the party's history. Mark reveals the role of several senior ALP figures who he claims were closet communists. Two of these, senators Arthur Gietzelt and Bruce Childs, approached me after the Labor defeat of 1975 to join some group which was bent on retaining Labor's socialist commitments. I wish I could remember more, but to be honest the men seemed already relics of an irrelevant past, and at the time I was caught up in the romance of gay liberation and the democratisation movements at Sydney University. Of course, if ASIO had done its job better I might be able to check the details of these approaches, and indeed possibly of others. If Mark is right, I overlapped, worked and possibly slept with communists without any awareness of the fact. Either I was remarkably naïve or, as I prefer to believe, they were remarkably inept in exercising much influence on most of us.

Thus a list of participants at a 1971 moratorium rally – 'Stop work to stop the war' – at which I was present includes a range of leading communist and ALP figures such as Laurie Aarons and Lionel Murphy, as well as others who, as far as I know, were not members of any party. The obvious point is that proximity does not, by itself, determine influence, just as extensive lists of names proves little except that people were together at a meeting. My own opposition to our involvement in Vietnam began when I was a graduate student at Cornell in the 1960s, and owed nothing to local communists, whom I regarded as one might slightly boring aunts, certainly not inspirations for my thinking. I was briefly at Monash University in the late 1960s, at the time of the infamous drive to collect blood for the Viet Cong, and I think I irritated the leftists by my refusal to see North Vietnam as any less nasty than the puppet regimes in the South.

So was I duped? I suppose one could find evidence in these files that I attended, and even spoke at, events that local communists organised. Thus one CPA meeting is recorded as identifying a number of people who were 'available speakers' for an anti-apartheid rally in 1971, including lawyer Garth Nettheim and myself. But if the CPA helped organise some of the events at which I spoke, this shows no more than a common interest, and it is just as arguable that those of us who were not members of the Communist Party manipulated those who were.

This is not to deny a certain degree of political naivety on my part. According to these records I clearly consorted with known communists, even if I didn't know it at the time. To be honest, I was far more interested in known homosexuals, and while there were a couple of people who fitted both categories, I barely thought about their actual political allegiances. Those of us in our twenties then thought of ourselves as a radical generation, largely uninterested in old-style party politics, though I was a gut Labor voter, and shared the hopes of so many that Whitlam would change Australia radically.

In the late 1980s, when I settled in Melbourne after four years living in the US, I spent several years as a member of the Socialist Forum, which brought together a mix of disillusioned communists and Fabian socialists, and, again, it is hard to say who was manipulating whom. The most successful product of the Forum is, of course, Julia Gillard, who has become reflexively pro-American to a degree that none of us would have accepted when we spoke in the most genteel terms of the need for a radical critique of the reforms of the Hawke Government.

The last entry in the files to date comes from September 1978, a record from Immigration authorities that I had arrived in Sydney on Japan Airlines flight 771. I am grateful for the reminder – much easier than hunting through tattered old diaries of my own – and mildly flattered that ASIO cared. There is no evidence they had any interest in why I was in Japan, or even that they knew it was a stopover en route from Paris, where I had spent much of 1977 and '78. It would be interesting to know if there is any record in the files of the French national security service of my time in Paris, which included encounters with such subversive figures as Michel Foucault, William Burroughs and a motley collection of gay liberationists and Australian expats. One of my best friends there was Guy Hocquenghem, who was a central figure in the French gay movement, and undoubtedly had among his acquaintances a range of far more subversive figures than I was able to meet.

There is something quite endearing about the earnest amateurism of the ASIO files. I suspect they were far less intrusive and nasty than some state police, particularly in Queensland, as Andrew McGahan reminds us in his novel *Last Drinks*. In the current environment, government surveillance is far more sophisticated, although not necessarily more relevant. For the real question is surely what sort of surveillance into political activity is necessary – or desirable – in a democracy.

In the current environment it would be futile to argue against all forms of surveillance: September 11 and Bali settled that. But one wonders how much of the presumably extensive surveillance now in place is rather like banning real knives from airline meals – when steel forks could actually do more damage. Only a tiny proportion of what is listened to and monitored relates to genuine threats to 'national security', if by that we understand attempts to harm people in the service of other states or anti-democratic ideologies.

The enemies have shifted, and become more amorphous, since the 1970s. It is hard to believe that current security officers would bother noting, as a file entry on a university friend does, that he 'was a force in every club or society that was then considered "bohemian"'. But one suspects there is the same obsessive collection of irrelevant data, which tells us more about the prejudices of security officials than it does about any real risk to our security. If there are such risks – and regrettably I think there probably are – I hope very much that current surveillance is a lot more focused and useful than that to which I was apparently subject.

ROWAN CAHILL

1967   2013

Rowan Cahill was born in Sydney in 1945 and educated in state schools. While a student at Sydney University, his marble was drawn in the second conscription ballot in 1965. He became a conscientious objector, and went on to become prominent in the anti-Vietnam War, student, and New Left movements. Variously arrested and charged, he avoided prison courtesy of civil liberties lawyers. Formative journalistic experiences during the 1960s were gained working on the Sydney University student newspaper *Honi Soit* under the editorships of Hall Greenland and Keith Windschuttle.

In 1967 Rowan was a founder of the innovative Free University in Sydney and in the early 1970s was a member of the editorial board of *Australian Left Review*. In 1970 he began two years' employment as a historian with the militant Seamen's Union of Australia (SUA); there he was influenced by its leader EV Elliott and by SUA journalist Della Elliott. This was the beginning of a long and continuing association with Australian maritime unionism.

Rowan has variously worked as a teacher, freelance writer and agricultural labourer, and for the trade union movement as a journalist, historian, and rank and file activist. Prior to its winding up in 2006, he was 'Picket Line Correspondent' for the NSW Labor Council e-weekly, *Workers Online*. Rowan has published widely in labour movement, radical, and academic publications. His books include, as co-author, *A History of the Seamen's Union of Australia, 1872–1972*; and *Twentieth Century Australia: Conflict and Consensus*; and as co-editor, *A Turbulent Decade: Social Protest Movements and the Labour Movement, 1965–1975*. Most recently he was co-author with Terry Irving of *Radical Sydney: Places, Portraits and Unruly Episodes*. Currently Rowan is teaching at the University of Wollongong. In 2013 he was awarded a doctorate for his thesis on journalist Rupert Lockwood.

JOINING THE DOTS: C/58/63

by Rowan Cahill

In Australia during the Vietnam War, the charge was frequently made that domestic opposition to the war and to conscription was variously organised or manipulated by communists. On the international stage Prime Minister Menzies claimed this, for example, in 1965 in an address to the Australia Club in London. However, as Ann Curthoys has pointed out, while the Communist Party of Australia (CPA) was important as an organising force in the anti-war movement, it was only part of a loose coalition of forces opposed to the war. Apart from trade unions, churches, and political parties, there were at least 146 organisations actively opposing conscription and the Vietnam War during the period 1964–1972.

For ASIO, however, dissent and opposition were the conspiratorial products of communists and radicals, a view that was then fed to the government. The anti-war movement, and all that flowed from it, according to a July 1968 ASIO analysis, was at root a machination of Soviet Union foreign policy; the less communists were seen as an active presence or as an initiating agency, the more that proved their sinister guile. Research papers generated by ASIO were provided to right-wing journalists. Between 1962 and 1972 ASIO supplied sixty-seven sets of briefing papers to the Australian press, the bulk of them about the Communist Party. ASIO research materials were also provided to anti-communist organisations like BA Santamaria's National Civic Council and the Congress for Cultural Freedom.

I enrolled in a Bachelor of Arts degree at Sydney University in 1964, the same year the conservative Menzies Government announced the introduction of a selective conscription (National Service) scheme for twenty-year olds. I was conscripted the following year in the second call-up ballot, a fate shared by one in twelve of my vote-less male peers. In May 1966 I destroyed my call-up notification (the so called 'draft card') and began a political trajectory that brought me to prominence in the emerging and developing anti-war, student protest, and New Left movements.

My radicalisation commenced in high school during the late 1950s and early 1960s, as a tentative and developing liberal unease with the stifling conformity of Menzies-era Australian society and culture. It was an unease that delighted in the pages of the new satirical *Oz* magazine, the first issues of which I enthusiastically devoured with some of my peers in the school playground during my last year of schooling in 1963.

Conscription brought this liberal, middle-class unease face-to-face with the power of the state in a personal way, and compelled me to focus on a war I previously knew little about. During 1967 ASIO began its surveillance of me and I became ASIO file C/58/63.

The rebellion of youth against conscription and the Vietnam War concerned ASIO, generating a mixed response within its ranks. Particularly troubling was the New Left of the late 1960s, a multi-dimensional leftism that variously blended moral and cultural nonconformity with the leftisms developing in Europe, the US, and the Third World. It was hard to classify, and, according to David McKnight in *Australia's Spies and Their Secrets*, this left 'older (ASIO) officers cold'. According to a 1970 ASIO research paper, the New Left comprised a range of people: the offspring of old leftists, radical Christians, career rebels (who spurned regular employment in order to protest), anti-draft activists, and 'drug using beatniks and other social deviants'.

The rebellion and its complexity intrigued younger ASIO officers. Reports and background papers were generated within the organisation and it was claimed that Australia was headed for 'internal war'. An ASIO view was that orthodox Australian communism was wedded to an insurrection or coup d'etat; the new radicals sought nothing less than the complete restructuring of society through the use of urban guerrilla warfare. As McKnight has pointed out, in developing this understanding ASIO tended 'to accept at face value' some of the left's 'wilder fantasies'. Another ASIO fear was that international Trotskyists and anarchists would push the politics of the Australian left further to the left, so that revolutionary politics would become part of regular political discourse.

Alarming also for ASIO was that the CPA was changing, transforming ideologically from its traditional authoritarianism and conservatism and moving away from its links with the Soviet Union. Particularly worrying about this transformation was that the party was seen to be building relationships with other people and organisations seeking what ASIO described as 'great' and 'fundamental' social change.

Opposition to the Vietnam War, the youth revolt and attendant intellectual ferment boosted ASIO organisationally. Staff numbers increased, it moved into new purpose-designed premises in Melbourne, its areas of specialisation increased, and state Special Branches became 'official adjuncts'. Students were recruited as informants; university intellectuals were targeted because of their role in contesting political conservatism; and break-ins, along with phone-taps, became tools for collecting raw intelligence data. From 1969 to 1972, an operation code-named 'Operation Whip' concentrated on the anti-war movement, a major part of its brief being to target student activists with a view to establishing their links with the CPA.

ASIO regularly released material to selected parliamentarians who then used it in their parliamentary speeches. As mentioned above, selected journalists also received ASIO materials. In 1969–70, ASIO produced a paper on the anti-war militancy of secondary school students. There are close parallels between this material and a widely sold booklet *Student Power* (1970), published under the name of journalist, author and NSW state Liberal parliamentarian, Peter Coleman.

ASIO file C/58/63 was generated in, and reflects, this broad ideological context. The file is catalogued by the National Archives of Australia as beginning in 1967. However, the first folio of the file has been withheld from the public arena, so the circumstances of the file's origins remain unclear. Folio 2 is a copy of a leaflet in which I am mentioned, published in March 1968 by the Sydney University-based Students for a Democratic Society. All up, for the period 1967 to 1972, the file comprises 171 folios; eighteen of these are totally exempted (withheld) from public scrutiny, and sixty-eight are partially exempted (censored) with the blacking-out of words, names, and bureaucratic numberings/references that could possibly assist cross-referencing and checking by independent researchers. The exemptions were variously made by ASIO under the exemption categories described by Section 33 of the Commonwealth of Australia *Archives Act 1983*.

The content of the file has apparently been gathered through bureaucratic research (for example, of birth and car registration records), personal and photographic surveillance, the contributions of informants, media monitoring (newspaper clippings where I am mentioned; selected published items I authored), and postal and telephone intercepts. I was amongst those targeted by 'Operation Whip'. The surveillance/informant material largely concerns associates, people met (their names cross-referenced to other ASIO files), meetings attended (and sometimes what transpired), and finally demonstrations/protests attended.

In common with many other ASIO files now in the public domain, C/58/63 is little more than a collection of raw information and data, with a chronological structure, about a particular person. There is no specific overall biographical narrative, little in the way of commentary or analysis, and the material included is selective. However, as Fiona Capp has argued in *Writers Defiled*, ASIO surveillance files constitute a form of biography compiled while the subject was alive, with a 'narrative' that is implied. In a sense the files are 'works in progress', constructed parallel to the life of the subject as it was being lived. The existence of a file is evidence the subject was under surveillance, bringing with it implications of being guilty of something, of being a dangerous social type, of being subversive. The files are not comprehensive 'literary' biographies, but constitute what Capp termed 'an incriminating biography … the inverse of hagiography', the intention being to conjure up 'the diabolic rather than the saintly'. To this end only aspects of the subject's life are recorded, akin to a collection of episodes or 'snapshots'. Fact, falsity, gossip, legend can all form part of the data, the material reflecting the subject not as a full human being but as a political being. The ideological forces that have shaped, and shape, the collector/agency frame the data collection process. For the reader-user, a file is a biographical resource from which an 'imagined enemy' can be constructed.

So who was the subject of C/58/63 as seen by ASIO in 1967–1972? Rowan John Cahill, aka John, Rohan, Roland, and Rowen Cahill, was born in Cremorne, Sydney, in 1945. Correct, except for the suggestion of multiple identities; these were due to mistakes by ASIO field operatives and/or ASIO transcribers. Cahill was variously described as being either 5 feet 4 inches or 5 feet 9 inches (for the record, the correct height was 5 feet 6 inches), with fair to brown hair, of medium build, a youthful appearance, and with 'pointed features'. He owned and drove a 1961 green Volkswagen sedan, its registration details dutifully recorded by ASIO. This detail was important for tracking Cahill during surveillance operations.

Cahill was an undergraduate, then a post-graduate, student at Sydney University; at times ASIO was confused, describing him as an academic. According to surveillance reports, he was a frequent presence at protests and demonstrations, sometimes addressing them, and sometimes getting arrested. Media monitoring indicated he also wrote, and authorised, leaflets; he was frequently published in the left press; and he edited the Sydney University student newspaper *Honi Soit* (which in fact was not the case; he was its publisher). ASIO regarded him as a student leader.

In August 1968 Cahill was prominent in the capture and detention of two NSW Police Special Branch officers, including the branch head. The officers were observed in an unmarked police Mini Minor, covertly tape-recording a student meeting on the Sydney University campus. Students surrounded the car and immobilised it. Tyres were deflated, the electrical wiring system was wrecked, sugar was put in the petrol tank, and the car plastered with anti-war stickers. The officers were detained for two-and-a-half hours until the Acting Metropolitan Superintendent of Police agreed to come to the campus and sign a statement to the effect that in future, police would not spy on campus student meetings.

Following this signing, the officers were released, their car lifted and carried by students and dumped on Parramatta Road. Between the capture and the dumping, a large number of police assumed siege positions off-campus, while students erected barricades on-campus. The media dubbed the incident 'The Siege of Sydney University'. There is a two-page report of the incident in the Cahill ASIO file. While a large number of students were involved in the incident, only four were deemed of interest to ASIO; Cahill was one, his behaviour implicitly belligerent/inflammatory, and noted as 'abusive'.

In May 1969 an ASIO report noted that Cahill and others were planning to go into the Army and 'interpret the military laws in such a way that they could not be charged with treason or sedition, but could work effectively'.

Essentially correct. What the report failed to include was background and context. At the time the Commonwealth was steadfastly refusing to grant me status as a conscientious objector, for which I had applied; the issue was the subject of a long-running legal case. With the support of Ken Buckley, a founding member and leading activist of the NSW Council for Civil Liberties, and the assurance that he had organised a panel of supportive lawyers, the plan was to enter the Army should I be compelled, and work on behalf of the Committee for the Rights of Servicemen (CRS).

The CRS was convened by Ken, run on a need-to-know basis, and mainly comprised ex-servicemen like Ken. Its purpose was to familiarise servicemen, particularly conscripts, with their rights and civil liberties, disseminate anti-Vietnam War materials, and facilitate challenges to 'unlawful' military orders/commands. To date the CRS had only distributed leaflets to conscripts as they arrived on periodic intake 'recruitment' days at the Marrickville Army Depot (New South Wales), notifying them of the existence of the CRS. As it turned out, I was never put to the test; in August 1969 a district court judge recognised my status as a conscientious objector.

The May 1969 report brought Cahill to the attention of ASIO's B1 branch, the counter subversion branch that dealt with communist influence in trade unions and front organisations, with international communism, and with plans for the internment of left-wing Australians (which remained operational until at least 1971). 'Abusive', 'treason', 'sedition': C/58/63 was, arguably, an increasingly dangerous character.

By 1971 Cahill had been 'assessed' by ASIO as a 'Trotskyist sympathiser' and as being associated with prominent Trotskyists. He was also known to be a member of the Australian Labor Party, and in frequent contact and working closely with leading members of the CPA. He was even known, at least once, to have done a job of subterfuge for the CPA. (He had acted as a front man in the hire of the Sydney Town Hall for a lecture by visiting French Marxist intellectual Roger Garaudy on the Christian–

Marxist dialogue.) Cahill also was linked with numerous other left organisations. Amongst his contacts were left intellectuals (also the subject of ASIO files). He was involved in the development of political links between tertiary student radicals and trade unions, and seen to be interested and involved in the radicalisation of secondary school students and Aborigines.

In a sense, the Trotskyist 'sympathies' attributed to me were correct; but ASIO did not explain what it meant by the description, nor did it probe or elaborate upon these 'sympathies'. To a great extent my interest in Trotsky was intellectual. A study of aspects of Trotsky's life formed part of my history honours thesis in 1968; I was greatly impressed by Isaac Deutscher's three-volume study of Trotsky. Of special interest was Trotsky's later life and thought following his exile from the Soviet Union. Trotsky was a lens through which I explored the nature of the state, and the historical problems of what happens to idealism of a social justice kind when it becomes part of a revolutionary program, and later, part of the apparatus of state power.

ASIO's data correctly identified me as being close to the CPA, and in March 1970 described me as an intellectual with views to the left of the CPA and 'explicitly revolutionary'. While I was never a member of the CPA, from 1969–1973 I was a member of the editorial board of the party's theoretical/intellectual journal *Australian Left Review*. Part of a small group of young intellectuals, I was invited onto the board in an effort to widen the journal's readership and develop perspectives reflecting New Left and contemporary Marxist perspectives. According to a March 1970 ASIO analysis in the Cahill file, the CPA had a strategic master plan to utilise the intellectual resources of 'Marxist academics' and create 'Red Bases' in the universities from which 'the revolution' could then be 'exported into society'.

C/58/63 depicted Cahill as having a broad range of leftist contacts, and as working politically in a broad-left way. Again correct. However, ASIO failed to elaborate. Considering what we know of ASIO's political understanding of the time, it can be conjectured the organisation viewed Cahill's broad-leftism as part of an organisational conspiracy. In reality, however, my broad-leftism was personal and hard won. It emerged slowly out of my interactions with many people; and from my undergraduate studies of European and British history, which included studies of the English Civil War and of nineteenth century socialism. From these came understandings of the often crippling impact that competing egos, tactical issues, and ideologies had upon radical social movements.

The portrait of Cahill that emerges from C/58/63 mirrors the ideological concerns of ASIO during the period 1967 to 1972; essentially he is what ASIO wanted him to be. Of course the subject did contribute to this portrait by his actions/activities, but much of C/58/63 is a circumstantial construction of an imagined, possibly unpleasant and dangerous, political being, certainly more dangerous than he was in reality. No evident interest was expressed, nor time spent, by ASIO trying to understand C/58/63 as a human being, nor in probing the personal nature of his politics. For ASIO it sufficed to apply labels, and to join the dots. The pattern that emerged was pre-determined. Which begs the question: does the same, or similar, approach still apply in today's hydra-headed world of Australian spooks?

PHILLIP ADAMS

Phillip Adams began writing over sixty years ago – as a teenage film critic for Melbourne's communist *Guardian*. Since then he's been a critic and columnist for publications including *The Australian, The Bulletin, The Age, Sydney Morning Herald, Courier-Mail, Adelaide Advertiser, National Times, Nation Review, Launceston Examiner, Australian Business* and both *The Times* and *Financial Times* in London. With Barry Jones, he was the driving force behind the revival of the Australian film industry, chairing the Film Radio and TV Board, Film Australia, the Australian Film Institute and the Australian Film Commission. His twenty films include *The Adventures of Barry McKenzie, Don's Party* and *We of the Never Never*. He has published dozens of books including *The Unspeakable Adams, The Big Questions, A Billion Voices, Backstage Politics* and, most recently, *Bedtime Stories* – his account of twenty-two years as presenter of *Late*

Night Live. Robert Manne describes Adams as 'perhaps the most remarkable broadcaster in the history of this country'.

A foundation member of the Australia Council, Phillip chaired the Commission for the Future, the National Australia Day Council and was President of the Victorian Council for the Arts. Scores of board memberships include Film Victoria, Greenpeace Australia, Ausflag, both the Adelaide and Brisbane festivals of ideas, the National Museum and Families in Distress. He is currently Chair of the Australian Centre for Social Innovation. Honours include two Orders of Australia, four honorary doctorates, a Walkley, the Longford Award, the Human Rights Medal, Humanist of the Year and a fellowship in the Australian Academy of the Humanities. A 'minor planet' was named after him by the International Astronomical Union.

After quitting the Communist Party he joined the ALP – resigning after fifty years to protest the coups against NSW Labor premiers and a first-term prime minister.

Asked to identify what was 'wrong with the ABC', John Howard famously asked, 'Where's the right-wing Phillip Adams?' He remains the 'licensed leftie' at *The Australian* – and its longest-serving pundit.

I WAS A TEENAGE BOLSHEVIK

by Phillip Adams

I've been asking ASIO to show me my file for almost forty years. Having been a teenage Bolshevik, it seemed reasonable to assume one existed … probably a thick one. Though only sixteen when I became a card-carrying member of the Australian Communist Party, I hung around with many of the best-known comrades, wrote for the commo newspaper, worked for various 'front' organisations, signed all the angry petitions, marched on May Day, painted anti-war slogans in railway viaducts and often heard strange clicks on the phone. All this during the coldest years of the Cold War, when Menzies had tried to ban the party, heading into the McCarthy era.

But from the fifties to the mid-sixties, though they were bugging my phone, ASIO declined to return my calls. Or reply to my letters. Then, when times were a changin' in the late sixties, with my brief flirtation with Marxism-Leninism far behind me, they finally responded … and lied to me. They said 'you don't have a file', which made one wonder about their competence.

They said the same thing in the early seventies. But they would say that, wouldn't they? In the new political circumstances Lionel Murphy was raiding ASIO and, presumably, they'd been desperately shredding.

Many of my old comrades, who'd either left the party in disgust after the Hungarian invasion or Khrushchev's denunciations of Stalin – or had been expelled for expressing outrage over the Soviets' intervention in Prague – had become distinguished members of the ALP or academe. Some had even become MPs, or right-wing columnists … or members of the Liberal Party.

The seventies found me chairing a few government and cultural organisations, as well as writing for the ageing Sir Frank Packer and the youthful Rupert Murdoch. Despite confessing my political sins in early columns for *The Australian*, the teenage Bolshevik was now a semi-respectable member of the community. By the eighties I'd achieved such a high degree of stultifying dullness that the Governor-General invited me to pop in and collect an Order of Australia. And on that grand occasion I found myself in the curtseying queue with Harvey Barnett, the boss of ASIO, or more correctly, the Director-General of the Australian Security and Intelligence Organisation. I was vastly amused. He wasn't.

Not one to waste an opportunity, whilst we were partaking of post-gong nibbles with Sir Ninian, I asked Harvey (we were now, to his considerable annoyance, on first name terms) about my ASIO file. 'What makes you think you have one?' he asked. 'Well, I bloody well should!' I replied, tempted to tell him of the time I'd sent photographs of the Kew Tramway Depot and other military secrets to the KGB.

Time passed, but I didn't hear from Harv. As fellow members of the Order (it's a bit like being in Rotary, even the lapel badges are similar), you can be informal. Then, towards the end of the nineties, I was informed, in a letter, that, yes, I had a file. But I couldn't see it. Because it might reveal the identity of the various dobbers they'd had keeping an eye on me and my fellow subversives. Actually, the letter didn't say 'dobber'. I think it said 'informant', which is the official ASIO term for someone who dobs in his friends.

(After the fall of the Berlin Wall, millions of Stasi files, almost as extensive as those kept on Queenslanders by Joh's Special Branch, were opened to public scrutiny. And it emerged that almost everyone in that most paranoid of police states was dobbing in each other. Kids had dobbed in mum and dad, brothers had dobbed in sisters, neighbours neighbours, employees employers. Even more astonishing, revered dissidents, like Stefan Heym, whom I subsequently interviewed, had dobbed in other dissidents. So you could understand ASIO's sensitivities.)

That seemed to be that. I'd never get to see my file. The one they didn't have. Then, a few months ago, something extraordinary happened. I was asked to give a talk – on self-censorship in the Australian media – at that fine institution, the National Archives. Not as well-known or frequently visited as the National Library, the Archives is the principal repository of government papers and turned out to be a friendly and user-friendly place, full of fascinating displays and, yes, secrets. At least until they're unburdened by the 'thirty year rule'.

No sooner had I finished my talk than a charming archivist moved a vote of thanks and gave me a couple of prezzos. The first was a book they'd recently published. And the second was my ASIO file!

A lovely and unexpected gesture. Mind you, it wasn't the

whole file and many passages, especially names and signatures are censored. Where you and I might have a little bottle of whiteout, ASIO obviously has big jars, even buckets, of blackout. Nonetheless it was fascinating to see the material, with SECRET typed top and bottom.

The next day, someone who'd been in my audience emailed another page from the files, dated November 1957. This is one of the first entries. I was eighteen years old. My crime? I was projecting Russian films – Eisenstein and others – at the Realist Film Association, New Theatre, Flinders Street, Melbourne. Another letter, dated the third of July 1964, says:

> … one 'Phillip Adams' has come to notice from time to time. Attached is an electoral extract for Phillip Andrew ADAMS who is considered to be identical with this man.

(Good work ASIO!!) The rest, including the signature, is blacked out, but the notepaper belonged to the Regional Director, Victoria, and was marked SECRET. Some secret.

There's a handwritten note – another signature blacked out – dated 18.8.70 asking, 'Mr.B, do we have a file on PHILLIP ADAMS, newspaper writer for "The Australian"?' After more than a decade, you'd think they'd have known. Major party activities – even my membership – seem to have escaped our spooks. Instead there are pages of trivia – the various journals to which I subscribed, odd meetings I attended or chaired, with lists of those participating. Clearly the entirely non-political Humanist Society was under scrutiny, mixed up with 'front' outfits like the Congress for International Co-operation and Disarmament. As late as 1970, my membership of this harmless mob is being recorded, as is my involvement with the Victorian Fellowship of

Australian Writers. Amongst the fire-breathing members were Judah Waten, Oscar Mendelshon [sic], Judith Wright, Frank Dalby Davidson, AA Phillips, Jim Cairns, Barry Jones and – wait for it! – Geoffrey Blainey. Even to be on the Fellowship's mailing list was enough to have you listed as a fellow traveller. But to be fair to ASIO it's good to see that Bolshie bastard Blainey unmasked at last.

The next year, the clowns follow me to another Fellowship function, a seminar at the Microbiology Theatre, Melbourne University, where they have 'Philip [sic] Adams' chairing a session. Dangerous Stalinists involved included Bruce Petty (agent's comment: 'artist'), Barry Humphries (agent's comment: 'comedian') and, worst of all, the notorious Professor Leonie Kramer ('poss.VOF.566/54'). And to think they made this dangerous double agent a dame!

ASIO kept watchful eyes and ears on those amiable duffers in the Fabian Society, all passionate anti-coms, noting a story in BA Santamaria's journal *News Weekly* that Phillip Adams is one of the organisers of a Fabian conference themed 'Planning for Victory', a doomed attempt to help the electoral hopes of the ALP: 'Adams also appears on the list of speakers.'

Next year, ASIO surveillance of left-winger Jean McLean and folk-singer Glen Tomasetti led the spooks to a small concert in aid of Save Our Sons, some long forgotten anti-Vietnam group. A phone tap (so many clicks on so many lines) reveals that academic Max Teichmann will address the audience – and that someone has contacted 'a Phil Adams to help with publicity'. ('Probably Phillip Andrew ADAMS, VPF 11844'). So there's my file number.

Moving onto 1972, Headquarters Intelligence Report No. 602/72 identifies me as a member of the Australian Committee for a New China Policy. This traitorous affiliation is filed within days of Prime Minister Whitlam announcing a new China policy. Otherwise it's London to a brick I'd have been interned or disappeared. Instead of being ID'd as VPF 11844, the document identifies me as A/25/64.

Having worked out that I'm the same Phillip Adams that writes for *The Australian*, ASIO starts clipping out columns. Not all of them, but ones they see as significant, sinister or both. Thus 'Adam's Apple' for Saturday 15 August 1970 has been scissored from the paper – a mildly amusing account of my brief period in the Citizen's Military Force, aka the CMF. After my lack of competence stuffed up a small military exercise, the Army asked me to resign. As a true patriot, I agreed. Unimpressed by the column's cheery confession, ASIO clearly suspected that I was a Soviet saboteur.

Another column they filed from this era is a detailed account of my times as a card-carrying comrade. Headed 'Recollections of A Teenage Bolshevik', it came complete with rude remarks about ASIO:

> For decades ASIO has provided Australian politics with much needed humour and light relief, as their incompetence is staggering. One of my favourite memories concerns an historian, the late Brian Fitzpatrick, a man of leprechaunian wit and defiant left-wing associations. One day he arrived at the front door of ASIO's thickly disguised headquarters and demanded to see his dossier. The ASIO people were so stunned by this unprecedented request that they acceded to it, and Brian went through the papers with a blue pencil making corrections. Then, shaking his head in disappointment at their inaccuracies and ineptitude, he left.

Phillip Adams (right) visiting the Swinburne Film and Television School during the 'Life. Be In It' campaign, 1980. Alexander Stitt on left.

My column listed many of ASIO's sillier efforts, including a description of a 'Keystone sequence chasing ASIO men across a paddock after we discovered them hiding in a shrub under our lounge room window'. But the best proof of the agency's preposterousness comes in another heavily censored letter from my file. Scout's honour, this reveals that ASIO seriously attempted to recruit me. Dated 5 July 1965, just after my twenty-sixth birthday, the letter is the most heavily censored of all the documents, with just the odd sentence surviving the blackings-out. My employment details are listed, and various people, rendered anonymous, are asked for character assessments and to comment on my suitability for a discreet approach.

I am described by one agent as a 'highly intelligent and egotistical left-winger' (accuracy at last!) 'who lacks basic stability and could not be trusted'. An anonymous dobber adds, 'Adams would actually consider any approach by ASIO a huge joke.' (Right again!) In summary, the letter concludes:

> ... he would probably play along with us for a while but would be unable to resist discussing the matter with others. Adams gave the indication that he failed to treat with proper seriousness those loyalties we considered normal.

A third dobber has the last word: 'As regards asking him to assist us in our work he personally would very strongly recommend in the negative.'

This bitter disappointment, all the worse because it's only now I've learned about it, has blighted my life. I'm sure readers will now understand why I signed up with the KGB instead.

Please eat these top-secret pages after reading them.

Yours sincerely,

VPF 11844

JEAN McLEAN

1969   2013

Jean McLean was arrested many times, jailed twice, threatened with a charge of aiding the enemy and eventually became a Labor Member of the Victorian Parliament for fourteen years.

Born in London to a Russian–Jewish mother and a British father during the Depression, Jean moved with them to Australia. She was largely home-schooled by her parents. After a career in modelling, which she found boring, she opened a coffee lounge with her mother in the Melbourne suburb of Cheltenham. There she met her future husband, Eric, and for two years they roamed the world, returning to Australia to start a family.

She had joined the ES&A Bank after quitting school at fourteen, but in 'an early encounter with the pervasive world of spooks' she was sacked three years later and told that a banking career was not for her (probably because her mother was named as a communist by a mysterious 'Madam X' around the time of the Petrov inquiry).

In 1964 when conscription was introduced, Jean was horrified that Australia was going to force young men to fight in an illegal war in Vietnam. She found like-minded women in her suburb and they began Victoria's Save Our Sons anti-conscription movement. From 1965, for seven critical years, she was their convenor, which inevitably meant prison. A decision to see for herself what was happening in North Vietnam in 1969 resulted in the Commonwealth Police trying to charge her with treason for aiding and abetting the enemy.

Her long-time work around independence for the East Timorese led to her involvement with Victoria University to help its education program in that country, which she visits often.

She has received a Peace Medal from the Socialist Republic of Vietnam and an honorary doctorate from Victoria University.

MY LIFE IN A DISTORTING MIRROR

by Jean McLean

When I rang ASIO to ask for my files, a woman asked why I thought there would be files on me. Then she explained that most people think they have files and are disappointed to learn otherwise.

I assured her that there were files, because I knew someone who had seen them. She was soon back on the phone. This time 'Ms ASIO' was excited. Not only was I correct, she said, but there were nine volumes of files. For $500 I could have them.

My impression as I skimmed the mountain of documents with their constant little deletions, was the spies' absolute obsession with anything to do with what is called in all the files the COMMUNIST PARTY. There are myriad copies of the most excruciatingly dull minutes of CICD (Congress for International Co-operation and Disarmament) and the moratorium movement.

The fact that Bernie Taft was the Victorian Secretary of the Communist Party and also a committee member of both organisations ensured that our major spy body spent a fair amount of its highly paid agents' time, and that of their co-opted pimps, hanging around long dull meetings collecting roneoed sheets of minutes.

Occasionally, there are the spies' personal opinions about the strength of the speeches or otherwise, the age of participants of interest, or their clothing or dress sense. There are also long lists of the number plates of the cars parked outside the meeting halls.

I am fascinated to see in the earliest file that I was a member of the Eureka Youth League (EYL), the youth wing of the Communist Party. I joined, they say, in 1947. I was not a member of the EYL and never went to one of its meetings or camps. But my elder sister, three years my senior, did go to the EYL, having been told it was a useful place, in those socially barren days, to meet young people.

Our parents were members of the Communist Party from about 1942 until 1947 when they left because of the insular and undemocratic nature of the party at that time. Maybe a member of the family or friend put my name forward, but our spies never seemed to worry about checking their facts. I was never a member of the Communist Party, but somehow the fact that I served on committees with members of the party was enough to trigger constant surveillance.

There are innumerable files covering my involvement with the anti-conscription group Save Our Sons, the Stop Omega campaign, the Australia Vietnam Society, visits to Australia of a Vietnam trade union delegation and a Vietnamese women's delegation. There is mention of my jailing in Fairlea Prison a couple of times for opposing conscription. There is comment about my trip to Libya and who travelled with me; about my trip to North Vietnam in 1969 during the war; and to the Soviet Union for a peace congress.

Some of the gems in their reporting include comments of mine, such as, 'I won't say any more on the phone because I think it is bugged.'

Interestingly, there are virtually no documents on my involvement in the Labor Party, of which I had been a member since 1965 and which I represented in the Victorian Parliament from 1985 to 1999. One can only speculate that that was not their brief at that stage in history. Nor is there mention of my involvement in the arts.

So while the files make me seem one-dimensional, it is pleasing to think that the spies didn't pry past their anti-communist brief. They do state quite often that there was no proof of my membership of the Communist Party or direct involvement with other organisations, other than as a speaker or at a couple of Christmas parties – though I am projected into meetings that I did not attend and there are other minor discrepancies.

What does emerge, however, is how little of genuine importance there was for our agents to spy on, how small was our threat to security and how great the waste of money from a huge secret budget.

What is more, in October 1978 the Prime Minister, Malcolm Fraser, is noted in my file as ordering an investigation – 'a Prime Ministerial Inquiry' – into the political party affiliations of a group of people, including me, who signed a *National Times* advertisement protesting against Australia's military ties with ASEAN nations. All names are blacked out. To me, this suggests how threatened Fraser was at a simple statement of opposition to government policies in the region.

My plot to 'infiltrate sports and local bodies' came to the ears of ASIO courtesy of an unknown informant. He phoned the spy headquarters in May 1971 saying he had information on my husband, Eric, and me. The venue for the passing of this information was about as mundane and middle Melbourne as possible: the car park at the Hawthorn Bowl, Glenferrie Road, Hawthorn. There, an agent was told that Eric had a copy of a report of the Worker Student Alliance Conference of January 1971, which revealed the infiltration scheme.

'He initially thought that this report was emanating from the McLeans and this had prompted his call to ASIO,' says the agent's report. 'However, he has since learnt that this report, which consists of about forty–fifty pages, is being used as scrap paper within the [Worker Student Alliance] office.'

The informant, who is noted as having a nervous condition, is asked to collect the scrap paper. He returns to Hawthorn nine days later with about thirty sheets. Those 'of value' are in my file – four pages of them.

They consist of lists of books to be read by a Marxist–Leninist Study Group, works as diverting as Mao's *Problems of Strategy in the Guerilla War Against Japan* and *Carry Through the Struggle Against Khrushchev Revisionism*, and a plainly subversive and dangerous Albanian pamphlet, *Progammatic Proclamation of the Soviet Revolutionary Communists*, as well as works by the immortal Enver Hoxha, which are deeply fascinating studies on the basis of revisionism and tactical flexibility fronts.

This bizarre incident is not reported on further, although it is useful to add that Eric is a non-political person, a builder by occupation and the least likely person to have anything to do with such scrap paper.

My family is also roped in during another weird event. There is speculation in the files about whether Neil McLean, Secretary of the National Union of Australian Students in the

1970s, was my son or stepson. He was spotted handing out Maoist literature at Latrobe University. There follows a tortuous series of reports in which efforts are made to find out if we are related.

Firstly, he is confidently named as my son. Then the next report notes the names and birthdates of my two children and this comment: 'No record can been [sic] of a son of university age although such a person could possibly exist.' The third report says that, according to an informant, the student leader 'is related' to me. Almost a month after the first report it is suggested, on the basis of no evidence, that Eric may have been married before we were wed, and so, *voilà*, the young McLean may be my stepchild. To me, it would have been entirely simple to find who the student leader McLean's parents were. But, as is common, it seems, ASIO took the hard road and got nowhere.

Two months pass before a note goes to the State Regional Director of ASIO saying that Eric McLean had *not* previously been married. And further enquiries found that their Neil McLean had not been identified 'as there are a large number of persons of his name in the probable age group. It is considered that further details will be required to affect [sic] a positive identification.'

As I have said, my file opens with a mistaken statement that I was a member of the Eureka Youth League. My parents were members of the party until 1947 and it is, I suppose, possible that my name was wrongly put on a membership list. That being said, it is odd to read a confident report by ASIO that, at the age of fifteen, I was 'a financial and active member' of the league.

This 1961 report says that in that year my parents made an 'apparent statement' that I was 'still active' in the Communist Party – despite the fact that I never joined it. Nineteen years

Anti-conscription protest at the 1969 Melbourne Cup.
Jean McLean on left, Cice Cairns on right.

pass before another document clears me of ever being a member of the party.

Accounts of meetings of Save Our Sons in Sydney, a separate organisation from the one I was a co-founder of in Melbourne, are followed by a note that the communist journalist Malcolm Salmon phoned a woman asking for my number. Salmon is also phone-tapped being told that there are some lovely photos of my little boy (then aged three). Another communist journalist whose phone was intercepted, Dave Davies, is recorded ringing to find out about an anti-conscription demonstration and being referred to me.

My age is overstated by thirty years in a document that also falsely says I told a Sydney meeting of SOS that I 'had fifty women lined up for action, and was anxious to get moving on Save Our Sons'.

A 1972 document in the file, distributed to thirteen ASIO operatives, makes it clear mail was being opened. It's a copy of a letter sent by me to the Waterside Workers' Union boss, Ted Bull, at the union's West Melbourne offices, inviting him to a fundraiser to help pay for the bail and legal costs of draft resisters.

An ASIO officer reported on a lecture by author Felix Greene at the Assembly Hall, Collins Street, Melbourne in 1965. The agent comments that the meeting was taped by a female member of Save Our Sons. 'This woman had long blonde hair and wore knee-high boots.' The agent adds that the woman is 'probably' me.

A month later, back in the Assembly Hall, the Victorian Special Branch records me reporting on the Paris Conference of Women from Belligerent Nations.

An infiltrator reports on a meeting of the Victorian

Anti-Vietnam War march, Melbourne. Front row, left to right: Kevin Childs, Sam Goldbloom, unknown person, Jim Cairns, Tom Uren, Jean McLean, Clyde Holding.

Congress for International Co-operation and Development (CICD). This spy does not limit his or her report to facts, but talks of an 'unimpressive speech' by one speaker which 'only' made two points (against conscription and the Vietnam War). A minister of religion's talk was described as 'the most radical' of the evening.

Photographic surveillance is a consistent theme in the files. The photographers would have been busy because we protested every thirteen weeks for nine years at the Army Barracks in Swan Street, Richmond, at the intakes of conscripts.

In October 1968 I went to Burnie in Tasmania with a lawyer, Julie Dahlitz. According to a heavily censored account of our meeting there, one participant was cross and said the $80 used to bring us from Melbourne 'had been unwisely spent' because the aims of preventing war had been lost in a mire of other actions, such as opposing conscription and promoting civil rights. The agent's comments are blacked out – and we would not know who attended, except that the fourteen names are on another file, which also notes that I talked about why the women of North and South Vietnam opposed the war. The meeting received a glowing critique from the resident spy, who wrote that 'both speakers were impressive and well received by the audience ...'

Two months earlier a flurry of activity had erupted when ASIO's Regional Director for Tasmania was required to report to headquarters on 'communist influence in the ABC'. This arose because two of us were interviewed on TV while visiting Tasmania and a transcript was sent to ASIO headquarters. South Australian Premier Don Dunstan also visited Hobart and spoke at a rally, ensuring an urgent secret message from an agent there, saying that I was on the way there and 'left radical groups' planned to demonstrate.

This report notes that a memorandum the previous year listed those employed by the ABC in Tasmania. None were 'currently' known to be closely linked with the Communist Party. The communists were refused free air-time for elections and communists who appeared on Tasmanian television were 'visiting Mainland functionaries', such as party Secretary Bernie Taft, ABC television personality Corrine Kirby, and me.

Also in 1968, the file reports that Paul Hasluck, Minister for External Affairs, made inquiries about me before a scheduled meeting held that month. ASIO repeated the erroneous statement that I had been in the Eureka Youth League.

Newspaper clippings on demonstrations and copies of leaflets litter the files. Federal Opposition Leader Arthur Calwell is reported as marching in a 1968 demonstration. He is one of just eight people out of about a hundred whom ASIO could name.

My sense of humour was lost on the agents carrying out a phone tap in October that year as we planned a vigil in the city. I told fellow protestor Harry van Moorst that I would be wearing a wig and mask. He thought he would do the same because police warned him that if they caught him in any trouble they would beat him up. Jokingly I said this would be good publicity and suggested that he get beaten up where everyone could see it. The humourless agents entirely miss this joke in their report.

An indication of just how zealous ASIO was, is offered by a report in April 1969 after the arrest of nine of us, including federal Member of Parliament Dr Jim Cairns and the Reverend Terry Lane, later an ABC broadcaster, for breaking a city by-law by handing out pamphlets in the City Square. Phone taps on Cairns's office record an activist asking to speak to him that day and then calling van Moorst to tell him of our arrests.

Later that year ASIO opened and copied a long letter a friend and I sent to draft resister Brian Ross in Sale Prison, telling him he could possibly be free if Labor won the impending federal election and explaining how we could help him in his case.

Some ASIO codenames would please John le Carré. 'Hawke' is one such. Reports appear on Eltham sculptor Matcham Skipper in 1980 because he won a Churchill Scholarship. Skipper is noted in reference to the late folksinger Glen

Tomasetti, a close friend. ASIO names me as another of Skipper's friends, saying I was helping his visit to Moscow through the USSR–Australia Society.

The agents were again hard at work recording a talk on Christian–communist dialogue, a garden party and fete in Ascot Vale, tributes to Ho Chi Min [sic] in a St Kilda hall, and a meeting with Judith Todd, daughter of the former prime minister of Southern Rhodesia, now Zimbabwe. There follows a blacked-out section, ending with:

> [name censored] refused to visit the C.P. of A. Headquarters … because he believes this address is close to ASIO and he does not wish to be observed by ASIO entering Communist Party premises.

A message headed 'Secret, Priority' from Adelaide to ASIO headquarters reported that I boarded a TAA flight to go to a rally in Adelaide.

Special Branch officers ED Callaghan and Larkins were sent to the Richmond Town Hall on a Sunday afternoon in July 1971 when the Draft Resisters' Union met. They reported to ASIO that thirty-three people turned up, of whom eight were known. Another eleven were named because of the cars they drove. That event was true, but what is untrue is a report that I attended Marxist study groups organised by the Socialist Left of the ALP. I didn't need something that boring – and the Labor Party did not organise such events.

The famous baby doctor and anti-war activist, Benjamin Spock, spoke at Melbourne Town Hall in 1971. The phone of his assistant was tapped as attendance numbers and door takings are discussed. I am reported as having 'spoken quite well'.

The equally famous Greek composer Mikos Theodorakis is caught up in a phone tap when I call a Communist Party member to ask if he knew whether Theodorakis had just resigned from the party. ASIO would learn that this information had been gained from the television news the previous evening.

My file is littered with odd observations by ASIO's spooks as to the alleged level of interest, or not, generated by speakers at meetings. For instance, the late academic, Dr Max Teichmann, is described on Armistice Day 1971 as giving 'a long discourse' to a meeting of about forty people at the Assembly Hall, 'without saying anything which was novel'. The agent did, however, comment that Dr Teichmann's address was received with enthusiasm.

A significant theme running through these secret files is the detailing, in the style of a shopping list, of the issues discussed. The superficiality is startling, especially if one considers how much all this was costing the taxpayer. It is a clear indication that a security service operating without, at the very least, rigid parliamentary oversight, becomes a political tool, is clearly irresponsible and largely valueless.

For instance, because the moratorium movement operated as an umbrella group, whenever Bernie Taft, the local Communist Party head, contacted people such as me simply to discuss drawing up a petition to be published in the paper, his phone calls were tapped. Or it was just enough for my name to come up in a bugged conversation for yet another document headed SECRET top and bottom to record this fact and be circulated to five logs in Victoria and New South Wales.

Gough Whitlam got a guernsey in September 1971 when security purloined a copy of a report by the South Australian branch of the Union of Australian Women (UAW) about the

UAW's national committee meeting. Whitlam's name is listed under the heading 'Case Officer's Comments', with that of the one-time South Australian Governor, Sir Mark Oliphant, a priest and four women, including me. No more explanation is offered.

Even the national conference on feminism and socialism at Melbourne University in October 1974 was infiltrated. A female Spartacist League speaker said it was more important to work for the revolution than women's issues. 'The content of her address was not taken seriously by most persons present,' noted the agent, who also said the conference appeared to lack direction and was generally seen by those there as ineffective.

Whitlam is not the only politician mentioned. The late Jim Bacon, union leader and later Premier of Tasmania, makes an appearance in phone taps about the arrest of men opposed to being drafted for the Vietnam War; it is mentioned that Bacon's help as a unionist would be sought.

Minutes and reports of meetings, and financial records, including the most exquisitely mind-numbing minutiae, fill these pages. There are also pages of number plates of the cars of people attending meetings.

There is, however, a hint of shifting grounds in 1973 when an unattached agent (not paid by ASIO) reported that a CICD meeting was told that talks with the new federal Labor Attorney-General indicated that he was confident of being able to make ASIO a more suitable and effective organisation under his control.

During this period, protests against abortion laws, Chilean repression, the French nuclear tests in the Pacific, American aggression in Cambodia and proposed American spy bases are scrutinised and recorded.

The Victorian Police's infamous Special Branch was active on behalf of ASIO in an outstanding example of Commonwealth–state cooperation, reporting on demonstrations in Collins Street. Special Branch officers Detective Sergeant Sharkey and Senior Detective Gardiner popped along to the City Square for the annual 4 July rally in 1973. 'An attempt was made to record the speakers with a portable tape recorded (sic),' they told ASIO, 'but owing to heavy interference these speakers are practically indicipherable [sic].'

In keeping with the tradition of newspapers, the communist *Tribune* conference at the Collingwood Town Hall in 1973 was followed by dinner and, according to the ASIO spy present, 'much drinking'. This may be why the spy says that although the agent met many communists, 'I was unable to remember all of the names.'

More graphic details are forthcoming in a 'confidential' report of a meeting of twelve women in solidarity for peace in 1975. The informant present noted one woman was aged about sixty, 'gnarled looking, has long greying hair, has an ample figure, was of a scruffy appearance …' but Dianne, the domestic James Bond writes:

> … is of medium build, has dark short wavey [sic] hair, has very clear, well coloured skin, dark blue eyes, big dark brown eyelashes with dark around eyebrows and does not wear makeup … She recently raised $27.50 towards the Vietnam Rebuilding Fund in Victoria and is the girlfriend of a well-known middle-aged Professor.

Much alarm erupted among the forces of law and order in June 1977. The revolution, it seemed, was upon us … Our own Storming of the Bastille or October Revolution, perhaps. This arose through the Victoria Police Special Branch reporting that at a meeting at Melbourne University the now respectable academic, Professor Humphrey McQueen, said of a 4 July demonstration, 'We are going into a wing of the Defence Department.' A pamphlet included in my file announced a march on ASIO's office in Wellington Parade, East Melbourne, and demanded 'all files kept on Australian patriots'. A confidential report to ASIO's Director-General said McQueen may have been referring to this ASIO office, for the pamphlet also attacked interference by the CIA and the KGB in Australia. 'Victoria Police are taking action to ensure that demonstrators are kept at a safe distance from the Victorian regional office (ASIO).' Commonwealth Police were also called to the demonstration.

As it happened, ASIO offices were not stormed. Like much of the stuff in my files, it didn't happen. In the parallel world of spydom the distorting mirror is, it seems, the only reality.

My reflections on my ASIO files make me wonder if successive governments have lost sight of the rights of the citizen in this democracy. 'If you don't have anything to hide it doesn't matter' is a commonly heard view, especially when debates arise on issues such as a national identity card. Of course it matters. What could be more unsavoury than being followed, having your phone tapped, your letters opened and not knowing whom among friends and colleagues might be reporting on you? In this *Lives of Others* world, inhabited by those who use the powers of the state for political purposes, democracy is the loser. While I may not have been irrevocably harmed by what the spooks did and may still be doing to invade my privacy, society as a whole certainly is.

Clearly at the very least there is a desperate need for proper oversight of the security services to ensure our rights are not trampled on, and a genuine debate needs to take place about why we need such an all-pervading secret spying machine.

It seems our politicians are constantly hampered by their own shortcomings and insecurities and, instead of working as a government towards a society that encompasses the needs of the majority of its citizens, they opt for mechanisms that suppress dissent and acquiesce to policies that are in the main utterly inadequate and short-sighted.

One result is that any issues as seemingly straightforward as opposition to conscription for military adventures abroad, which was subject of a vote in the First World War, and rejected by soldiers at the front, becomes the subject of massive and intrusive domestic spying. We were continuing a noble tradition in opposing this sort of conscription and yet we were treated as dangerous enemies of the state.

JACK WATERFORD

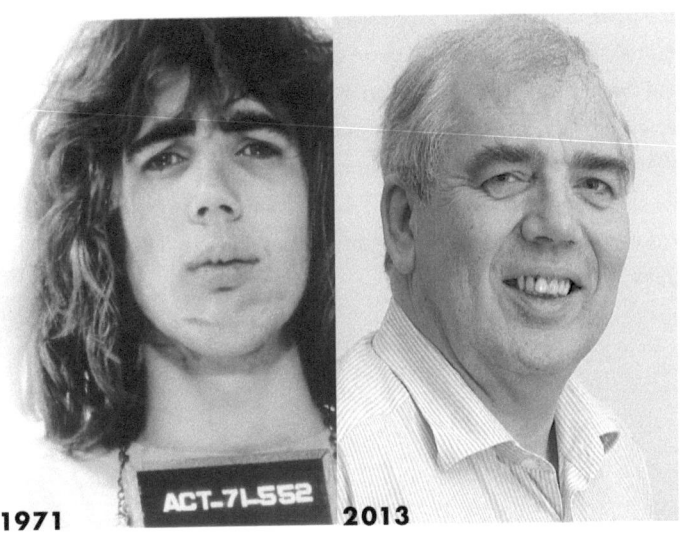

1971 **2013**

Jack Waterford is Editor at Large of the *Canberra Times*, having previously been Deputy Editor, Editor and Editor in Chief. As Editor at Large, he is relieved of administrative duties, and is back to reporting and commenting; more disrespectful staff call the job 'Editor at Lunch'. Jack graduated in law from the Australian National University and since 1972 has been 'more or less' with the *Canberra Times* which he joined as an openly draft-dodging copyboy. In 1977, however, he took a leave of absence for two years to work first with Aboriginal groups establishing Aboriginal medical services in Central Australia, and later as an organiser and report-writer for the Fred Hollows National Trachoma and Eye Health Program.

He received a Jefferson Fellowship at the East–West Center

in 1987, and has served on the board of the Asia Pacific Journalism Centre.

Jack received the Graham Perkin Australian Journalist of the Year Award in 1985. He was named a Member of the Order of Australia in the 2007 Australia Day Honours 'for service to journalism, particularly as a commentator on national politics and the law; to raising debate on ethical issues and public sector accountability, and to the community in the area of Indigenous affairs'. In March 2007, Jack was named Canberra Citizen of the Year. Presenting the award, ACT Chief Minister Jon Stanhope said Waterford was a champion of many causes and a leading figure in his trade.

SMASHING THE STATE

by Jack Waterford

The greatest affectation of my youth was imagining that we were all important enough to be followed around by ASIO, or that someone might be tapping our telephones. Sure, we were smashing the state, or liked to imagine that we were. But was the state collapsing? Did anyone notice even slight tears in its fabric? Was anyone actually treating us as anything more than trifling nuisances? Even in our own minds, could we imagine that we represented any clear and present, or even vague and potential, danger to Christian civilisation?

Of course we knew that we were the subject of some regular attention from police special branches, that our occasional demonstrations or 'agit-prop' sometimes resulted in arrests, court cases and public denunciations from the great and good – my favourite being Billy Snedden's comment, after the May 1970 moratorium march, that we were 'political bikies pack-raping democracy'. One imagined too that there were security chaps who were coldly surveying the student left and the international phenomenon of anti-Americanism; opposition to the Vietnam War; and anti-racism causes such as anti-apartheid action and Aboriginal rights. Were they wondering where the politics of the street might take Australian society or whether we (the demonstrators) represented any serious danger to the modern state?

There was more than the usual amount of Marxist talk, of anarchist talk, and talk of practical sabotage, and for some, passions were strong enough, and heartfelt. But few of us, in our hearts, thought either that the fields were just waiting for 'the spark' or that there was any organised body of people capable of seizing the moment or taking charge. Neither did we have the conceit of thinking that those who represented what we were fighting against (apart from each other) would overestimate our ability or our influence.

In the early 1970s I lived in a house in Canning Street, Ainslie, a nice middle-class suburban street where resided, besides the long-haired hippy louts at my house, one High Court judge, one police magistrate (invariably to be found drunk in our local pub after work), a number of intelligence analysts, a senior Salvation Army officer, and miscellaneous public servants, most of whom (other than the magistrate) were friendly enough. The house had been founded by a few office bearers of the ANU Labour Club, and had become informally the meeting place of people plotting demonstrations against conscription, Vietnam and various other issues of the day.

The Canning Street house, whose garage area was an effective second floor, housed at any one time between six and fifteen people, plus people crashing while travelling to and from Sydney or Melbourne. We had learned to silkscreen posters, and the house was the starting point for expeditions going out leafleting, postering or painting up the town – because of which, a police car was sometimes parked up the street, waiting for people to return home with incriminating materials, such as paint brushes.

We were, of course, familiar with the police Special Branch, whose head mostly gave the impression that he rather liked students and whose activities were generally focused on minimising rather than aggravating confrontations. If a march, say, from the ANU over Commonwealth Avenue Bridge, was likely, Sergeant Ron Dillon would suggest that if we confined ourselves to two south-bound lanes, leaving one free, there would be no trouble, perhaps even a motorbike escort.

Naturally some of us would actually want trouble – because some degree of confrontation was the essence of attracting publicity to the cause – but generally the police stuck to deals and arrested only those who had more or less wanted to be arrested. It was only with the 'Day of Rage' in 1971, the Springbok game at Manuka Oval, and later the Aboriginal Embassy protests, that relations with the police broke down. In these instances there were indiscriminate arrests and violence on both sides. In due course I was to discover that the breakdown followed, in part, breakdowns of command within the police, with some senior officers itching, against adamant Special Branch advice, for an all-in brawl with students and other long-haired troublemakers.

In the very early days of the Commonwealth *Freedom of Information Act*, I obtained a copy of the ACT Police Special Branch file on me – unwittingly causing all of their other old files to be destroyed. The FOI Act had created a right to obtain documents dating back up to five years – to about 1978 – and when I asked for my file, I was told smugly that there were no files on me later than 1973, well outside this period, and thus I could not get access. I appealed, and during a preliminary hearing, outlined the argument I would put: that the Australian

Federal Police (the result of the amalgamation of the ACT and Commonwealth Police forces) had come into existence in 1979, and that documents of the old bodies had, in effect, 'come into existence' when brought together as a result of the amalgamation; they were thus to be regarded as less than five years old. The police urgently got legal advice that I was right; they then extracted my file, destroyed all the other ones, and handed mine over. Now no other files could be accessed.

I have long lost these files, but they prepared me for my look over ASIO's shoulders. The Special Branch files were by and large accurate, if written in an exceedingly dull and impersonal police-ese sort of way. They were not excessively judgmental. They recounted incidents, many of which I had long forgotten, but was now able to recall with hoots of laughter. In this sense, they would be, if I could retrieve them, fabulous for help in writing a memoir, but shed very little real light on the human condition, or the state of the body politic circa 1970.

The best blast from the past came from a number of reports dealing with an incident near the Commonwealth Club on a moonless night at about 1 a.m. in 1971. A favoured evening activity in those days was painting graffiti – usually the words 'SMASH APARTHEID' – on the wall beside the gate of the South African Embassy, about 50 yards through the bushes past the Commonwealth Club. These words appeared on the wall virtually every morning, and every morning the Australian Department of External Affairs apologised to the South Africans and sent a crew from the Department of Interior to paint over them. We reckoned the wall was an inch deep in paint. The local newspapers gave the police heaps for their seeming incapacity to catch the vandals involved – generally lads from Bruce Hall at the ANU.

ASIO surveillance photo from Jack Waterford's file: Jack Waterford with bullhorn, anti-Vietnam War demonstration, Canberra, 30 June 1971. Names listed on the back of the photo: 1. Tony Wilson 2. John Waterford 3. Noelle Pratt 4. David Hirst 5. Lawrence Somos.

But it was a communal activity for anyone bored after a long and tedious meeting, or a day smashing the state, and one night another lad and I drove the old bomb (which had its South Australian registration painted on a piece of masonite, and a papier-mache boot) off Commonwealth Avenue, down Kaye Street and into Forster Crescent. As we came up the hill towards the Commonwealth Club, a police car passed us so we proceeded cautiously until we were out of its sight, then stopped. Suddenly about four police cars converged on us, one with a spotlight. An inspector of police strolled over, 'G'day Jack. G'day Bill. Now what are you doing here?'

I explained that we were on our way to Curtin and had got lost. This was not strictly true, or even probable, but I was not on oath.

We were invited to get out of the car. Three policemen began searching it. A fourth looked at the number plate, then at the rego sticker, then climbed under the car to check engine marks and so on. The cops removed the back seat and searched under it. They opened the boot, so far as it could be opened, and removed various pieces of newspaper and firewood. Another looked under the car, and the bonnet. Infuriatingly, no paint, or brush, or spraycans could be found. More carloads of cops came. More standing around. Another team of cops began repeating the search. Out came the back seat again. Out came the firewood.

After about ten minutes, another inspector arrived. Again it was 'G'day Jack, g'day Bill' and 'I wonder what you are doing here', and again our simple explanation. This inspector walked to the passenger side to look in the car, and his brother inspector said there was no point – the car had been searched thoroughly, and there was no paint. The inspector opened the glove box, pulled out two spraycans and put them on the car bonnet. He looked at me. I walked over to the bonnet, picked up both cans putting my fingers right around them (so as to account for any fingerprints should anyone check) and said, 'My goodness me.' The inspector said, 'Now, fuck off, Jack and Bill'. And we did. No charges ever eventuated.

The documents recounting this were addressed to the officer in charge of Special Branch, and began something like, 'I have to report that on the 11th May I was proceeding in a southerly direction down Forster Crescent when I saw a person I know as Jack Waterford.' It skipped over the failed searches, saying merely that 'a search of the car revealed two cans of spray paint' before saying that 'It was my opinion that the two characters had been intent on committing malicious damage on the walls of the South African Embassy' but 'unfortunately there was no evidence or admissions which would prove this'. It ended, 'Perhaps this report could be stored in Special Branch records.'

As it turned out, ASIO had a few records about it too, as a result of our telling everyone over the phone about our close shave. Alas, after having my fun with the Special Branch documents, I lent them to a young ANU student who wanted them for a history essay. She never returned them, and I have long forgotten who she was.

By the time I got to see my ASIO files, I was rather more aware of ASIO in practical operation. As a young journalist I reported, from close quarters, the 1973 Bijedic affair (there had been concern within the government that ASIO may withhold information on threats to the Yugoslav Prime Minister, Dzemal Bijedic, who was about to visit Australia), including the two raids by Attorney-General Lionel Murphy on ASIO, and played some role in making it such a fiasco for Labor.

A year or two later, the head of ASIO reported to the Prime Minister, Gough Whitlam, that he had reason to believe that a well-informed story of mine in the *Canberra Times* about whose telephones were being tapped by ASIO, had been sourced from a minister (whom he named) who had almost certainly allowed me to read an ASIO report.

I reported on aspects of the 1983 Hope Royal Commission into security services, including the Combe–Ivanov affair, and, later, on the release by ASIO and other agencies of the Petrov

Royal Commission files. By now I knew that I had been under formal ASIO notice in the early 1970s – indeed by now I knew some of the ASIO people who had followed me around in those days – but still had no idea of the range of files they had kept.

They had been tapping my telephone. What an honour – if what a bore for them! ASIO had three volumes of files on me. The Aarons family, the royal family of Australian communism, only had ten – and they may have received a bit of Moscow gold, which is more than I ever did. Indeed a number of the intercepts of my telephone conversations contain tedious discussions of the state of the movement's bank accounts, or about cheques for $10 being bounced for want of funds, or someone's urgent need of $25 to pay a printing bill.

If the files are a blast from the past, recording many events I have long forgotten, they have not once told me a thing that I never knew, or provided a surprise, whether about myself or anyone else. If there was a certain untidiness about our lives and relationships of the day – and the records contain hints of this if one knows where to look – the files are hardly gossip sheets, and if anyone was using the organisation for honey traps, blackmail or exposure, we must have been too strait-laced – or perhaps there is another layer of files to which I have not been made privy.

A great many of the files given to me were reports of telephone calls. The prosaic transcription style suggested that scores of people must have, over the years, lived lives of utter tedium punctuated by short bursts of not very interesting activity. To this were added a host of newspaper cuttings, including cuttings from radical and student newspapers, a vast array of leaflets, and a number of essentially straight ASIO situation reports. There is little analysis evident in any of the material, and when there is, it is mostly commonplace.

A typical transcript might say:

INTERCEPT REPORT : ACT W801/52
1835hrs 11.1.71
John Edward O'Brien WATERFORD Intel70/1124
Kenneth John McLEOD m/52/25

Ken (Kenneth John) McLeod (ACT File 3/2/299) spoke from Sydney to John (Edward O'Brien) Waterford (ACT file W/i/122). Waterford apologised for not attending the National Coordinating Committee.

2. Ken said he would be in Canberra the following day (12.1.71) and suggested he have a talk with WATERFORD. Ken said he would be attending the Orientalist Congress in the morning and would see WATERFORD in the afternoon. WATERFORD agreed.

3. Ken asked after Kel (Kelvin Mark) O'NEILL ACT (file 47/2/2-2138). WATERFORD said Kel was going to be editor of 'Woroni' this year. Ken said he would also like to see Kel while he was in Canberra.

This riveting information was earmarked for distribution to:

1. WMF
2. HQ WMF
3. -5 HQ
6. The Ken McLeod file
7. The John Waterford file
8. The Kel O'Neill file
9. B branch
10. ASIO New South Wales

Or another:

> WOMENS LIBERATION MOVEMENT
> Diedre (Diedre Margaret) HUNTER ACT File H/1/162 asked John (Edward Obrien) WATERFORD ACT File w/1/122 if he knew that the Womens Liberation had now moved to Turner. He said he did. Hunter said they had a good meeting last night and were trying to decide whether Womens Liberation would join the Moratorium or not. It was a big problem because Womens Liberation now included women who were not anti-war. They then discussed the booklet Concerned Asian Scholars of North America. They would use article for this booklet for the next issue of Woroni on Moratorium.

Thirteen separate copies of this document were distributed, including one each for the Waterford and Hunter files.

Or another:

> MORATORIUM COMMITTEE 1600hrs 12/5/71
> A male (u/i) told a female named Syl (phon. fnu) that nothing much had been happening except that at the Moratorium meeting they decided to drop Street theatres until June 30 and said that a group of them had decided to go around the churches. He said they were doing other things but nothing really spectacular. She told him that Kathy McInnes (phon ui) got into some trouble over that. He told her there was a lot more planned for just the Moratorium. She asked what had been planned. He said the apartheid thing. That is the Springboks. She then asked if he was calling from Canning Street. He said yes. She said, 'I was wondering why you were

being so restricted, so you can't really tell me anything about it.' He said no and they would have a meeting about it.

It's hard to deduce much from the materials. There was certainly someone who was reporting to ASIO who was attending moratorium meetings, and I could probably work out who it was if I cared, which I don't. As it happened we had put the Director-General of ASIO, Brigadier Charles Spry, on our mailing list at his home address in Melbourne as a joke, and even if we used a wee bit of phone security – if it occurred to us, and if we could sustain it – there was little that was said that was in any real sense a secret, or which amounted to any criminal activity. There was a certain amount of merry prankster activity – spray-painting raids, for example, planned from the house, and, sometimes broadcast from the telephone, but from the records it did not seem to excite much response from ASIO, beyond the passive record.

Like most left-wing addresses we were very puritanical about drugs on the premises, for fear that it would give the cops further excuses for raids, and hardly any of the transcripts make references to drugs. But one reference to them (a veiled warning to a person to make sure that any he had were removed, because we had reason to believe a police raid was imminent) was recorded without the meaning being understood.

There is a certain amount of household business, referred to elliptically, which was recorded, possibly as 'mysterious', which seems to have gone completely over the heads of the listeners-in. But I expect there were also hundreds of calls of a personal nature, possibly compromising one party or another, which did not make it into transcript form.

I have at times tried to put on my indignant face, pretending outrage about being monitored and taped, but must confess that I am not greatly concerned, for the two reasons of having some record of the past and of being able to share stories with old comrades I have run into, who are themselves preparing some form of memoir.

I do have to record that ASIO has had the last laugh, of sorts. About twenty years ago, I was invited, as editor of the *Canberra Times*, to chat to an intake of young ASIO employees about the press, attitudes to government secrecy, leaks and so on. I am invited to give such talks to public service groups all the time and regard it, more or less, as a public duty. In any event, I went, I chatted, I was cross-examined. They were a bright lot, and not particularly scary. I was presented with some engraved ASIO glasses – with a scorpion motif – and, in due course, a cheque.

In the ASIO annual report for that year, I was listed, by name, as a consultant to the organisation. Talk about professional suicide!

FRANK HARDY

1957 **1982**

Frank Hardy was born in western Victoria in 1917 and grew up in Bacchus Marsh. He left school at fourteen and worked as a messenger, bottle washer, potato digger and fruit picker. He married Rosslyn Couper in 1940 and had three children, Frances, Alan and Shirley.

Because of his experience of poverty during the Depression, Frank joined the Communist Party in 1939. He enlisted in the Army in 1943 and was posted to Mataranka in the Northern Territory. He wrote and edited a unit newspaper for the Army and was employed as an artist for the Army journal *Salt*.

He continued to work in journalism for most of his life, often under the pseudonym of Ross Franklyn. He wrote many books including *The Four-Legged Lottery*, *The Hard Way*, *The Yarns of Billy Borker*, *The Outcasts of Foolgarah*, *But the Dead Are Many* and

The Needy and the Greedy. However, it was his first novel, *Power Without Glory*, self-published in 1950, which led to instant fame and a celebrated court case when he was arrested and charged with criminal libel. *Power Without Glory* became a classic of Australian literature and in 1976 the ABC adapted it as a 26-episode television miniseries.

In 1966, Frank travelled to the Northern Territory and took up the cause of the Gurindji people of Wave Hill who had come into conflict with their employers, the Vestey pastoral company, and had been led out on strike by Vincent Lingiari. Frank wrote *The Unlucky Australians* to publicise their cause and became involved in the long campaign which culminated in Gough Whitlam returning their land in 1975.

Frank was broke for much of his life and remained in a constant battle with some of the Communist Party leadership over his way of life and his growing opposition to the Soviet Union. He remained a member of the de-Stalinised party and at the age of seventy-six stood for Parliament in the 1993 election as an independent to support the unemployed 'because someone has to do it'. He died in January 1994.

THE HARDY WAY

by Alan Hardy

It was quite a daunting task to deal with my father's file. It consists of some 1500 pages, covering 1943 to 1972. I first set eyes on the file in 2009 and when I was asked to write this chapter I wasn't sure how to approach it or where to begin. So many pages – most of it banal and irrelevant – but enough of interest to keep me reading.

ASIO's interest in Frank appears to date from World War II. Then it follows him through the Victorian Royal Commission on Communism, the *Power Without Glory* trial, his championing of the Gurindji and finally his disillusionment with the Soviet Union in the late 1960s. Throughout, they also track his attempts to make a living as a novelist.

When I first began reading, it was fairly random. Most of it I knew but there were a few surprises. ASIO's attitude to him was not a surprise – their obvious desire to write up anything that showed him in a bad light was very clear.

But as I watched my father's life unfold before me I realised there was an unintentional consequence of ASIO's attention. By reading in sequence I was able to track my father's ever-fluid life circumstances and his gradually altering political beliefs.

So I found the best way to deal with all this material was to track the changes and comment on ASIO's commentary along the way.

1940s: THE EARLY DAYS

At the beginning they began looking at him when he was still in the Army during World War II. ASIO reports a 'Communist Party Meeting on the Yarra Bank 13.6.43. PRIVATE HARDY spoke'. I was unaware he did that during his Army service. And amazingly, even my painfully shy 24-year-old mother spoke too! (One of the best bits I learned from the file.)

Then they included some transcripts from the 1949 Victorian Royal Commission on Communism. There is evidence about Frank 'setting up communist cells in the armed forces'.

When Frank started writing seriously in the late 1940s he used the *nom de plume* Ross Franklyn. This intrigued ASIO at first and it took them a while to figure out who it was. There were several notations asking for more information on him. When *Power Without Glory* was published, the cover read, 'written by Frank Hardy – (Ross Franklyn)' because he thought people might know him better by that name.

EARLY 1950s:
POWER WITHOUT GLORY – PROMINENCE

The book quickly became notorious and ASIO were onto it. They included an article from the Melbourne *Guardian* (the Victorian communist newspaper), which was a report of a Yarra

Bank meeting. Frank 'challenged John Wren to sue him if he thinks he is identified in *Power Without Glory*'. (Careful what you wish for, Dad!)

When Frank was arrested and charged with criminal libel, ASIO asked for, and was given, by the Victorian Police, minute details of everything in his pockets – even unsuccessfully trying to decipher his handwriting (something only my mother could do).

In 1950, the Frank Hardy Defence Committee was formed to raise profile and money for his defence on the criminal libel charges over *Power Without Glory*. The interesting part for me was that, though rarely are agents' names revealed, in this case the agent's name was given — N. Spry. (Any relation to ASIO boss Brigadier Spry?)

Frank travelled the country for the Defend Hardy Committee. And on one occasion in Sydney an ASIO agent arrived at the New Theatre premises and reported Frank asleep on one couch and Wilfred Burchett asleep on another. (Two of the most notorious Australians of their day – both had their passports taken at later dates.)

Later when they woke up and everyone went to the pub, Frank told the agent he had 'very little chance of winning the "Power Without Glory" case'. (I'm pretty sure that's correct. Frank always thought he would lose and be jailed for many years.)

But he was found not guilty and ASIO did not take it well. In July 1951 the Director-General of ASIO gives an extraordinary directive: he asks for a list of the jurors who acquitted Frank and to check if any have ASIO files.

Frank and Ross (my mother, Rosslyn Hardy) travelled overseas in 1951. This was arranged by the party for them to attend a World Youth Festival, but the family always believed they just wanted to get away from all the post-trial attention. As a small child at the time, it was devastating. My sister and I were sent to live, virtually in hiding, with a communist family in Gippsland for six months – a lifetime for a five-year old. ASIO reports that Frank and Ross couldn't leave their ship, the *Oronsay*, in France as they could not get a visa. They couldn't get off until the United Kingdom.

In 1951 ASIO gets hold of a translation of an article Frank wrote for a literary gazette in Moscow in which he attacked bias by the judge in his trial. ASIO thought they might bring it to the attention of the Victorian Attorney-General for possible contempt of court! (Anything's worth a try.)

In 1951 ASIO also reports letters from Frank being intercepted by US and Australian military intelligence.

MID 1950s: STRUGGLING

In this period – and really throughout his life – Frank's finances were always in a bad way. ASIO reports that staff at the People's Bookshop were complaining of Frank 'pocketing the money for sale of his books – but then wanting second payment.' (I have no idea whether or not that is true but I know from firsthand experience and from reading his diaries that when he was desperate for cash he would try anything.)

Around this time an interesting event is reported – handwritten information about Frank was obtained during a raid on Bert Chandler's home. Bert was one of three communists charged with sedition over an article in the *Communist Review* criticising the British monarchy. At this time the ASIO files also show Frank as a very strong Soviet supporter.

In 1953 Frank was reportedly drunk at a New Theatre party. (Frank could be a heavy drinker – though not an alcoholic. ASIO loved reporting items such as this. Was it to denigrate him – or to finger him as unreliable?) At the party the agent reports rather snobbishly that Frank's speech 'was grammatically incorrect indicating a lack of education' but he had to admit that 'he had an amazing mind'.

Between 1954 and 1955 ASIO reports that Frank had his passport withheld (allegedly by Harold Holt) and was applying to have his passport returned. It was eventually returned in 1955.

In 1955, Frank was spied driving a Holden – which, of course, turned out to belong to someone else. ASIO later reported that Frank finally had a new car – his own this time. At this time he was also reported as 'drinking heavily during State Election campaign'.

LATE 1950s: STRAIN

By 1957 ASIO reports Hardy's health under strain. They report him as saying that Russia is the only place he can get printed. They also report him as critical of the Hungarian Uprising – he was still following the Soviet line.

In 1959 his file includes a report from inside the party of a criticism of Frank's manuscript for 'Up the Garbos' that he was desperately trying to get the party to support financially. But it was rejected. They said it made fun of the communist character, the 'Red Dean' and treated the issues with 'patronage' and 'disdain' and 'too much larrikinism'. The report claimed 'Frank's unstable way of life has contributed to wrong ideas of the Australian Worker'. The internal report even suggested that

Frank 'put his pen aside' and go and get a job in 'basic industry where hordes of workers are employed in a disciplined fashion'. (How tough to be an author and a communist.) The subsequent novel – far more outrageous than 'Up the Garbos' – was printed successfully as *The Outcasts of Foolgarah*, but not by the party. (Frank felt an outcast from all sides of society – both communist and capitalist.)

In 1959 it was reported that Frank did not attend a Brookvale party branch meeting as he had a 'heart attack', however he was seen the next night in the Harbord Hotel!

EARLY 1960s:
UNDER ATTACK FROM BOTH SIDES

On 8 April 1960 an agent reported after an Australasian Book Society meeting at Frank's Manly home that the flat was 'well furnished and they have a television'.

At this time the file includes a weird story from a 'Minnie Wilson'. Frank had left a parcel in a cab. When it was returned to the address where he had picked up the cab, the Wilsons opened it and discovered 7000 names of party members, including 'some very interesting ones'. (Extraordinary!)

In 1960 the file includes a report from a small CPA branch meeting of barely eighteen people. (How many agents did they have?) In October that year the informant at a party branch meeting reports the following random information: Frank was reported to be thinking of going back to sea; Ross reports girls at her work are not 'communist-minded'; and Charlie Begg reports on two new recruits, 'One is seventy-six and the other English'.

In August 1960 Frank is reported trying to borrow seventy-five pounds to publish a book. Another source said Frank had been at that game for years: 'He'll never be a success.' In December 1960, Frank is reported as being a seaman – 'but had done his back and was on compo'. Frank describes himself as a genius at beating the tax people. He has 'beaten them down from 2000 to 200 pounds'.

In 1962 there are various reports of Frank in the Soviet Union. Frank is reported as 'stirring older Soviet Writers to the pleasure of younger ones'. One 'Eugene Bugaev' notes he met Frank and son Alan in Moscow. Bugaev reports Frank was a 'fine chap who loves horse racing and lost a lot of money. Lived a poor life and sometimes had to work as a sailor.' In late 1962 Frank was reported as being in a sanatorium in Russia – 'possibly mental' (it wasn't).

Also in 1962, ASIO took note of the car number plates of people attending Frank's lecture at the Australasian Book Society. They then obtained their names, presumably from the police. (Spying on the Australasian Book Society? Sure, it was a publisher of left-wing books – but it was quite open about it.)

In 1963, ASIO reports Hardy was recently described by a leading CPA member as a 'degenerate bourgeois' who goes around borrowing money and not paying it back. (They didn't seem to understand it was impossible for a serious writer to make a living in Australia at the time – and Frank was what we would today call a 'gamblerholic'.) Criticism was levelled at him for 'sending his wife out to work to keep the family'.

Also in 1963 Frank came under severe criticism (a great Communist Party word) for his actions in 1961 and 1962 for borrowing money and trying for a loan to hold off legal action for debts to the tax department and for the house loan (we'd had to sell our house in Narrabeen). Hardy was instructed to report regularly to the Central Disputes Committee on the repayment of his debts. At one stage when author Judah Waten was asked how Frank coped financially, Waten replied, 'He borrows money.'

During a phone intercept in June 1963, Judah Waten talks to the painter Noel Counihan, who is to do a mural for the CPA headquarters in Sydney. Counihan says the older brigade was the biggest problem. However, Frank Hardy is on his side. They then discuss whether it's sometimes better not to have Frank on your side.

ASIO quotes Elsie Leyden at a party conference saying that some time ago she and her husband had criticised Frank Hardy's book *Journey into the Future* and he would not talk to them over it. She was glad to see that today: 'at last he has seen our point'. (Source's comment: 'Hardy became very upset at this point and attempted to speak but was not allowed to do so by the chairman.')

In March 1965, Bert Keesing asked Charlie Begg to request the return of money Frank Hardy had owed him for some time. Begg said he would speak to Rosslyn as she was more responsible.

At this time, Hardy is censured by the party for a statement he had made regarding authors being too easily led down the Soviet line and 'had made outrageous claims during a series of lectures'.

In June 1966 a sad episode occurs. Communist Party activist and author, Roger Milliss, rings Frank to discuss work at the ABC for his wife Susë Milliss. Frank says he has talked to Allan Ashbolt (ABC producer) and Susë should ring him. Frank adds that he is very friendly with Allan Ashbolt. A second intercepted phone call is Roger Milliss speaking to Susë. He tells her he's spoken to Hardy who referred him to Allan Ashbolt. (Frank had done very little except put the kiss of death on Susë.) Susë says she's already been told not to have Frank talk to Allan about her. (It is now known that ASIO intervened to stop Susë Milliss working at the ABC, although she was amply qualified for the job for which she had applied.)

There is a random file note on Hardy being a member (in his youth but it's true) of the Catholic Campion Society with Bob Santamaria. There are also snippets of reports about Hardy's doubts about communism and that he feels it can be of use to him. He is reported as understanding that 'the CPA is not happy with him and he doesn't care'. He regards Laurie Aarons as the only worthwhile person in the party.

In December 1966, after recording another phone call, ASIO reports Frank trying to borrow money from the party against a future expected writing cheque. Desperate times and so on, 'if there is a million to one possibility I would get Alan (!) to come in and get it ...'

MID-1960s:
FRANK HARDY AND THE GURINDJI

In 1966 there is a significant (as it turned out) report of Frank's journey to Darwin and then to Sydney via Adelaide.

> In accordance with instructions full surveillance was carried out on FH whilst in transit at Adelaide airport 2/7/66! He waited, made a phone call, wrote in a note book ...
>
> Report on FH trip and return to Darwin. Trip follows phone intercept in which FH rang CPA HQ and requested they pay for an airfare for him to return to Sydney to discuss an extremely important matter.

ASIO noted that Frank's interest in Aborigines may include the demand for equal pay now rather than in three years' time.

> This is further supported by the fact that FH is staying with Cecil Holmes who has been active in respect to Aborigines. Returned to Darwin approx 4/7/66.

The ASIO agent reported from a Darwin meeting of the Communist Party in July 1966 that Hardy 'predicted he would stir industrial trouble amongst aboriginals'.

(Quite right. He went to Darwin to get away from his money troubles and his writer's block ... to try and find himself. He felt that, even if he'd lost the ability to write, he could still write a pamphlet.

Of course history tells us that Frank then found the Gurindji, an illiterate people who needed a man of words to write their story – and Frank needed a story to write. The Gurindji got their champion, Frank wrote *The Unlucky Australians* and eventually the Gurindji got their land.)

In Darwin ASIO reported the local Communist Party branch was very critical of Hardy: 'Trying to stop him.' But Frank went to Wave Hill and wrote the articles in *The Australian* which brought the plight of the Gurindji to national prominence.

Despite this, the ASIO agent reports: 'Hardy is most unpopular with CP Darwin Branch Members' (the feeling was mutual). 'They regard him as a bludger and a go-getter.' Frank is reported as saying 'there were only four members of the Darwin CP Branch and they were all "half mad".'

On 13 September 1966 Frank Hardy camped with the Gurindji at Wave Hill:

More stockmen coming out. Hardy MOST unpopular with NTCAR and CPA. They regard him as an objectionable intruder who has no right interfering in the matter and trying to organise where he has no right. They are talking about contacting HQ to complain. All local CPA members sick of him.

(Thank God they didn't succeed in stopping him – otherwise *The Unlucky Australians* may never have been written, the Gurindji may never have got their land, and the song 'From Little Things Big Things Grow' might never have seen the light of day.)

In April 1967, ASIO reports Frank was almost flat broke when in Darwin recently. He borrowed $100 from Jo Cunningham and gave her a cheque, which bounced.

In July 1967, CPA secretary Laurie Aarons said Frank had been very useful in the Northern Territory but in view of his recent activities it would not be desirable for him to return there. In February 1968, ASIO reports a meeting by unknown persons to discuss *The Unlucky Australians*. It was agreed it was most inflammatory.

There follows a report of a letter from Hardy to someone (name deleted) who passes on information about Social Security using the trick of offering Gurindji jobs at full pay then cutting off their dole if they refuse to take them. Hardy thinks they should get a letter signed by prominent people in support of the Gurindji.

By 1968 the file records, 'The Gurindji did not know the difference between a Communist and a Capitalist. They think Frank Hardy is a wonderful chap'. (They still do.) And a prescient agent comments, 'I believe the hard core will stay there [at Wattie Creek] until doomsday if they have to.'

LATE 1960s: A PUBLIC FIGURE

In 1968 there was much ASIO commentary about the CPA's interest in broadcasting, particularly the ABC. They note Frank as 'being old friend of Clem Semmler (Asst Gen Mgr)'. They reported they would discuss this with the ASIO Director (obviously considered important). Later that year the file contains a Sydney *Sun* report that the ABC boss Talbot Duckmanton had banned Frank from appearing on a radio show.

ASIO notes the CPA's reaction to Frank appearing on *This Day Tonight*. An intercepted phone call records two communist writers, Judah Waten and Alan Marshall, talking about how they thought Frank was awful and he would never be able to go back to Russia and he wouldn't have a lot of friends.

On 18 June 1968 there is another phone intercept of a conversation between Bill Brown and Laurie Aarons. Brown curses Aboriginal activist Ray Peckham who 'failed to get Aborigines to the meeting at the BWIU. Refused to hand out the leaflets in La Perouse.' Brown stated that there was a trade union group out looking for Hardy who had denounced the movement at a union-sponsored meeting. Aarons says Hardy is mad and Brown says they won't support him again.

LATE 1960s: QUESTIONING BELIEFS

In December 1968 ASIO reports from a meeting of boilermakers that Frank 'was unsure of his political convictions and was having second thoughts'. They thought he was 'partly instrumental' in encouraging the striking Gurindji stockmen to squat at Wattie Creek. ASIO thought that if the Gurindji got their land it would be a victory for the CPA and Frank Hardy!

In December 1968, ASIO reports that *The Heirs of Stalin*, a series of sensational articles by Frank Hardy, has appeared in the *Sunday Times*. By 1969 ASIO reports that Frank had gone on the radio program *AM* and spoken critically of pro-Soviet forces within the CPA.

In February 1969 an ASIO informant at a party branch meeting in Manly witnessed heated arguments. My mother declared her intention to resign from the party because of personal attacks on Frank. The agent describes all members as hard-liners (thus enemies of Frank).

In 1969, ASIO tapes a phone call from an *Age* journalist, Michael Richardson, to Dave Davies at the CPA. They mainly talked about the support Frank had in the party, which they believed to be about 75 per cent and believed him 'unlikely to be expelled'.

Later the file includes newspaper clippings from the *Sydney Morning Herald* headed 'Red Hard-Liners Move to Oust Frank Hardy'. (Even the *Herald* reports Frank's writing has moved from a pro-Soviet line to an extremely pro-Australian socialist line.)

> Phone Intercept 4/3/69 Hardy tells Mavis R that his dues are paid up till the end of 1968. She says that it's been rumoured that his dues are unpaid and said that Laurie A would hate it if someone tried to get him on a technicality.

A note is included that Hardy is 'rethinking his views on communist doctrine in light of the return of Stalinism'. In January 1969 there is a memo that Ivan Stenin, presumably from the Soviet Embassy, is upset and that the embassy is arranging for a Soviet reply. Then there is:

> ... gossip that L Aarons had said that Hardy had gone off the rails and had an ego problem ... Jim Mitchell says that Hardy was required to appear before the Nat C/tee and that he is a dangerous man but he is a brilliant man with a wide following.

Another phone intercept records Ted Bacon speaking on the draft proposal about Hardy to go to the National Committee on 25 January 1969. Bill Brown talks about trying to avoid anything which looks like a collision course with the USSR. Brown goes on to say that they should either put up evidence that the Soviet Embassy is seeking to set up a separate (pro Soviet) party or not. He says he has spoken to the embassy about this and they gave him a denial. A handwritten ASIO officer's note in the margin says that Molotov gave a somewhat similar reply to a question by Dr HV Evatt in 1954 concerning Soviet espionage activities in Australia.

Brown advises that they consider the moves they make in relation to Hardy very carefully. Says that they shouldn't go the old route of blackening the name of a member who does something wrong by the party. Then Brown says how Hardy has set himself on a course of gaining kudos in the capitalist press. He mentions his unprincipled behaviour, money troubles, and complaints (alleged) from the Gurindji: 'he's not a principled person'.

Judah Waten has information about 'how much money Hardy made'. (For his *Sunday Times* articles?) They note that Hardy can be 'foolhardy' but also that he has displayed extraordinary courage and boldness particularly around questions like Aborigines and has given an example that many comrades might well emulate.

An ASIO minute paper of 22 January 1969 notes that most of Hardy's statements seem to have come from Yevtushenko. The agent queries whether it is possible that Hardy is wittingly or unwittingly being used to spread disinformation. It would be of value if sources could be questioned about whether Hardy's disillusionment is genuine. If it is not genuine is he clever enough to write convincing articles expressing views he does not hold? Is he capable of sustaining the role in his social, professional and party contacts?

The agent quotes sources (names deleted) that don't believe that Frank's articles are part of Soviet disinformation. Because of Hardy's intemperate background he didn't believe that the Soviets would entrust such an important mission to him. Both sources believe that Hardy can continue as a journalist under present CPA leadership. If the leadership changed it could lead to his expulsion.

In February 1969, Laurie Aarons reports to a Melbourne meeting about the National Committee decisions. ASIO notes that the general policy of the CPA towards the Russian invasion of Prague is that they should stay out of it and Aarons publicly reprimanded Frank Hardy for his articles in *The Bulletin* (reprints of *The Heirs Of Stalin*). There was support for Hardy from the floor and a majority supported the Czechs.

There are reports from many different branch meetings and their discussions around the Czechoslovakia/Hardy affair. The files report how the issue has gone around the whole CPA and caused discussion regarding party democracy, direction and the generation gap. In 1969 I appear again in a phone intercept: 'June Hearn to Dorothy Gibson. Re background on Allen [*sic*] Hardy.' (Looks like I was applying for something.) 'And they don't want him if he's like his father.' Mmmmm …

ASIO surveillance photo from Frank Hardy's file, captioned *March against Racism demonstration, Chifley Square, Sydney 3 December 1971 – 1. Denis FRENEY 4. Dennis WALKER [HG3368/25]*. In the front with ASIO number 2 is Frank Hardy.

In July 1970 the first large Gurindji demonstration occurs in Sydney. The file contains a press cutting about it and the arrests in George Street. Paul Coe and Hardy are noted as in attendance. There was a heavy police presence and a very tough response to demonstrators. Two hundred people were present and forty-three were arrested. Mavis Robertson rings Carol Aarons to say that Laurie Aarons has been arrested, almost certainly the same for Brian Aarons, didn't know about Mark and that Hardy had been 'marvellous'. Wendy Bacon was also arrested. Pat Healy had been thrown to the ground. Laurie had a black eye. Later, in another intercepted call, Hardy and Laurie Aarons discuss whether the prosecutions are going to go ahead – maybe there's an adjournment. Hardy says the campaign is becoming a strain for him.

In a later call, Hardy (ever the opportunist) asks whether Aarons would consider publishing 'Up The Garbos'. Aarons says he wouldn't mind but money is the problem. Hardy says it could be a profitable venture. Aarons will have a think. The charges arising from Hardy's arrest at the Gurindji protest are dismissed. Hardy says the police acted like Keystone cops. Judge says he has his doubts about the whole thing.

MY COMMENTS

From his early twenties Frank was a communist and remained one to his death at seventy-six. He said towards the end of his life that he was the last genuine one in existence. He was anti-Stalinist from the early sixties. He had previously been much more hardline and had spent a long time travelling in the Soviet Union. (It was also cheap for him, as any money he earned from the sale of his books in the Eastern Bloc had to be spent in the Eastern Bloc.) In 1962 he travelled extensively with a view to writing another book about his experiences. (He had written *Journey into the Future* in the early 1950s, which was a view of the communist state that Stalin would have loved.)

But he found in 1962 that he could not write the proposed book as he was so concerned about what he saw. The last straw was the Prague Spring and the invasion of Czechoslovakia by Soviet troops. This caused him to write *The Heirs of Stalin* for the *Sunday Times* and all hell broke loose. Most of the ASIO entries around this period focus on attacks on him and attempts to expel him from the party. (Why would ASIO be interested? Doesn't this mean he was no longer a threat? But one reference from an agent suggested he might have been trying to fool people into thinking he had changed.)

Some entries appear to be opinion and gossip rather than facts. I was outraged by ASIO's glee in denigrating him, in always finding the nasty jibe. It was some of the more malicious gossip that seemed to make the file. Though occasionally praise crept in for who he really was and what he stood for.

I don't know that the surveillance had much effect on our lives. We always joked in our house about how we were probably being spied upon by ASIO and just took it in our stride. It never worried us. But I noticed in a file note a report about a photograph of our family. My sister Shirley, then sixteen, is mentioned as being employed by the ABC (and doesn't yet have a file of her own). A chilling handwritten comment is added, 'Please find out employment details of Shirley Ann Hardy at the ABC.'

I am proud of who my father was – despite ASIO's attempts to make him appear a lesser man. They seemed to thrive on any unpleasantness, anything derogatory said about him – and there was plenty. He made many enemies – he was egotistical, self-promoting, always broke and borrowing money that he always struggled to pay back (and often didn't). But he also wrote *Power Without Glory*, and he is revered by the Gurindji for his huge part in helping them get their own land. Even in the last year of his life, he stood for the Senate at the age of seventy-six as an independent to help the unemployed 'because someone had to do it'. The strain undoubtedly contributed to him suffering the stroke and subsequent heart attack which killed him six months later. I wonder if ASIO put that in their files?

The ASIO file is also fascinating in that it traces my father's developing and ever changing political views. For that I thank them. The unexpected consequence of their interest is that it presents me with a snapshot of his very full life. I got a sense from the early part of the file that they had a genuine fear of communists and what they might do to the country … and Frank was becoming one of the best known. But it quickly became clear that Frank Hardy was not any threat to the security of his country. Sure, he was a bloody nuisance to the Establishment with his campaigning for what he believed in, but not a threat. While he admired the Soviet Union and believed in the communist state, he was an Australian – who wanted what was best for Australia. Capitalism had failed him and his family during the Depression. There had to be a better way.

I know from growing up in our household he was all about support for the workers – better wages and conditions. He was pro-peace and anti-war. He was for equal rights for Aborigines and any people of colour. This is what I was taught as a kid –

nothing about overthrowing the government by force or spying for Russia. You had to wonder. Clearly there appeared to be ASIO agents in the New Theatre, the local party branches – even in Darwin. Was it like the USA, where there were more FBI agents in the Communist Party than communists?

ALAN HARDY

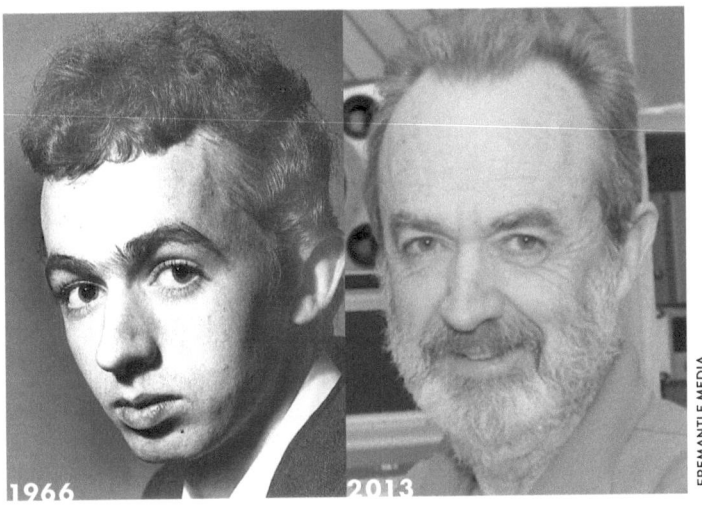

Alan Hardy is Frank's son and has been involved in show business in Australia for most of his working life as an actor, writer, script editor and an AFI Award-winning television producer.

His credits include, as an actor, *The Chant of Jimmie Blacksmith* and *Mad Dog Morgan*, and as a writer and script editor, *Home and Away*, *The Bob Morrison Show* and *City Homicide*. He has produced *All the Rivers Run*, *The Sullivans*, *Embassy*, *The Wayne Manifesto* and *Something in the Air*. He is currently the producer of *Neighbours*.

VERY INTERESTED IN THEATRICS

by Alan Hardy

My file is a rather embarrassingly small seventy-nine pages (ending in 1968). Originally I imagine I was only awarded the honour of my own file as the son of author and communist Frank Hardy (over 1500 pages up to 1972), probably the best-known communist of his day.

My file began when it was proposed that I go as a delegate to a World Youth Festival in Finland and I sought a passport to transit through Czechoslovakia, Poland and the Soviet Union.

I don't recall that I was ever serious about going. My family – and I'm sure the Communist Party – thought it would be a good idea. It was even contemplated I attend university in Moscow. Fortunately I was a high school dropout only interested in becoming an actor. So Moscow disappeared from the agenda.

But I was now on file. Then my mother, sister and I did go to the Soviet Union in 1962 to visit my father who was working there at the time … as ASIO dutifully reported.

The most interesting – and unexpected – part of a dull

document was that I was placed on a security risk list when I was a sixteen-year-old clerical assistant in the public service pushing a trolley of files between floors. I was in the Repatriation Department (now Veterans' Affairs) and it was noted: 'He has access to ex-servicemen's files,' and 'It is probable that it is only his youth that keeps him from being a member of CPA'. Tagged a security risk at sixteen!

Back then I suppose I was a communist, but really in name only – I was not an activist – and apart from May Day marches and Ban the Bomb rallies I did little. But I was an active member of New Theatre, considered a 'communist front' organisation at that time.

The ASIO reports from New Theatre committee meetings were very detailed. I was there and I knew all those people, so who was the agent?

New Theatre production of *On Stage Vietnam*, circa 1966. Alan Hardy in the centre; second from left, Christine Shaw; on Alan's left in striped shirt, Pat Hickey; to right of Alan at back, Bruce Gibson.

There were very few communists in the New Theatre. I became one of them when I turned eighteen and actually attended a party faction meeting at CPA headquarters where suddenly we all called each other 'comrade' ('Comrade John ... Comrade Alan'). I joined the party, but I don't recall paying any dues, and attended a handful of meetings – including a local branch meeting with my parents. I did nothing to help the cause.

I was not a joiner. In my ASIO file I am constantly listed as a member of the Eureka Youth League (EYL) – but I never really joined it. My family and the party were clearly very keen that I join but it just didn't interest me. I appeared in an EYL satirical revue, went to a camp – which I hated (I hate any form of camping) – and other jolly events. But ASIO always listed me as a member. I remember each 'tent' at the EYL camp had names – I was in 'Leika', named after the first dog sent to space by the Soviet Union.

It is very weird reading your own file. I discovered that one ASIO informant (name blacked out) was at the New Theatre conference in Sydney in 1962. I was described as '16 years of age and very thin', true but hardly flattering. The informant is quoted as saying: 'In conversation Alan Hardy told me ... about living in Manly, leaving school, working in Repat and travelling to the Soviet Union.' Who was that person? I have no idea.

So ASIO was aware of who I was – or were they?

Two descriptions of me:

1. 'Alan Hardy is a blond haired, tattooed truck driver working for Dalgety's.'
2. 'Alan Hardy is very thin, lives with another boy in Kings Cross and is VERY interested in theatrics.'

One completely inaccurate but hilarious account (no.1) and one accurate (no.2) … but is it ASIO-speak for *gay*?

It's not the accuracy that's the issue – it's the intrusion. They sought details of my new wife's totally innocent family and placed them on record. They were Jewish refugees from Nazi Germany and had suffered enough from being spied upon, so I wasn't very impressed reading that.

I only started thinking about the people who spied and reported on me and my family when I first read my file in 2009. We, in the Hardy family, had always assumed we were being spied on – phone taps, being followed, mail intercepted. That was a given. It didn't worry us, as I recall. I was brought up not to like ASIO or what it stood for. To my communist family, ASIO were spying on innocent people like us – people who wanted to help our fellow man. We were for the workers, the unemployed, the Aborigines and world peace. How dangerous was that! And for those beliefs our country didn't trust us.

But it's too long ago to be outraged. Today I'm not active in any way, but I'll always be on the left and will never vote conservative.

And today I think ASIO is mainly interested in 'people of Middle Eastern appearance', which rules me out. Though looking at some of ASIO's earlier descriptions of me … you never know.

LEX WATSON

Lex Watson was an academic in the Department of Government at Sydney University from the 1970s until his retirement. He has been interested in gay politics since he was a teenager, taking note of the reports of the UK Wolfenden Committee and its aftermath. He joined the ACT Homosexual Law Reform Society soon after it was formed in 1969 and in 1971 joined the Campaign Against Moral Persecution (CAMP) at its formation and was involved with its organisation of the first gay and lesbian demonstration in Australia. Subsequently he and Sue Wills were the first co-presidents of CAMP in New South Wales.

He was involved in early moves to amend the *Crimes Act* in the ACT and New South Wales through his membership of the Council for Civil Liberties and the Humanist Society in New South Wales. He later became Secretary of the NSW Council for Civil Liberties.

Lex was a founder of the AIDS Action Committee in Sydney, was the first President of its successor, the AIDS Council of New South Wales (now ACON) and a community member of the federal government's National Advisory Committee on AIDS when it was established in 1984.

He was co-founder of the Gay Rights Lobby in Sydney in 1981. Over the years he has been involved in numerous campaigns and submissions federally and in the states and territories concerning law reform, anti-discrimination and other policy areas. He has done innumerable media interviews. He was the first openly gay person on SA TV and his starring role in an ABC TV *Monday Conference* episode in Mt Isa in 1976 is still remembered and often re-broadcast as an example of homophobic attitudes of the period.

Lex is now involved with the Pride History Group in Sydney, contributing to the recording of those events and the documentation and dissemination of the history of the gay and lesbian sub-cultures.

MY OWN 'PINK FILE'

by Lex Watson

As someone who grew up politically aware and became a gay activist, being considered a potential security risk has always been part of the furniture. Somehow I knew of the activities of Senator McCarthy, and his equation linking homosexuality, communism and security risks. The scandals surrounding the defection of Philby, Burgess and Maclean and the allegations of blackmail were all over the papers and hard to miss.

Being a politics student and lecturer at Sydney University meant that ASIO was an issue, especially if you were thinking of a career in the public service. Received wisdom, quite widely held, was that being gay – in those days 'homosexual' – excluded you from Foreign Affairs and ASIO. Requiring a high-level security clearance was the specific barrier. Some of us used to occasionally wonder which of our students might be reporting back to ASIO or even which of our academic colleagues might be sounding boards for security references for our students.

So when CAMP (Campaign Against Moral Persecution), our first gay and lesbian organisation, came along in 1970, the issue of surveillance was very much there. Several of us – three university staff and a friend – set off to CAMP's first public meeting in February 1971, but one of my colleagues opted out at the last minute, fearing that ASIO or other security people would turn up and note down our car number plates, faces and the like. It was probably not fanciful.

In October 1971, CAMP held the first ever gay and lesbian demonstration in Australia in Ash Street, Sydney, outside the NSW Liberal Party's head office. When we arrived there were a dozen or so uniformed NSW Police and none other than Freddie Longbottom, head of Special Branch, the state's

CAMP demonstration outside ABC studios after ABC management had banned the broadcast of a *This Day Tonight* segment on gay lib, 11 July 1972. Lex Watson in centre, Frank Taylor on right, Mark Diment behind. Lex would like it known that he has long since quit smoking.

political police. As we had had no dealings with the police over the demonstration beforehand, our suspicions were reinforced. Longbottom introduced himself and suggested we contact him about future demos and marches. As a result, and to our amusement, that ended in him actually leading the first gay and lesbian street march through Sydney the following year.

Not surprisingly, there was considerable speculation about who around CAMP and other gay and lesbian groups was a 'plant', spying on our activities. It was a puzzle, we thought, how someone could do the job satisfactorily if they were not allowed to participate, so to speak, in what we were up to sexually. Who was celibate, we wondered. There were one or two candidates, some of us thought. Even so, few were worried. There were numerous people in highly ranked positions, in Foreign Affairs for instance, who were confidently believed to be homosexual and who appeared to be secure. The picture was mixed.

The Hope Royal Commission into our security agencies in the mid-1970s should have seen an end to much of this concern, though its recommendation, eventually implemented, was a touch quixotic: if you were openly gay, it was OK, but if you were closeted, it was not, as you were still potentially subject to blackmail. However, some police surveillance probably continued. There was a little man who turned up at some of the demonstrations outside NSW Parliament House in Macquarie Street during the homosexual law reform activities of 1981–84. He looked out of place with his long overcoat and his attache case, which he periodically realigned as though he was recording the speeches. On one occasion we invited him to come closer to the truck with the sound system so the recording would be better and, astonishingly, he did.

It was the so-called 'pink files' affair in South Australia that widened and sharpened gay concern about spying. The South Australian Police Special Branch, the state's security police, had been keeping files on people, and those started for gay people purely because they were gay, were coded pink. The South Australian Premier Don Dunstan became aware of this and was assured by the Police Commissioner, Salisbury, that those files had been destroyed. When it was found that this was not true and the Premier had been misled, the Police Commissioner was sacked.

Dunstan had been sensitive to this issue for quite some time. As Attorney-General in the late 1960s, he was proposing to appoint John Bray as Chief Justice of the Supreme Court of South Australia. He was approached by the police who suggested this was inappropriate. Why? Because police records suspected him of being homosexual. The evidence? He was known to sit in coffee shops reading and writing poetry. Dunstan, himself bisexual, appointed Bray to the post. Bray, as it happened, was indeed homosexual.

Special Branch political files in other states became an issue, an extension of concerns about who and what was properly a matter of police surveillance. In New South Wales the Premier, Bob Carr, opened Special Branch files to the public and to those individuals on whom files had been kept. Naturally I applied for mine. If the routes of our marches through the streets of Sydney had been worthy of Freddie Longbottom dealing personally with me, then clearly I would have a file. Alas no, I was told. No record, nothing.

So I was surprised, when ASIO files were opened up, to find I had a file. Surprised but also a bit flattered. Surely with all the homophobia in some quarters of the police and security forces I would have had a file. The wait was long, over a year and a half, and then came the news that it was a large file, and that photocopying would cost double the standard rate. And so it eventually arrived and consisted of the following documents:

1. a copy of a letter about homosexual law reform I had published in *The Australian*;
2. a copy of a seven-line ad for a public meeting at which I was one of the speakers (it had been in *Tribune* but had nothing to do with the Communist Party); and
3. a two-page report on a gay march in Sydney in 1972. This piece of intelligence gave the date of the march, its route, and its destination. It reported that there were two speakers at the end; me and another whose name they didn't know. What we said was not reported. The report was supplied to ASIO by the NSW Police Special Branch and signed by no less than four officers.

My hopes that I would find out things I had said or done long ago and since forgotten, as others had in their ASIO files, were dashed. The challenges, the game of trying to guess who had been informing, was denied me as there was no information. Not even a marginal note saying 'Harmless', or 'Mostly harmless' to deflate my ego. Nothing to exercise the black obliterating pen and hide the unrevealable. What an anti-climax.

WENDY AND JIM BACON

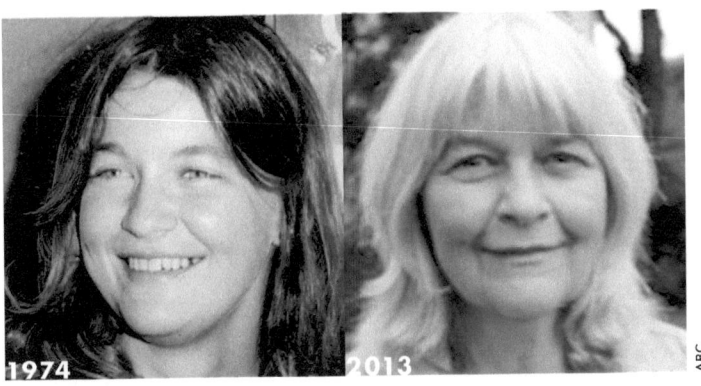

1974   2013   ABC

Wendy Bacon grew up in Melbourne and studied Arts at Melbourne University before moving to Sydney in 1966. She joined the Sydney Push and was active in the Libertarian Society. While studying sociology at the University of New South Wales, she was elected as an editor of the student newspaper *Tharunka* in 1970. The editors launched a campaign against censorship laws which resulted in numerous charges against them under the New South Wales obscenity acts. Wendy was arrested and convicted for exhibiting an 'obscene publication' during a court protest in which she and others dressed in nuns' habits. She was twice held in remand in Mulawa Women's Prison during these censorship campaigns, which led to her involvement in the prison reform movement, especially Women Behind Bars.

She was involved in the Australian publication of the children's rights' book *The Little Red School Book* and the underground newspaper *Thor*. She was arrested during protests in support of Aboriginal land rights and against apartheid and the export of uranium. She squatted in Victoria Street, Kings Cross, when it was threatened with demolition. She completed a law degree but was prevented from practising law by a 1981 Supreme Court finding that she was not a 'fit and proper' person. She then worked on Channel Nine's *Sixty Minutes* and *Sunday* programs, SBS's *Dateline* and for the *National Times* as an investigative journalist. She received a Walkley Award in 1985 for her reporting on corruption in New South Wales.

From the early 1990s onwards, she taught investigative journalism at the University of Technology, Sydney, where she became the Director of the Australian Centre for Independent Journalism. She is currently a contributing editor of *New Matilda*.

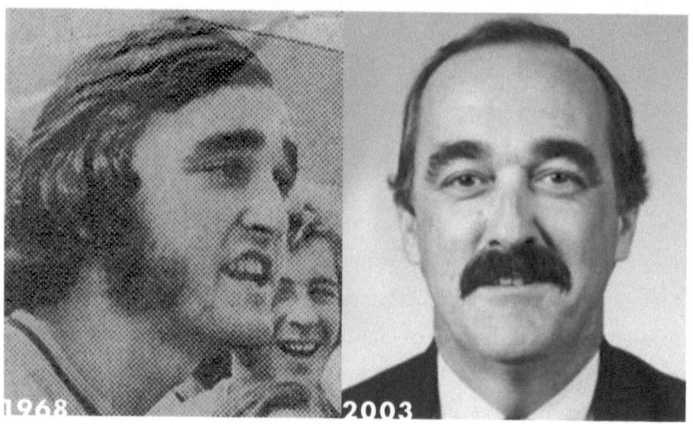

Jim Bacon was born and raised in Melbourne. He was educated at Scotch College and Monash University, where he became a Maoist student leader, and left before graduating. He moved to Western Australia where he became an official with the Builders Labourers' Federation. The union sent him to Tasmania where he became secretary of the Tasmanian Trades and Labor Council.

He abandoned Maoism and was elected a Labor member of the Tasmanian Parliament in 1996. He became Labor leader in 1997 and won the state election in 1998. He won again in 2002 in a landslide.

He was a hugely popular premier, introducing important social policies and increasing tourism. He died prematurely of lung cancer in 2004.

A BACON FAMILY AFFAIR

by Wendy Bacon

When I heard that people who had been involved in left-wing politics in the 1970s were applying for their ASIO files, I assumed that I would have one, but was in no great rush to access it. After I was asked to submit a chapter for this book, my first surprise was to find that there was no need to apply for access because someone had already paid for my files to be digitised and published on the National Archives website.

I asked National Archives who had paid for this public service but was told that the identity of the person was a confidential matter. This seemed ironic because the file contains a myriad personal details about hundreds of people. Not unexpectedly, many redacted passages still protect informants and agents by blocking any information that could identify them, and anything else ASIO prefers us not to see, even forty years later. So if someone decides to apply for your file and have it made public, don't expect to be notified.

The first document in my own file is a pamphlet and conference program produced by the Sydney and Kensington Libertarians for distribution at Sydney University in 1969. The Sydney Libertarians were linked to the Sydney Push, which from the early 1950s onwards had revelled in parties, pubs, bohemian culture and in challenging restrictive sexual values. The Libertarians were opposed to all states, including socialist ones. They called themselves 'pessimistic anarchists' rather than revolutionaries and preferred 'being free by acting free', direct action and critical inquiry.

I had joined the Libertarians when I moved to Sydney at the end of 1966, after studying at the University of Melbourne. By 1969, when my file starts, I was a postgraduate student and tutor in sociology at the University of New South Wales, where several of us started a miniscule offshoot group called the Kensington Libertarians. At the end of that year, I was one of three students elected to edit the UNSW student newspaper, *Tharunka*.

The ASIO agent who collected the pamphlet noted that this was the first he or she had heard of the Libertarians for a while. Like other older left-wing groups, the Libertarians were being stirred into action by the emergence of New Left activism. The pamphlet, which today's students might regard more as an essay than a leaflet, had been hurriedly roneoed on an old Gestetner. It was about events sparked by a May Day protest against Sydney University Regiment's guard of honour for a visit from the New South Wales Governor, Roden Cutler. Cutler had been jostled and hit with a tomato. This sparked outrage from conservatives, with Rupert Murdoch's *Daily Mirror* reporting that the Liberal Premier Robin Askin was threatening to withdraw funds from the university if it failed to discipline students.

Our Libertarian pamphlet's academic authors were scathing about the silence of fellow academics who failed to speak out in defence of the university's role as a base for independent thought and inquiry. Our leaflet pleaded,

> But the real aim of the government is to render the university as an institution less complicated, more tractable; to damage not the flow of graduates but the functions of inquiry and dissent.

ASIO's informer noted the names of several Libertarians who had previously come to notice, including anthropologist Ian Bedford, wharf labourer and anti-conscription activist Darcy Waters and well-known writer Frank Moorhouse. My name, which was on the conference program, was noted for indexing.

Meanwhile, the old left parties were also engaging with the New Left. I attracted further interest when my name cropped up during conversations recorded on phones tapped by ASIO at the Third World Bookshop and the Communist Party of Australia (CPA). Within the CPA, the role of bureaucracy in socialist states was being questioned and I was invited to talk as an anarchist at a youth branch meeting about the 1968 student protests in Paris. Author Frank Hardy, who was a member of the CPA, was invited as well. Agreeing with the plan to link with younger activists, he is reported to have remarked, 'nothing else will save the organisation'. In another conversation a CPA member described me as 'quite good but a bit mixed up', which may have been a reference to my anarchist views. Soon, I had my own personal ASIO file, which by 1981 consisted of hundreds of pages arranged in three volumes.

Another intercepted conversation in my file involved my younger brother, Jim. Jim later became Labor Premier of Tasmania but was at that time a second year student at Monash

Jim Bacon (right) addressing student protestors, Monash University, 1971. Albert Langer on left.

University, where he was a leading member of the Maoist-influenced Labor Club. Jim planned to visit me in early 1970 and was keen to attend the national conference of the CPA, which was to be held in Sydney. Mavis Robertson, a CPA organiser, rang me thinking it was me who wanted to attend.

Although the conference was already full, Mavis found room for Jim, who never joined the CPA, instead becoming part of the smaller underground CPA (Marxist–Leninist) until the early 1980s. Over the next eleven years, ASIO developed seven volumes of files on Jim, which track his career from student activist to union official with the Builders Labourers' Federation to Secretary of the Trades and Labor Council in Tasmania.

Exploring these files was a mixed experience. Having an ASIO file is a bit like discovering a long lost personal clippings service, reintroducing me to forgotten articles I had written or for which I had been interviewed, as well as agent reports that refreshed my memory of life back then. Most of this information had been routinely passed on to ASIO by the NSW Special Branch, which carried out a massive surveillance operation on all sorts of protests and political meetings. Along with uniformed police and detectives, you could always expect at least one Special Branch officer at protests, taking photos and talking on a walkie talkie. It also gave me insight into the much more intense scrutiny applied to those, like my brother Jim, who were actively involved in socialist parties.

Political activists were aware of surveillance and soon learned to expect that phones were tapped. We wondered if our groups were infiltrated by spies but reassured ourselves that we were being overly paranoid. I know now that we were not being paranoid. Both ASIO and Special Branch had far more informants and agents than we ever suspected.

By April 1970, ASIO had worked out that the 'Jim' who attended the Communist Party congress in Sydney was probably my brother. In order to confirm the connection and find out about any other subversive influences in our family, the Victorian branch of ASIO was asked to prepare a report.

The report included the date and place of birth of each family member and the details of what each of us (aside from my deceased father) had been doing the previous year. This involved making calls to the house in which my sister Janet, who was then a medical student, was living, and identifying the school attended by my fifteen-year-old sister. At this stage, the only basis for these inquiries was that Jim and I were interested in communism and libertarianism, respectively.

It was this background report that provided my most surprising discovery in the ASIO files. To understand why, I need to explain that like nearly everyone I knew who grew up in the 1950s, I did not conceive of my parents as involved in politics. These were the days when 'respectable people' did not discuss 'politics, religion or sex'. We lived in a new suburb of Melbourne, Reservoir, where my father Frank practised as a doctor until he died of a heart attack aged forty-two in 1962. When asked previously about my parents' attitudes to censorship, I remembered that they had unexpurgated editions of novels banned in Australia hidden out of reach on the top shelf of their bookcase, and attended a concert by black American singer and activist Paul Robeson when he visited Australia in 1960. But I can remember little talk of elections, and only later learned from my mother that my parents voted Labor rather than Liberal like most of my friends' parents. It would not have occurred to any of us that our family had come to the notice of ASIO before the late 1960s.

Annotated against the names and dates of birth of each of my parents in the ASIO 'family report' were the letters VOF. This stood for Victorian Organisation Files. I asked National Archives if I could obtain these files. I was initially told that there were no files, but I then supplied the numbers and received small files that were a collection of documents retrieved from other files. (For this reason, I suggest that those activists who are surprised to find they do not have file, look for a number against their name in another file and use that to access ASIO documents referring to them.)

The earliest document records an ASIO interview with my father on 26 July 1954. According to this record, Frank had contacted ASIO the previous week to tell them that he was concerned that he had recently received two copies of a 'Russian magazine'. He also acknowledged receiving a copy of the CPA newspaper *The Guardian* for some years. A week later, Frank was interviewed by an ASIO officer at our home. The notes of the interview record him explaining that an old frail patient had given *The Guardian* to him on a regular basis and that he had once paid him 10 shillings after the patient told him that otherwise he would have to pay it himself. The agent found that my father appeared 'sincere' but that even allowing for his sympathy for the patient, he had not 'altogether satisfactorily explained' his receipt of the paper over such a long time.

It is an indication of the suspicious mindset ASIO had at that time that the agent concluded that Frank may have been 'somewhat sympathetic towards the working class' when he first 'squatted' in Reservoir after the Second World War. He or she also noted from other records that Frank was in charge of a 'native hospital' in Borneo during the war.

I am unlikely to ever discover the truth about the circumstances in which my father contacted ASIO, however, it made more sense when I realised that these events occurred during the hearings of the royal commission into the defection of Vladimir Petrov. This was the highpoint of Australian Cold War hysteria about communism, which paralleled McCarthyism in the United States.

Frank perhaps feared – or knew – that his name would appear in documents seized by ASIO. Fearful of the consequences if this became public, he may have decided to get in first, or perhaps he was tipped off that ASIO might have seized information. Whether his anxiety was justified or not, it shows how threatened Australians with progressive sympathies may have felt at this time.

Seven years later, Frank and Joan Bacon came to notice again when they appeared on a list of about forty other people who supposedly belonged to the 'Kew Peace Group'. At the time of writing, I have been unable to track down details of this group. An informant had supplied ASIO with a list of members and their addresses, phone numbers and occupations. The women were all listed as 'home duties'. Several members, although not my parents, had personal ASIO files. The informant divided the list into three categories: the key organiser, those who were 'moderately interested in peace', and those who were only 'occasionally interested in peace'. My parents were in the last group, which I assume meant that they attended fewer meetings. To an outsider, it might appear odd that the more interested in peace you were, the more dangerous you were perceived to be.

Back in the 1970s, we tended to see our politics as a rupture from the past and a rejection of the culture and beliefs of our parents. The discovery of these documents led me to think more deeply about my own roots and the influences acting on me as I grew up. There is no doubt, however, that our political views evolved rapidly in the late 1960s.

The files provided me with a chronology for events that had become a blur. I was reminded of how quickly Jim's and my clashes with authority came in a rush at the same time. I reflected, in a way I did not do back then, on the impact of these well-publicised events on my mother and other siblings. Our files, and many others, also document the intensity of life in 1970, a year of huge moratoriums against the Vietnam War, anti-apartheid protests, land rights marches, student occupations and growing women's and gay liberation movements.

In March 1970, Jim was one of many students who occupied a building at Monash University in protest at the university inviting companies which were profiting from the Vietnam War onto the campus. He and a few others were charged with breaches of university discipline. On August 18, Monash suspended the students, who were described as 'militant extremists'. Jim was suspended for a year. He and fellow activist Michael Hyde, a student teacher, were reported by ASIO as warning of 'unrest and militant behaviour' in response to the decision.

Later that day, Jim was recorded talking to my mother, Joan. She seemed resigned, saying 'she did not think they could do anything', while Jim said he was 'shocked' but was reassuring, explaining that they would appeal and apply to get admitted to other universities. Jim never completed his degree.

Within days, I was arrested during a Gurindji land rights demonstration. My memory of police being particularly brutal at this 1500-strong demonstration was confirmed by phone intercepts in which CPA activists mention that the demonstrators tried to stop police 'grabbing' musicians and speakers, an eye was blackened, a protestor was thrown to the ground, ribs were bruised and police said things like, 'What are you worrying about those black b—— for?'

Just a few days later I was again arrested in a protest, this time in support of my fellow *Tharunka* editors, who had been charged with publishing obscenity. I was one of a group of anti-censorship campaigners who dressed up as nuns with slogans from an anti-Christian poem sewn onto our habits. I was later convicted and spent a week in Mulawa Women's Prison, which sparked in me a long-term interest in prisons.

These events, including our names, were widely reported and understandably shocked my family. My mother would often recount how she went to visit my Presbyterian great-aunts during this week, anxious about their reaction to this negative publicity. Although then in their eighties, they consoled her by telling her 'not to worry', as the sixteenth-century Scottish protestant reformer John Knox had been put in prison for his views.

But today as I read the files, I can still hear an anxious note in my mother's voice in several other conversations with Jim that ASIO recorded. As her middle-class expectations for our futures crumbled, Joan, in contrast to the parents of many other activists of my generation, was supportive. Many of her acquaintances, unlike the elderly aunts, shared ASIO's view that the movements that we were a part of were a threat to national security. Our activities cost her friendships, including a surgeon acquaintance who said at one dinner party that Jim and his friends 'should be put up against a wall and shot'. She too was influenced by these events and later in the year took my youngest sister out of school for a day to attend the massive Vietnam moratorium.

Later, in an intercepted conversation, she says she has 'heard on the news' that student leader and Maoist Albert Langer had got off a criminal charge, and that this was 'great news'. In another tapped conversation, Jim told my sister Janet that he thought he might be expelled, but not to tell his mother. A couple of weeks later, he was taped telling Joan he would be moving out of home into a group student house. She inquired how the disciplinary proceedings were going. Jim said that they would not be turning up to the hearing, which would scarcely have allayed her fears.

Joan would have been unnerved to think that someone was listening to her conversations, although she did have doubts about the genuineness of a minor break-in at her Hawthorn home during this period. Having called the police, she was bewildered to watch detectives removing political literature and other belongings from Jim's room. She heard nothing more. There is no mention of this incident in the file, although ASIO and the state Special Branches were known to do the odd break-in. There is mention, however, in Jim's file, of her house being selected for photographic surveillance in a project called 'Operation Sweep'.

One wonders what ASIO may have thought of the small grey-haired woman in her sixties who regularly carried green garbage bags from her car into the house (these were full of eucalyptus leaves that she was using to experiment with for natural dyes for weaving). They may also have seen the Maoist barrister Ted Hill, whom she described as 'such a very nice man'; she invited him to dinner as part of getting to know Jim's friends. Much later, ASIO placed her tiny home in a narrow Prahran lane under surveillance while tracking Jim on a visit from Perth, where he had become a union official in the building industry.

There are a few incidents in the files that I had completely forgotten. In 1970, an informant recorded that during the planning for a Vietnam moratorium, I suggested that we should purchase some old cars, or 'bombs' as we used to call them, and drive them onto the Sydney Harbour Bridge and abandon them. The idea was that this would be an inexpensive and peaceful way of drawing public attention to our protest. An ASIO agent considered this to most probably be 'an idle thought' and unlikely to eventuate, which was correct at that time. I have no memory of making that suggestion in 1970 but I must have, because much later in 1978, during a successful campaign to shut a draconian New South Wales prison punishment block called Katingal, I helped organise a small motorcade of Prisoners' Action Group and Women Behind Bars activists who stopped the traffic on the Harbour Bridge in exactly that fashion.

By 1972, I had been through two obscenity trials and imprisoned for brief periods in Mulawa Women's Prison. I wanted to see the much larger student movements and hippy revolutions for myself. ASIO became aware that I had applied for a passport and planned to travel to San Francisco for a holiday. When my application for a US visa was refused, I was told by someone in the United States Embassy that this was because I had created a 'national furore' by saying 'fuck' on Channel Nine's *A Current Affair* during an interview about the distribution of free copies of the *Little Red School Book*, a handbook on children's rights.

At the time I was disappointed but amused that anyone would think that I could be a threat in San Francisco, where there were thousands of people like me. When I read my ASIO file I found that my CPA friend Mavis Robertson had been recorded as saying she had arranged for me to meet a communist friend in the US and to interview the black activist Angela Davis for the CPA newspaper *Tribune*.

The files are a huge historical resource, especially now that they can be digitised and searched. But future researchers should be wary of relying on even minor details in the files without independent verification. I have a friend whose file contains material about another person of the same name. My dark-eyed brother was recorded as having blue eyes and my hair, which was dark brown, was described as fair. For years, ASIO admitted that they had no up-to-date photo from which to identify Jim. At particular stages, we were both recorded as likely members of the CPA, which we were not.

More significantly, at the height of student activism at UNSW, an agent decided that the 'most dangerous group' on campus was the 'Counter Culture Club' which he or she concluded had seized control of the campus newspaper *Tharunka*. I was supposedly a member of the group and Graeme Dunstan (who has since admitted working for ASIO at Melbourne University), the leader. Neither I nor Dunstan, who these days is well known for his Peace Bus campaigning around Australia, have any memory of this group. Possibly no one told the agent that the counter culture was not the name of a group, but the term used for a wide and amorphous cultural and social movement.

As others have previously written, ASIO's activities were underpinned by deep social conservatism and a Cold War obsession with progressive political organisations, especially the CPA, but also Trotskyist, Maoist and anarchist ones. This also means that the files tend to exaggerate the influence of the organised communist parties during this period. Action groups that were often more radical in tactics but more fluid and open in organisation were harder to pin down. Judging from my own file, this was particularly so in relation to groups influenced by less authoritarian forms of organisation, such as the prisoners' movement and the women's liberation movement, which was also of interest to ASIO.

In an early CPA phone intercept report included in my file, feminist and CPA organiser Mavis Robertson's young son Peter contacted his mother about the death of his guinea pig. In the course of the conversation, Mavis asked him to get a file – 'one of the smaller ones, labelled Women's Liberation' – from a cupboard and to read her a list of names. He dutifully read out fifty-six names, of which I was one. While some of these women were members of the Communist Party and already had ASIO files, others were not.

It would seem that the groups including these women were under more surveillance than many other groups which were just as radical in ideas and actions. There is a detailed record of a meeting of a Working Women's Group 'Yak Session' held in a home on Sydney's North Shore which was included in my file because I was in Mulawa Women's Prison at that time and a planned demonstration outside the prison was discussed at the meeting. For some reason, the list of names of people who attended this meeting is entirely redacted, although quite a few individuals are mentioned in the notes.

The agent, who was clearly unfamiliar with the milieu, commented that no one had introduced her to anyone, suggesting that perhaps she was under suspicion. Her notes describe a meeting which planned a number of future actions and featured a discussion about 'childhood experiences with sex'. Despite this, she reported that 'there did not seem to be any organisation of the meeting' and there was no chair or 'correspondence secretary'. This was, of course, not unusual for feminist meetings.

The agent gave a description of each woman, including an academic who she said was wearing a black wig with 'black hair peeking from under the wig' and had pajamas and toiletries in a bag. She noted that some were living in a commune. After the meeting, the agent was de-briefed by her case officer, and identified Mavis Robertson and four other women who attended the meeting as being identical to women in ASIO photographs.

In April 1972, an agent was also present at a meeting to form a Women's Media Group. Thirty women attended this meeting, including me. The agent supplied a list of all the names, drawing particular attention to two women, one of whom worked for the *Daily Telegraph* and another whom she had noticed at two anti-war rallies. No one knows what happened, if anything, to such information, but once in the hands of ASIO it would have been easy to pass it on to employers.

ASIO agents, both male and female, were quick to pass judgment on the appearance of women, who were 'petite', 'plain-faced', 'dumpy' or 'mannish'. The presence of homosexuals was worthy of special mention by both agents and intelligence police in what were still the early days of gay liberation. For example, my file contains a report of a protest about the poor treatment of girls in Parramatta Girls Home, which was addressed by left-wing MP George Petersen. The report includes the names of twelve men and women, most of whom had ASIO files. The rest of the 150, some of whom were the key organisers in this campaign, were simply lumped together as 'lesbians', as if they were an alien race. Similarly, in 1976 when 1200 people protested in favour of abortion law reform, individuals and groups were identified simply as 'gays'.

ASIO also carried out surveillance on anarchist and Libertarian conferences. At the end of 1971, an ASIO agent was dispatched to a joint Libertarian and anarchist conference over a weekend in Minto, just outside Sydney. He (I assume he was a man because of the way he described women) was one of only fifteen people who arrived on Friday night, which was not enough for a planned party. The agent did not have much fun, explaining that he had been served the most 'atrocious' meal he had ever eaten and that three meals consisted of 'frankfurts camouflaged in three different ways'. His chief job seemed to be to identify and describe as many participants as possible. There was an 'unattractive woman whose only saving grace was her friendliness', a friendly woman with an 'illegitimate child', a man with a large brown 'Marxian' beard, a 'weedy man' with a 'slavic expression' and another 'sandy haired man' who was described as being 'secretive' for refusing to give his second name. I was described as being a 'loud mouth' and a 'self-professed member of Women's Liberation'.

According to the agent's report, I was part of a discussion about whether women's liberation was consistent with human liberation, which included a debate about whether we were in favour of the nuclear family, which I was not. The speaker who most impressed the agent was journalist Paddy McGuinness, who, while being a 'big drinker', was 'not biased to either side' in his talk on Cuba. McGuinness, who correctly told the agent that the Libertarians were in decline, later became a prominent member of the Australian right.

The agent concluded that 'apart from intellectual discussion' the purpose was to have a 'good weekend' – a fair assessment. 'Sex and drugs were blatantly displayed and there were rumours of quite a bit of swapping going on.'

Overall, ASIO's operation in Victoria appeared to be much better organised and intense than elsewhere in Australia. This could have been because ASIO's headquarters was in Melbourne or even because radical movements were larger in Victoria than in Sydney at that time. One ASIO report of a Melbourne meeting to organise a single American Independence Day rally says that it was attended by 250 people, with thirty on the communications group and eight on the poster group.

Two months before the election of the Whitlam Government, 200 people, including my brother Jim, attended a meeting 'in defence of Australian Democracy' at the Unitarian Church in Melbourne to discuss concerns about the growth of the far right in Australia. ASIO prepared a detailed report of the speeches and recorded the names or car numberplates of as many of those who attended as possible. Of those on the list, many had ASIO files, including the chair, Dr Jim Cairns, who later became a Labor deputy prime minister.

As a Maoist, Jim was an enthusiastic member of the Australia China Society, another key ASIO target. This did not seem surprising as our grandmother Jessie Bacon had campaigned within the Presbyterian Church for China to be accepted into the United Nations during the long years when Cold War fears meant that Australia and other Western countries refused to recognise the government in mainland China. ASIO monitored the meetings and the entire membership of the society. An agent was on the plane when Jim led a delegation to China via Hong Kong in 1972. This surveillance continued even after the Whitlam Government recognised China. For example, included in Jim's file is a full list of Australian health workers, including my sister Janet (who used Chinese medicine in her medical practice), who visited China in 1977.

For ASIO, each event left a trail of car number plates, descriptions and names to follow up. Sensing the future, a Melbourne anarchist had raised the issue of computers at the Libertarian conference, warning of how much easier they would make surveillance. These days, ASIO can instantly track down people using mobile phones. Back then, intelligence work was slower and more tedious. When Jim moved to Perth, local operatives asked for a contemporary photo to be sent by mail so they could recognise him.

In the early days of activism, people were aware of the possibility of being monitored but it was at best a background issue. But gradually, ASIO and police Special Branches became an issue for the left in their own right. Jim became involved in a campaign, led by Labor activist Joan Coxsedge, to focus attention on ASIO. This meant that ASIO agents were now attending meetings which planned marches on their own premises. This must have been an odd experience for the agents.

Suspicion increased as more information emerged about the role of the CIA in the affairs of other countries, including Australia.

In 1978 I joined the campaign for the release of the three Ananda Marga members suspected of involvement in the Sydney Hilton Hotel bombing. (One of them, Tim Anderson has written about his experiences in this book.) The NSW Special Branch had introduced an informant, Richard Seary, into the Ananda Marga, and Special Branch was closely monitoring the campaign. Once again, I was caught up in intercepted calls. This campaign, which was linked to a larger campaign against New South Wales police corruption, eventually led to a judicial inquiry, which found there had been a miscarriage of justice and that Seary was an extremely unreliable witness. The Hilton bombing remains an unresolved mystery with many rightly or wrongly suspecting that ASIO and the NSW Police Special Branch had some knowledge of the planted bomb.

By this time, I was working at Channel Nine as a journalist, having been refused admission to practise as a barrister after the New South Wales Supreme Court found that I was not 'fit and proper' to practise law. In a low-key way, ASIO followed that case and my continuing investigations of the cases against the Ananda Marga and consequent police corruption.

Meanwhile, by July 1981, Jim had moved from Perth to Hobart where he was working for the Builders Labourers' union. To assist with surveillance, ASIO in Western Australia sent a ten-year-old photo. Hobart advised that he was spending a lot of time in the office and that for 'operational reasons' it would be unwise to carry out surveillance, which was also difficult to do at his home because he lived in a cul de sac. It would be interesting if I could ask Jim if, after years of being watched and followed as a Builders Labourers' official, he chose this house deliberately.

I only accessed our files up to 1981. Over twelve years, ASIO had accompanied Jim, me, and many others on our political journeys. I have only touched on some highlights. There are also agents' reports on the interminable discussions about protest tactics; safe printing presses; editorial policy for publications; and dissent inside the Worker Student Alliance, the Builders Labourers' Federation and the CPA (Marxist–Leninist).

Our generation saw our political activities as a decisive break from the past. 'Don't trust anyone over thirty' was the phrase coined by San Francisco activist Jack Weinberg to express how younger activists wanted to throw off suggestions that they were influenced by the Old Left. Reflecting on these files has made me think more about continuities with the past, both within the family and in broad social and political contexts. In our different ways, Jim and I tended to adopt hard line stances, perhaps reflecting the moralism of our Protestant past. We were fortunate to engage in social battles of our own choice. One consequence of this is that we were monitored by ASIO, but this surveillance was marginal to our activities and the paths we followed in life. We had many advantages which others who have come to ASIO's attention, then and now, may not have had.

I continued on to become a journalist and academic. Jim joined the ALP and eventually was elected and re-elected Premier of Tasmania. He counted amongst his contributions the legalisation of homosexuality and the securing of Aboriginal land rights in Tasmania. Reading ASIO's reports on me and my family has led me to start research for a book on the social history of our family – the continuities and discontinuities between my generation and our forebears back to white settlement as we experienced and confronted the contradictions of our times.

MARK AARONS

1975　2013

Mark Aarons is an author and former ABC Radio National broadcaster and political advisor. He has written six books and published feature articles in many of Australia's major newspapers and magazines.

His last book, *The Family File*, is the story of four generations of the Aarons family and their activities in the Communist Party of Australia. It is told through a unique combination of oral histories stretching back to the beginning of the twentieth century, and the largest single collection of security files in Australian history.

Growing up in a prominent communist family, Mark became politically active in his early teenage years in the mid-1960s, campaigning against the Vietnam War and apartheid and in support of Aboriginal rights. After being active in communist youth groups, he joined the CPA when he finished school in 1969, by which time his personal ASIO file already contained 300 pages. It eventually grew to nine volumes.

For two decades, beginning in the early 1970s, Mark worked at Radio National, first on the original *Lateline* program and then on *Broadband*. He was the founding executive producer of the network's investigative documentary program *Background Briefing*. He was also an official of the ABC Staff Union and active in many campaigns in defence of the independence of the national broadcaster.

From 1996 to 2011 Mark was a senior advisor to NSW Attorney-General and Minister for the Environment Bob Debus and NSW Premier Morris Iemma, developing policies to combat climate change, to conserve our limited water resources (both rural and urban) and to preserve our natural landscapes, especially through the expansion of the national parks network.

He has written widely on war crimes, East Timor, the Catholic Church and the Middle East, including bestselling books *The Secret War Against The Jews*, *Ratlines* and *War Criminals Welcome*.

STATE AFFAIRS AND LOVE AFFAIRS

by Mark Aarons

Having an ASIO file was congenital, like the flat feet that my grandfather passed to my father Laurie and then on to me. In my infancy I made cameo appearances in Laurie's file because he was a national leader of the Communist Party of Australia (CPA). In March 1954, for example, ASIO intercepted Laurie's telegram from Darwin, sending his love to my mother Carol, my older brothers Brian and John, and to 'Marf', surely a mistake, as an ASIO officer perceptively commented.

Laurie's security file commenced in 1931 when he was fourteen and the NSW Police Special Branch began recording his subversive activities. I beat this record when I was thirteen. In March 1965 ASIO opened my personal dossier, noting that I had already 'come to adverse notice'. By early October ASIO's agents had filed their first 'Q reports' on me. (ASIO's Q branch ran agents inside target organisations.) By then I was active in the Junior Eureka League, taking my first step on the road to CPA membership, another family DNA strand that passed from my great-grandparents down succeeding generations, eventually reaching me.

My first agent reports noted, prosaically, that I had run in the 100 yards and 220 yards sprint races at a JEL sports carnival. By the time I finished high school in 1969, my file had reached 300 pages. But I was never destined to take Laurie's record as the single most spied-upon person in Australian history. My modest nine volumes pale compared to his eighty-eight, accounting for more than 14 000 pages.

ASIO occupied a special place for communists. It was an article of faith that ASIO's malign presence stalked our family, even haunting our political nightmares. It was widely held that it was a conspiracy against progressives; a force we labelled 'stumblebum' that nonetheless crossed over from being a security service to participate effectively on the conservative side of politics. Many otherwise mysterious things were attributed to ASIO's 'unseen hand', including wrecking people's careers.

There are indications in my file that such fears were well founded. Furthermore, there is considerable evidence in its massive personal and organisational files that ASIO's actions did have adverse consequences for honourable people. There is also a discernible pattern of active assistance for the conservative side of politics during the Cold War that crossed the boundaries of a professional security service.

My perspective is somewhat different in 2014, as the heat of Cold War controversies has passed into history and many once closely guarded intelligence secrets have been declassified. It is now possible to judge 'conspiracy theories' against known facts. Files released under the relatively liberal archive rules of the United States, Britain and Australia have confirmed leftist critiques about Western involvement in covert operations to overthrow democratically elected governments, and even in assisting mass killings, as in Indonesia in 1965–66.

The release of secret files after communism's collapse in Europe in the late 1980s and early 1990s has, however, confirmed the immense scale of killings and repression behind the 'Iron Curtain'. It has also been confirmed that Soviet espionage was widespread in Western nations, including in 1940s Australia. This was the immediate background to Ben Chifley's decision to create ASIO in 1949.

By the time I became politically active in the mid-1960s, much had changed. The CPA had set itself on a new course after Laurie became National Secretary in mid-1965. After the Soviet-led invasion of Czechoslovakia in August 1968, the CPA adopted a democratic program to achieve a transition from capitalism to socialism by peaceful means, culminating in a 'declaration of independence' from Moscow. This was the CPA I joined in 1969, proudly committing to the role of revolutionary, like my father before me, his before him and his before him.

During the Cold War, ASIO had two briefs: counter espionage and counter subversion. For over three decades most ASIO operations focused on political subversion, a function that was discontinued in the mid-1980s on the recommendation of Justice Robert Hope following his second royal commission report.

Much of ASIO's well-deserved reputation for political bias and, in some cases, malevolent activities that adversely affected innocent people, can be traced to its obsession with subversion and its incoherent definition of what this actually meant. As a consequence, it categorised many who were merely exercising their rights to hold legitimate viewpoints and engage in normal political activities, as dangerous 'subversives'. Mostly the causes taken up by such people (including communists) seem normal today, including opposing racism and the Vietnam War or supporting the struggle of the East Timorese against Indonesia's illegal occupation.

But ASIO did not embark on such counter-subversion operations without political direction. Subversion was a major element of the brief Labor gave ASIO in 1949; this persisted for the following twenty-three years of Liberal–Country Party governments. In fact, conservative politicians avidly encouraged such operations and sometimes utilised their results for partisan political ends. However, there is no doubt that many ASIO counter-espionage operations were instigated as a result of actual Soviet spying. This coloured its counter-subversion operations and could perhaps be seen as a mostly unreasonable prism through which to view the legitimate political activities of thousands of Australians, but our spy-catchers believed espionage was at the core of their purpose.

It cannot be denied that ASIO's operations had adverse effects on real people. The clearest examples in my file occur in the crossover between the personal and the political. ASIO took an extraordinarily close interest in my youthful friendships and romances, regularly dispatching officers to warn the middle-class parents of my friends that their sons and daughters were in danger of contamination from my subversive ideas. In typically Aussie fashion, ASIO was mostly told to mind its own business, as I have learned from several friends over the years. But just being close to me was sufficient to draw ASIO's ire.

In 1969 I fell madly and rapturously in love with Pauline Johnson, the daughter of Brian and Betty Johnson, both ex-CPA members. Brian was a gifted electronics expert who worked at Amalgamated Wireless Australasia (AWA), which specialised in radio communications and aviation systems. Brian believed that his career had been stymied because of their political beliefs, especially as Betty had worked in the CPA's national office in the late 1940s and early 1950s. Brian had been refused access to classified material, severely limiting his career and confining him to middle management when he deserved promotion.

By 1969 Brian hoped that this was behind him, but suddenly Pauline's and my romance blossomed. ASIO recorded our young love, including the madcap adventure when we ran away from home after Easter 1969, in response to Brian's edict to reduce the frequency of our trysts. There are dozens of phone intercept reports of Pauline's and my conversations over the following years and agents' reports concerning our political activities and personal affairs.

Our ASIO files starkly demonstrate how our relationship adversely affected Brian. The Department of Supply's Security Branch worked closely with ASIO on defence-related security matters and cultivated a network of agents at AWA who kept Brian under close observation. In early 1969 ASIO passed on the information that Pauline and I were linked romantically to the Security Branch, which recorded that she had 'eloped with Mark AARONS, son of Laurie AARONS, C.P.A. National Secretary'.

It is a recurring theme in my file: to my own sins as a political agitator is often added my sorry status as 'son of Laurie', infecting those with whom I came into contact. In Brian

Johnson's case it was enough to reconfirm his 'untrustworthy' status. The Department of Supply's correspondence is filed in Pauline's and my ASIO dossiers, confirming that Brian was still on the 'X' list (restricting his access to classified information) in late 1974, long after our relationship had finished and many years after he had left the CPA.

The danger I posed to 'national security' is graphically illustrated by the consequences of an ASIO telephone intercept report of mid-May 1969:

> 1. During the above period, Robin MELROSE contacted Mark AARONS at the latter's home and invited AARONS and some of his friends, including John MacCALLUM [sic] to his ... second wedding anniversary party. AARONS said he would attend providing he and Pauline ... were not going to the ballet that night.
>
> 2. MELROSE asked if 'we' are too old to join the Young Socialists and was assured by AARONS that they could join.

A fortnight later ASIO's New South Wales counter-subversion branch filed an assessment that concluded that 'MELROSE is a personal security risk'. This arose in part from his 'reported anti-conscription activity in 1965/1966 which culminated in his burning his Army call-up card', but when he applied for an appointment as a graduate clerk in the Commonwealth public service this was not considered by ASIO as 'adequate grounds for the refusal of a security clearance' to access classified government material.

This now changed. ASIO's national headquarters prepared a minute paper in early July 1969 which recorded the reason he would be refused a classification clearance:

> ... the 9/12th May 1969 intercept report indicates that MELROSE is friendly with Mark AARONS and the probability that MELROSE and his wife are now members of the [Young Socialist League]. MELROSE made overtures regarding joining the Y.S.L. and AARONS would be unlikely to let the opportunity of obtaining two new members go by.

So ASIO wrote to the secretary of the Public Service Board advising that as he 'has an adverse security record' it 'is considered that to allow MELROSE access to classified matter would constitute a security risk'. Among the reasons given was that he was 'reliably reported as a friend of Mark AARONS, the son of Laurence AARONS, National Secretary of the Communist Party of Australia'. Robin Melrose's public service career was stymied before it had even begun.

The scandal worsened a few weeks later, when ASIO learned that Melrose's wife was the sister of a budding diplomat, David Reeve, who coincidentally had been at school with my brothers Brian and John. Reeve's connection to Melrose started a new security scare that went right to the top of his own department and ASIO, which commented that Reeve was 'a young External Affairs officer presently serving at the R.A.A.F. School of Languages, Point Cook', who was about to commence his diplomatic career in Australia's Jakarta embassy.

By late August 1969 ASIO's national headquarters had prepared another minute paper:

> It is recommended that ... the Department of External Affairs be informed that Susan MELROSE, nee REEVE, the sister of David REEVE, and her husband, Robin MELROSE, are reliably reported to be close friends of Mark AARONS, a member of the Young Socialist League and the Communist Party of Australia, and a son of Laurie AARONS, General Secretary of the Communist Party of Australia. In May 1969, Robin MELROSE is reliably reported to have made enquiries about the eligibility of himself and his wife to join the Young Socialist League. Recently Susan MELROSE is reliably reported to have said that the last time her brother David was in Sydney she and her friends got in his car with balloons saying 'Bring back the troops from Vietnam' and 'Stop the war' as a result of which her brother was 'hauled up before External Affairs'. The Department could be asked whether they are able to confirm this statement by Susan MELROSE and should it be true, whether they would agree to an interview of David REEVE using this information as a pretext. Our enquiries have been unable to establish the degree of association between REEVE and the MELROSES and Mark AARONS and an interview would assist in this regard.

ASIO had recorded the incident in Reeve's car during a telephone conversation between Susan Melrose and me. This was clearly a mischievous exchange especially for the benefit of the eager ears of ASIO. Having said the words recorded in the minute paper, Susan then said, 'so I've jeopardised his whole career – isn't that good? I'll have to join the Communist Party on the strength of that.'

ASIO, however, did not see the joke. The intercept report recorded that the 'following conversation then continued':

AARONS: ... Isn't he [David] a secret undercover agent?
MUNROSE [sic]: Oh yes, basically ...
AARONS: ... Out to destroy the right-wing Government in Indonesia.
MUNROSE: Yeah ...
AARONS: What's the world coming to when they find out revolutionists like David.

With such casual humour David Reeve's career was put in jeopardy and ASIO went into overdrive to establish whether a secret communist cell was operating within the Department of External Affairs, as one had in the 1940s.

In early September 1969 ASIO Director-General Sir Charles Spry directed that Reeve be interviewed in the presence of the Deputy Secretary of the Department of External Affairs in order

> to ascertain REEVE's own attitude to Communism and to ellicit [sic], if possible, the degree of his association with the MELROSES and Mark AARONS; and if any such, the security implications of same.

In 2013 David Reeve was astounded to learn that he was ASIO's target at this interview. He recalled that his interrogators' line of questioning was focused solely on his sister's relationship to me. For forty-four years he believed they wanted him to inform on us, which outraged him. He had no idea he was the target, which outraged him all over again.

ASIO surveillance photo from Mark Aarons's file showing Mark Aarons and Lynda Boland outside the CPA's Brisbane headquarters as part of Operation Shiver (ASIO's attempt to identify all visitors to CPA headquarters), 20 December 1970.

My personal life had a habit of infecting 'national security'. When I was nineteen I took a year off my university studies and went to work for the CPA as a youth organiser. In May 1971 ASIO filed the following telephone intercept report:

> AARONS contacted John McCALLUM on 92.4694 and spoke about his girlfriend, Belinda ROBERTSON ... AARONS

said that ROBERTSON was working at the [Students' Representative Council] office at Sydney University.

(NOTE: The above is submitted for the identification of Belinda ROBERTSON.)

John McCallum was a close friend from our days at North Sydney Boys' High School. His parents had been summoned by ASIO and warned of the dangerous company their son was keeping, but John's mother Ann gave them short shrift.

I had met Belinda Robertson at university and in mid-1971 we had a brief but passionate romance. I had no idea that it would cause another security scare. Soon after my phone conversation with McCallum, I visited Belinda's home and met her her parents, who invited me to visit them while they were holidaying at Avoca, north of Sydney. This was recorded in my telephone conversation with Belinda, along with the following:

> Belinda ... said that her mother had been 'quite nice' about Mark ... and added that 'the only thing they worry about is their friends and also Mum was worrying that I might be a security risk to Dad ...'

Belinda's mum Betty was right to be concerned about the threat I posed to her husband Doug. ASIO went to enormous lengths to track down Belinda's family, dispatching an officer to interview people believed to have contact with them and eventually making 'a discreet call' to their telephone number. ASIO quickly determined 'that Douglas ROBERTSON ... is employed by [the Directorate of Military Intelligence] in a very sensitive area'.

ASIO had discovered that Doug Robertson served in the intelligence corps of the Army Reserve. In mid-August 1971, ASIO's investigators reported to New South Wales headquarters. The report's overtly religious tone suggests it may have been written by Catholics who judged Belinda's affection for me to be a 'mortal sin'. They had missed the fact that our romance had already ended; for them the security scare was just beginning:

> 5. Birth particulars of ... Belinda Jane ROBERTSON born 22.2.52 are attached, this shows that she is the daughter of Douglas Webster ROBERTSON who is the subject of Top Secret clearance NTS 1/8985, and who is apparently attached to D.M.I., Victoria Barracks.
>
> 6. We can not [sic] visit the sins of the daughter on the father but obviously further enquiries are justified, possibly to the point of an interview with Douglas ROBERTSON as a prophylactic exercise, if for no other reason.
>
> 7. As a number of sections will be interested in this case you may care to instruct how this case should be progressed.

By early November the case had reached ASIO Director-General Peter Barbour, who wrote to the Director of Military Intelligence:

> Douglas ... ROBERTSON was cleared to you under Top Secret Check No. T.S. 35934 on 22nd November, 1967 ...
>
> 2. Reliable reports indicate that Belinda ROBERTSON, a daughter of Douglas ROBERTSON, is deeply involved emotionally with Mark AARONS, a member and full-time

functionary of the Communist Party of Australia. Mark …
is a son of Laurence AARONS, the General Secretary of the
Communist Party of Australia.

3. It is understood that ROBERTSON is aware of his
daughter's association with AARONS and his political
affiliations.

4. It is considered that you will wish to carefully consider
the foregoing against the background of ROBERTSON's
Top Secret clearance. If a review of that clearance is to be
undertaken there would need to be some prior consultation
between us.

It is noteworthy that my CPA activities at this time involved entirely legitimate political campaigns, mostly focused on issues such as anti-racism (supporting Indigenous rights and opposing apartheid); education reform; and opposing the Vietnam War. But ASIO considered CPA members to be subversives, committed to overthrowing the constitutional order and creating a socialist society (by 1971 this involved a democratic alternative to capitalism, not the Soviet or Chinese models involving dictatorship and mass repression).

In the examples discussed here, ASIO was obviously focused on the possibility that my relationships with Pauline Johnson, Robin and Susan Melrose and Belinda Robertson posed threats to national security: Pauline's father might have access to defence-related secrets through his colleagues at AWA; Susan's brother was joining the diplomatic service in a sensitive post; and Belinda's father had access to military intelligence secrets.

It must be presumed that ASIO's interest harked back to the KGB-controlled espionage ring that operated in Australia in the

1940s. By 1971, however, ASIO had mountains of intelligence demonstrating that relations between the CPA and Moscow were poisonous. In the highly unlikely event that I had gleaned some scraps of top secret information through my relationships, there was no chance they would reach Moscow.

The fact is that I never obtained such intelligence, let alone passed it on to a foreign power.

From 1973 ASIO's surveillance focused on my work as an ABC Radio National broadcaster. In March 1975 I accompanied a fact-finding delegation to Portuguese East Timor, producing a documentary for the original *Lateline*. As a consequence, I became a lifelong supporter of East Timor. In 2014 this is unexceptional, but between 1975 and 1999 successive federal governments – Labor and Liberal – demonised those who believed that Australia's national interest lay in opposing Indonesia's illegal invasion. We were treated as subversives.

My ASIO file reflects the Whitlam and Fraser governments' warped national security priorities. For example, after the 1975 invasion, immense effort was expended on penetrating the CPA's operation to maintain an illegal radio link between the besieged internal resistance and its external representatives. This provided a steady flow of accurate information about Indonesian war crimes and a vital link between the resistance and diplomatic and solidarity activities abroad. It was especially important between early 1976 and late 1978 as Indonesia had effectively sealed off the country.

There are dozens of telephone intercept reports in my file about the operation, along with accurate agents' reports on the tiny group of CPA members involved. It is impossible not to be impressed by ASIO's penetration of our clandestine activities, including foreknowledge of my April 1976 trip to Mozambique to illegally import $US40 000 to finance the link. Given the tiny group involved it is maddening to read the detailed agents' reports revealing ASIO knew the fine details of our plans in real time. It was obviously a high priority to gather such intelligence to protect the 'national interest' as it was then defined: to maintain Australia's 'strategic relationship' with the mass killers who ruled Suharto's Indonesia.

In 1977 I commenced an investigation which also became a lifelong cause: exposing the many war criminals who have made Australia home over the last sixty-five years. ASIO was an eyewitness to the genesis, recording my telephone calls with Yugoslav diplomats seeking information about the Croatian, Serbian and Slovene Nazi collaborators and war criminals who came in the post-war mass immigration program.

It is ironic that several years later I became one of the first researchers to use the *Archives Act* to access thousands of pages of ASIO files on ex-Nazis and collaborators. I used these in ABC radio documentaries and several books which exposed ASIO's complicity in protecting such people and, in some cases, even recruiting them as agents.

ASIO's interest in my contacts with Yugoslav diplomats had been piqued by my 1977–78 Radio National programs on the Croatian Ustaše, quoting ASIO's own records that had been tabled in federal parliament in 1973 by Attorney-General Lionel Murphy. These indicated that ASIO was an important link in a wider Western program to utilise this fascist group which had ruled Croatia from 1941 to 1945, using such unbelievable cruelty in a campaign of genocide against Jews, Gypsies and Serbs that even the Nazis were frequently shocked.

In March 1979 ASIO headquarters was deeply concerned at my connections with diplomats from communist Yugoslavia, following a New South Wales office report that I would be:

> ... travelling to Yugoslavia on 27 March 1979 ... returning before 29 April 1979. He is also travelling to Austria and England.
>
> 2. The purpose of his visit is to obtain details of people now resident in Australia who collaborated with the Nazis in World War II.

ASIO was unaware of my face-to-face conversations with consulate staff to arrange access to material held in official Yugoslav archives. But they recorded a telephone conversation with Ante Barbir, a Yugoslav diplomat who later became a senior foreign affairs official in the post-communist Croatian Government. ASIO's report stressed our 'friendly greetings' and recorded that during my forthcoming trip I would be visiting Slovenia and Croatia. Barbir stated that my 'programme will be arranged there and [I] will have access to the material [I] requested'.

The ASIO officer who transcribed this telephone intercept commented on the ominous fact that it 'appears that arrangements between AARONS and BARBIR prior to this conversation must have happened in private'.

ASIO's antenna was alert to this sinister development. Indeed, one officer believed that I was involved in a communist intelligence operation. When David McKnight was researching his history of ASIO (*Australia's Spies and Their Secrets*) he interviewed a former ASIO officer who insisted that I must have been an agent of the Yugoslav security service, UDBA.

In fact, I located most of the material about Nazis in Australia cited in my books (*Sanctuary*, *Ratlines*, *The Secret War Against the Jews* and *War Criminals Welcome*) in Western archives. These also document Western intelligence operations utilising Nazi collaborators and war criminals as anti-communist agents. The agencies involved included the British Secret Intelligence Service; the US State Department, Central Intelligence Agency and Federal Bureau of Investigation; and ASIO.

ASIO may have been a junior partner, but it was party to Western operations that recruited notorious Ustaše war criminals and terrorists in anti-communist operations. Indeed, the earliest terrorist actions in Australia (in the 1960s) were organised by such people. There are massive organisational and personal ASIO files from the late 1940s to the late 1970s which document the Ustaše's Australian and international terrorist infrastructure (directed by fugitive war criminals). These expose ASIO's myopic notion of Australia's 'national security' during the Cold War. ASIO's largely indifferent attitude to the terrorism threat posed by such groups demonstrates its congenital blindness in the 'right' eye.

On the other hand, ASIO's obsession with largely non-existent 'subversive' threats from the left led it to concentrate considerable resources on the crossover of my legitimate political activities with my youthful romances and friendships, elevating me to an unjustified level of national security risk. My ASIO file records my earnest efforts to overthrow capitalism and replace it with a democratic form of socialism. It is also crystal clear that my activities were mostly legal and unexceptional. They scarcely threatened revolution. Sadly, capitalism and the Australian Constitution were safe from me.

KEVIN COOK

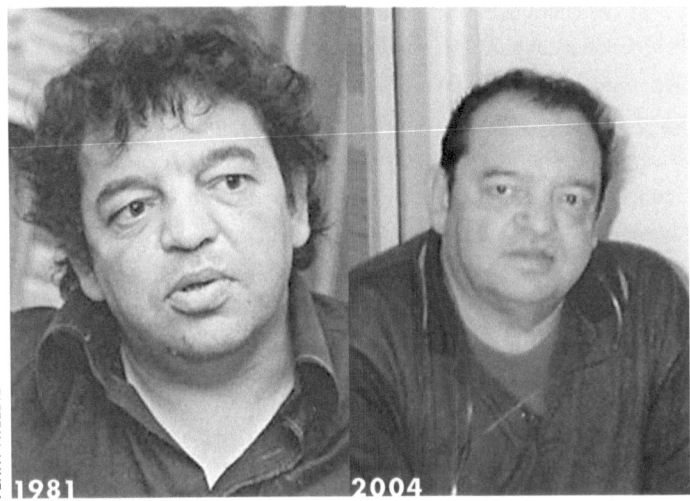

Kevin Cook was elected as the first Chair of the New South Wales Aboriginal Land Council in 1983 and continued to play an active role in local and regional land councils for many years. He is a Wandandian man who was born in 1939 near Wollongong. During the early 1970s he became active in the Jack Mundey-led NSW Builders Labourers' Federation and became an organiser during the tumultuous years which saw the beginnings of environmental unionism through the famous green bans.

From the mid 1980s, Kevin was the first Aboriginal General Secretary of Tranby Aboriginal Adult Education Cooperative. He expanded the college's programs with community outreach, union and university teaching support, and began active campaigning for causes such as an end to black deaths in custody. During the 1990s he worked with Macquarie University and UTS to build the capacity of these universities to offer appropriate education for Indigenous students. Throughout the 1970s and 1980s, Kevin played a key role in New South Wales and national organising for land rights, building links between scattered rural communities and across state borders.

With other unionists, he took the Indigenous voice to the International Labour Organisation (ILO) in the mid-1980s, pioneering the networks which would carry his Aboriginal and Islander colleagues to the United Nations later in the decade. As Chair of the Aboriginal Advisory Committee of the Australian Council of Churches, and of the Trade Union Committee on Aboriginal Rights, and as a founder and key supporter of the Building Bridges collaboration between black and white musicians, Kevin has had a vision of Indigenous and non-Indigenous Australians working together in mutual respect to develop an Australia where all people could live freely and with dignity.

THEY JUST DIDN'T CARE

Kevin Cook with Heather Goodall

When I saw my files I couldn't believe it – there were lots of pages but there was nothing in them. The whole thing was just a *nothing*!

The files covered the period from late 1979 to late 1983, when the campaign for land rights in New South Wales was really going strong to try to get some legislation to recognise our rights in land. The NSW Parliament's Select Committee brought down its report in 1980 and recommended that the government move to grant land rights before it did anything else. The Wran Government got re-elected at the end of 1980, on a promise to follow the recommendations of the Select Committee, but nobody knew what they'd do. Wran announced a new Ministry for Aboriginal Affairs – that nobody had asked for ... and no-one knew who Wran would appoint to be the minister or to implement these Select Committee reports.

So there were big meetings about land rights all through 1980 and 1981 ... but you don't hear anything about that from these files!

The ASIO agents just seemed to be interested in the Socialist Party of Australia (SPA) and the International Socialists (IS). Hannah Middleton was the Secretary of the Trade Union Committee on Aboriginal Rights (TUCAR), which kept unions in touch with Aboriginal politics. Hannah was also in the SPA and so were a lot of the unionists I'd been working with for many years in the building industry, long before TUCAR got started.

They seem to have had Hannah's phone bugged, because most of the reports are from agents listening to her phone conversations. We had no phone in the TUCAR office – it was just a little room in the Trades Hall. So Hannah often worked out of the SPA offices and used their phone for TUCAR business. The ASIO file reports her ringing me up a lot, but they never have transcripts of me ringing *her*. And they didn't know the names of people at Tranby (the important Sydney Aboriginal co-operative training college). When I wasn't there once, they said there was an 'unidentified man' who explained I was away. And another time they mentioned a 'Brian' but didn't know his surname. No-one else from Tranby was even mentioned. So it seems they weren't interested in my work at Tranby or in Tranby itself, and the Tranby phones weren't bugged. But Hannah's phone at the SPA office certainly was.

The funny thing is, they just got to record people ringing up Hannah as TUCAR secretary, to ask her about fundraising … they wanted to know how to get in touch with unionists so they could organise fundraisers and donations and publicity.

The other thing the ASIO agents used to do was sit in on IS meetings at Enmore in New South Wales. They didn't seem to have too many clues about what was going on there, but they used to copy down the agenda religiously and report on who said what. None of this was very interesting – everyone at the time thought ASIO was bugging everything so it doesn't come as a big surprise that they actually had people at meetings.

I wasn't too worried about ASIO at the time because we expected they'd be everywhere. If you went to a demo you could probably tell who the ASIO agents were – but nobody was worrying about it. Builders Labourers' Secretary Joe Owens knew – he went right up to one ASIO agent and confronted him.

And from these files it's clear they were at *everything*. They were even at the memorial service of a young Builders Labourer who'd been killed in an industrial accident. There are 'agent comments' scattered all through these files, so apart from the whole summary, they've got a separate box as well to have their say. At this particular memorial service, instead of listening to what had happened – all about how bad the industrial safety conditions were which was *why* this bloke got killed – the agent was making sly comments about the people there.

Like this one about a woman: '… very slim build, black straggly shoulder length hair, would not weigh more than about 8 stone'. Or this one about a bloke: 'slim build, grey hair receding. He speaks as if he is very sure of himself.'

Or about another bloke: '… about 5' 5", short, stocky build, short thick sandy coloured hair, wears silver rimmed glasses … He looks like a nasty kind of customer. 30 Jan 1979.'

But I didn't know anyone who was worried about ASIO or who *hid* anything. There just wasn't anyone who was doing anything secretive. And people assumed that ASIO would know about whatever was going on. Everyone expected it.

What surprised me was how little there was in the file about land rights … I was involved in lots of campaigning at that time,

Kevin Cook with Barbara Flick at the NSW Aboriginal Land Council rally, 30 October 1981.

from 1979 up to when the *Land Rights Act* was passed in the middle of 1983. It was a really big movement and a very new thing for many people all over New South Wales. But there was just nothing in the files about the actual campaigns or what we wanted or what we did! They just wanted to know who came to the meetings and what organisations they were affiliated with – like the SPA and IS. They didn't want to know about the Aboriginal politics that were raging at the time.

The only time they reported anything about what Tranby did (and they kept calling it 'Tramby') was in September 1982 when they heard Brian Doolan talking about the Commonwealth government's decision to slash the funds to Aboriginal adult education in New South Wales. At least the ASIO agent could tell that Brian was 'upset' about it. They reported that he said that Tranby and the Aboriginal Dance Company would have to 'cut' up to fifty courses over the next few months. But after that, they didn't report a thing about what we did about it. We had a huge protest about those cuts but there was nothing in the ASIO files about it.

They didn't even have much about the Commonwealth Games demonstrations in Brisbane at the end of September 1982. But there were thousands of us up there. Joh Bjelke-Petersen made out that Aboriginal people and their supporters were a threat to the whole of the country. That's why he banned us marching. And they arrested hundreds of us. And yet ASIO just wasn't interested. They put in a few details about SPA and IS meetings in the lead up, where people were trying to raise money to fund buses going up to Brisbane for the Games demos, and then all the confusion about who should go, and who shouldn't. ASIO were reporting that it was only 'Blacks' who were making the decisions.

But they weren't interested in *why* we were going up, they just say it's about land rights but nothing about the 'Queensland Act' or Joh Bjelke's ban on street marches or anything.

All they said about me was in October 1982 after the Games, when they reported that I'd been arrested but that they had 'no information' that I 'advocate or support the use of violence'. And then after that they really didn't seem much interested in me at all.

But they did get a lot of information out of those Games and they kept it in their files. The Queensland coppers gave ASIO the names of every single person – all 314 of us – who got arrested up there in Brisbane. They gave them the full names, addresses and all the details they had. And then ASIO looked them all up and put them in the files. Here's what they said:

> Where an individual is recorded in ASIO, details of his or her current and former membership of subversive groups have also been included. Of the 314 people arrested in the three demonstrations, 32 are recorded in ASIO. Twenty-seven of these could be considered adversely recorded. ASIO has no information to indicate the racial origins of those arrested, although an estimate based on those arrested in the Demonstration on 7 October 1982 indicates that 38% are Aboriginals.
>
> On the information available in ASIO, the demonstrations were initiated by Aboriginals and backed by white activists. There was no violence attempted and the protests were designed to achieve publicity for the Aboriginal land rights cause. While the International Socialists (IS) consistently supported all demonstrations, the increased number of Communist Party of Australia (CPA) members arrested in the demonstration on 7 October is of significance. It is likely that after the Games, the CPA and IS will organise national campaigns designed to exploit the arrests of their members and the land rights issue. (Note for File, 9 Oct 1982 … from an Agent [name blacked out] in the 'Games Operation Room')

The only funny bits in here are the reports of some of the meetings in the lead up to the Commonwealth Games. There was an open meeting that IS organised in Cope Street, Redfern. The agent obviously didn't have a clue about how grass roots organisations ran, where everyone gets to have a say. So there was an Aboriginal bloke there who seemed to have been drunk. The agent was still trying to follow what he said. And even apart from that, the agent just didn't really seem to understand what was going on – not because it was secret but just because they didn't know anything about the people or the issues. On the other hand, the meeting did sound a bit like it came out of *Life of Brian*. Here is the report with the 'agent comments' where he or she typed them, in between their own summaries:

14 September 1982:

Report of a meeting in Cope St Redfern on 8 September 1982:

Lists the 36 people there – (with phone numbers where they had them and cross-referenced to the files that ASIO already had on them).

Agent comment: of the thirty-six people, only three were black. According to HIRST, there were three or four Socialist Workers Party (SWP)/Resistance members present.

Agent's summary: General discussion took place on the organisation of buses to transport aboriginals to Brisbane during the Commonwealth Games. This group has a bank of $600, of which $340 is already committed to the costs of printing posters and handbills.

Agent comment: These handbills were handed out at the rally outside the Queensland Government Tourist Bureau on 9 September, 1982.

Agent's summary continues: It was stated that it was hoped to hire four fourteen seat buses to travel to Brisbane on 23 September, 1982 … At the meeting, it was asked who would be availing themselves of the use of the buses. Two hands went up.

Agent comment: This obviously does not look to be a terribly successful venture.

Agent's summary continues: They went on to say that the return cost per person would be $41 as the buses cost approximately $500 each to hire.

Agent comment: It seems to me that the cost of petrol has not yet been considered. It seems as though there is an outlay of $2000 odd just for the buses, let alone petrol, yet there is only $200 or so in the bank.

Agent's summary continues: There was another additional suggestion of booking one hundred seats on the train. Someone suggested that if there were vacant seats, then the Aboriginal community would welcome the opportunity to use them.

Agent comment: (i) Apparently the aboriginals will go if someone else pays for them but not otherwise.

(ii) This whole meeting seemed a waste of time. Participants are really in 'cloud cuckoo land'.

(iii) Two participants later stated that the IS was completely opposed to the concept of travelling to Brisbane.

Agent's summary continues: X [the drunken Aboriginal man] read out a letter which he was going to send to George Negus of the '60 Minutes' Television programme.

Agent comment: I honestly could not understand what he was trying to say.

Agent summary continues:

Composition of the group:

Agent comment: I guess that the bulk of the group are 'do-gooders' with a smattering of 'left' people present.

Agent summary continues:

Sub-Committees: It was reported that the group had four sub-committees:

a) Local Activities – This subgroup is responsible for the organisation of local rallies, dances and functions ...

b) Publicity

Agent comment: I have no idea what this group does.

c) Advertising

Agent comment: I don't know what the difference is between publicity and advertising.

d) ?? *Agent comment: unfortunately, no one could remember what the fourth sub-group was.*

But there wasn't much really in any of these files. All ASIO wanted to know about anything, even the Commonwealth Games demos and arrests, was who was in IS or the CPA.

The only really weird thing was that they had a report on the Australian Council of Churches Aboriginal Committee. They had a little history of when the ACC got involved in Aboriginal Affairs and who was secretary when, and how much the ACC gave to support the Aboriginal Embassy in the 1970s. And they had recorded the funding from the ACC for the Aboriginal and Torres Strait Islander Development Fund, set up in 1975.

They must have been listening on the phone all the time. Everyone at the time thought that ASIO was bugging everything anyway – so there wasn't anyone trying to hide anything.

People were happy to talk about anything – and anyway it was all just straight up and down. There was no revolution going on.

But ASIO didn't have anything interesting to say. And they weren't taking any notice of the stuff that really *was* interesting.

After all, everything we did, everyone knew about it anyway. You didn't have to be an agent to get the information. A two-year-old kid could have got it.

All they had to do was read the reports we were always producing … or even read the newspapers!

COLIN COOPER

1958   2013

Colin Cooper was born in 1941 and raised in Yagoona, one of Sydney's working-class western suburbs. He attended public schools in the local area, and at the age of ten became part of the Junior Eureka League (JEL). He joined the Eureka Youth League (EYL) when he was sixteen.

Colin started work with the Postmaster-General's Department (PMG) as a telegram messenger in 1957 and, after training, became a senior technician in 1965. During that time, he was an active member of the union, the Postal and Telecommunications Technicians Association, and in 1966 was elected as its New South Wales Assistant Secretary. In 1973, he was elected Branch Secretary and held that position until 1995, when he became the National President of the Communications Division of the newly amalgamated Communications, Electrical and Plumbing Union (CEPU).

As New South Wales Branch Secretary and Federal President of the union from 1970, he was involved in all major industrial campaigns and negotiations. These included the establishment of Telecom and Australia Post; the shorter hours and nine-day fortnight agreement of 1975; the staffing and technology disputes that arose from the introduction of new telecommunications technology, and all wage negotiations. Other activities included campaigns against the establishment of 'other than government telecommunications carriers' and against the privatisation of government enterprises. He led major campaigns against the privatisation of Telecom.

In 1973, he became a member of the New South Wales board of the Trade Union Training Authority and was an active supporter of trade union training. At the international level, Colin was an executive member of the Asian division of the international affiliate organisation, the Post Telegraph and Telephone International.

Colin served as a full-time senior union official from 1966 to 2007. In 1995 he was elected as the National Divisional President of the Communication Division of the CEPU and held this until July 2007. On his retirement, he completed an honours degree in history and industrial relations at Sydney University.

ASIO AND THE POSTMASTER-GENERAL

by Colin Cooper

The first thing I saw when I opened my ASIO file was their concern about my clothing. The garment was not outlandish or obscene; it was a simple khaki shirt with the letters PMG in red above the breast pockets. I was wearing it at home during the period ASIO had my parents under surveillance and, unbeknown to all of us, we had an ASIO agent as an invited guest. ASIO was clearly worried that the son of a member of the Bankstown branch of the Communist Party, who was also a member of the Eureka Youth League, was employed by the Commonwealth Public Service in the Postmaster-General's Department. It was enough for them to begin a process to verify who I was and to notify my employer.

ASIO became aware of my PMG employment on 24 January 1959. The shirt I wore was a remnant from my first job as a telegram boy in 1957. In 1958, I had transferred to become a technician-in-training, and at the time of ASIO's enlightenment, I was employed at the GPO in the Overseas Radio Terminal (ORT).

The ORT was the gateway between the PMG and the Overseas Telecommunications Commission (OTC) and included the international manual telephone exchange. At the time, public international telephone traffic was by radio telephone, and because of the varying quality of radio signals, calls were often required to be monitored by technicians.

If ASIO is still concerned that I might have heard clandestine conversations I should not have, I can assure them that the only call I remember was made during the making of the film *On the Beach* by Stanley Kramer in 1959. The conversation that Ava Gardner had with her friend in the US provided a level of insight into the life of an American film star that was very new to me, and was probably not appropriate for an innocent seventeen year old.

In June 1959, ASIO notified itself that I was a category B security risk. In an internal memorandum, they had made an educated guess as to why I had a PMG shirt (they discovered I was once a telegram boy) and recorded my employment at the ORT as a technician-in-training. Over the previous six months of inquiry, they had become convinced that in fact I was Colin Cooper, the son of Alan Cooper, and a member of the EYL. Surprisingly, they amended my real date of birth (20 June) to 30 June, and this error seems to have been maintained throughout my file.

On 24 November 1959, the ASIO Director-General asked the New South Wales Regional Director to again establish I was Colin Cooper son of Alan, as they proposed to send an 'appropriate summary of information' concerning me to both the Public Service Board and the PMG. On 27 November, ASIO New South Wales again confirmed that I was the son of Alan and a member of the EYL. In a minute dated 27 January

1960 on ASIO notepaper, four short points were made that comprised the 'summary of information' that was considered suitable for passing on to appropriate authorities. Firstly, I was a member of the EYL; secondly, my father was an active and longstanding member of the CPA; and thirdly, my siblings were also active in the EYL or the Junior Eureka League. It appears that this was the basis of correspondence dated 2 February 1960 sent by Director-General Spry to the Public Service Inspector. The Spry correspondence stated in part:

> Cooper has recently come to the attention of this organisation and were he to be considered for employment with access to classified information, I find I would be unable to grant a security clearance.

The correspondence constitutes no more than ninety words and provides no evidence of any wrongdoing by myself or my family. All justification is based on membership of legitimate organisations that, despite all the ASIO surveillance, were never found to have acted illegally or to threaten the nation's security. The justification for considering me or any other person a security risk based on our legitimate political activity should be of concern to all.

Reading this part of my ASIO file I recalled that it was about the time that I was transferred from the ORT to the Dalley Street trunk exchange. I now believe that the transfer was related to the ASIO report. Although at the time I was disappointed at being moved from a work force that I had come to like, the Dalley Street transfer proved to be of benefit when I became more active in the technicians' union, the Postal Telecommunication Technicians Association (PTTA). The Dalley exchange was the switching centre for the state's trunk network, and the establishment of communications on a technical and personal level with other technicians across the state was a natural consequence of the work. These contacts proved to be extremely helpful during the 1966 union elections.

Following my transfer the file seems to have become less intrusive, with no further entries until 24 April 1962, when my nickname and a short note on my attendance at the EYL rooms were recorded. It also noted the date and location of my twenty-first birthday party, which I am sure was of vital interest to those charged with protecting our national security.

The file then seems to get a burst of life in May 1963, when a document marked 'Secret' informs someone that I am employed in the PMG radio room in Dalley Street, Sydney. This information is obviously wrong, as to my knowledge no such place existed. The report prompted a response from the Director-General, who pointed out to the NSW Regional Director that I had been the subject of an 'adverse assessment' in a report dated 2 February 1960. The letter quoted my incorrect birth date as part of the identification process, with a request to be kept informed of the 'employment risk'. The response from the NSW Regional Director recorded my classification incorrectly but stated that I had 'limited access to Intra State trunk calls but it is considered that there is no employment risk'.

The inaccuracy of my classification and the claim that I worked in a nonexistent radio room indicates to me that ASIO did not have an informant among the people I worked with. If this is so, it does not surprise me, as generally the technicians helped each other and tolerated a wide range of views and opinions. The make-up of the workforce included many repatriated World War II defence force personnel, and most of the technicians and trainees came from working-class backgrounds.

It is from this point that my ASIO file seems to concentrate on personal, and what I consider, irrelevant information, such as who attended my 'buck's party' and the wedding celebration held at my parents' home. Someone also went to the trouble of compiling a list of the vehicles that were parked in the street, and details of the registered owners of the cars. When I told someone about this 'party list' in my ASIO file, they remarked how useful it was, as otherwise I would never remember who all the guests were.

The file at this stage simply contains lists of people who attended meetings, picnics, film nights and May Day balls, and again its relevance to national security is a mystery. It merely appears to be an attempt to compile a list of my associates who met ASIO's undefined definition of subversives or undesirables.

At this time I was starting to become active in the union, but there is little mention of this on my file. An exception was a response to an enquiry, apparently from ASIO to the PMG, when an article appeared in the *Sydney Morning Herald* on 21 July 1966, following my election as NSW Assistant Secretary in a union rank and file ballot. The *Herald* article was headed 'Postal Group Victory to the Left', and this appears to have stirred ASIO, who were informed after an inquiry from the Director-General's office that I had beaten 'a moderate' for the position of Branch Assistant Secretary.

In November 1969, the PTTA organised national midday mass meetings in support of wage claims. ASIO noted that the federal leadership was considered moderate, but that the New South Wales branch 'is militant to left-wing'. My pedigree was also mentioned, including that I was by then a member of the ALP 'left wing steering committee'. Following this there is

Colin Cooper speaking at Sydney Town Hall during a PMG wages dispute in 1979.

very little recorded until August 1970, when a copy of a NSW Special Branch report on an ACTU-sponsored budget protest rally at Wynyard Park was apparently provided to ASIO. In it, I was listed as a speaker representing white-collar postal workers in the Commonwealth public service.

The meeting contained a mixture of speakers from the left and right of the trade union movement and the ALP, and the motion to condemn the federal government's budget was moved by the then right-wing secretary of the New South Wales Labor Council, Ralph Marsh. This NSW Special Branch report was then sent by the New South Wales Regional Director of ASIO to their national headquarters.

After receiving this report ASIO commenced a re-evaluation of my security risk, with the Director-General recommending consideration of an 'upgrade'. Significantly, ASIO New South Wales recommended a downgrade from Category B to C, but that I be put on 'watch' on the basis that I was now believed to be a member of the ALP. I have the impression that the New South Wales region of ASIO at the time was either looking to offload work or, as the agents closest to the action, recognised the futility of what they were doing.

JUST WHO ARE YOU?

It was about this time that the New South Wales region forwarded a report to ASIO national headquarters about a telephone intercept on the Czechoslovakian consul in Sydney. The conversation appears to be between two PMG technicians (Ted and Tony), testing the telephone line between the consulate and the Double Bay telephone exchange. The transcriber of the telephone tap describes the conversation as 'phonetic' and quotes technical phrases such as '60 between' and 'clear condenser' as an example of the language being used. One of the technicians then states that 'Col Cooper' mentioned that 'They have a tape recorder across the line from time to time and this is apparently off now.' This transcript was then attached to a memo to ASIO HQ headed 'Intelligence Vetting of PMG Technicians', stating that I was the Colin Cooper referred to, and I was already known to the PMG Staff and Industrial Officer. The problem was that the PMG had two Colin Coopers; only one worked in the Eastern Suburbs telephone exchange, and it wasn't me. I am not sure if this ASIO confusion led to my namesake being misrepresented in other ASIO reports, but it does indicate a potential problem when their opinions seem to be the sole reason for labelling a person an 'employment risk'.

In its last few pages, the file lists the postal technicians who were members of the Association for International Co-operation and Disarmament in April 1971, and a confidential document listing presenters at a trade union training course on Postal Rationalisation in May 1972. A final document, dated May 1974, from the PMG Chief Security officer to the ASIO Director-General then provided an assessment of three officials of the New South Wales branch of the PTTA, including myself. The report is based on a senior PMG industrial relations manager's views of the individuals and hearsay regarding political affiliations.

TAP TAP, WHO'S THERE? AND WHO DID IT?

ASIO's tapping of telephones was well known to many PMG technicians, and it was generally achieved by connecting a line to a special junction cable that eventually provided a link to ASIO headquarters at Kirribilli. As I worked in the trunk exchanges, I did not become involved in this process, but I was aware of the 'Special Observation Room' on the fourth floor of the GPO that apparently provided a link between the PMG and ASIO. I understand that this interface was then moved to the Dalley Street local exchange, but after some problems with the staff and press publicity regarding ASIO line taps, it was moved to the North Sydney exchange.

If the technicians' rumour mill is to be believed, this 'running of the double jumpers' was undertaken by special security-cleared technicians who usually did the work after hours. Apparently their identities were generally known to many of the technicians, but it was accepted as part of their job. The requirement for a warrant to be issued under the *Telecommunications (Interception and Access) Act* before a telephone tap could be considered legal was an issue that the union highlighted at various times. The New South Wales police ignored the warrant requirements and undertook illegal phone taps over a sixteen-year period from 1967.

MY PARENTS

As my father's political activities were a major reason why ASIO justified my being seen as a 'security risk', I believe a few short comments on his ASIO file and his political history are warranted. I obtained a copy of my father's file as I hope to write the story of my parents' political activities.

My father arrived in Australia in 1927 aged sixteen, from a middle-class English family, as part of the 'Dreadnought Scheme', which sought to 'bring young men from British cities to be trained as rural workers on New South Wales farms'. It was through this experience that his political education began, as he found himself on a farm at Tottenham, New South Wales, where his wages were placed in a bank book held by the grazier. Like many other 'Dreadnought boys' they left their wages behind when they had had enough of exploitation and decided to leave for the city. Their method of terminating employment was to abscond during the night to avoid detection, taking very few possessions.

His contact with the CPA occurred while he was doing relief work digging stormwater drains in Bankstown during the Depression. According to his 1945 Army discharge papers, at the time of enlistment, in January 1942, he worked as a clerk at Arthur Yates. After the war he resumed his work at Yates, researching and writing for the *Yates Garden Guide*. It was a relatively well paid position that even involved the provision of a motor vehicle. His involvement in the Federated Clerks Union (FCU) as an elected central councillor was detected by ASIO, who dutifully notified his employer of his political activities. After this, my father was given the choice of resigning from Arthur Yates or the CPA. During this period, the left-wing leadership of the FCU was under attack by the right wing 'industrial groups' who eventually gained control of the union and I believe that ASIO was instrumental in aiding their success.

With the encouragement of the CPA, my father became a fitter's mate at the New South Wales railway workshops at Chullora, and eventually Secretary of the Combined Unions' Shop Committee. His railway job was a low-paid position and his main political activity was in local union actions and involvement in the Australian Railways Union (ARU). His ASIO file lists the campaigns and activities he undertook to raise the wages of railway workers and his support for the peace movement.

My mother bore the brunt of the political sacrifices made by her husband as she attempted to raise five children on the extremely low railway wage. To help the family budget, she took on full-time work in a Surry Hills shirt factory, and what we now call 'work-life balance' became a demanding and arduous task, without much 'balance'. Her main political involvement centred on the Bankstown Union of Australian Women (UAW), and in campaigns against rising prices and support for the anti-war campaigns.

THE EUREKA YOUTH LEAGUE

Although my membership of the EYL is used as a reason for my being considered a 'security risk', there is little mention in ASIO's files of the League's activities and its campaigns on issues that impacted the youth of the day. ASIO's knowledge of my twenty-first birthday party indicates they did have informants within the EYL, and if this is the case, it does disappoint me that there is no reference to the EYL's basketball and volleyball achievements. We were pretty good and very active in promoting 'men's rules' basketball among women in the 1950s. At the time, many considered that women should be restricted to netball, and women wearing anything other than below-the-knee skirts to play a team sport was deemed to be extremely radical.

The EYL also encouraged young people to become active in trade unions and it took up issues such as daylight training for apprentices, rather than them being forced to do technical college training at night, under the slogan 'The nights were made for love'. Again, these campaigns were political, and never a threat to national security. The EYL simply challenged conservative ideas and combated the influence of right-wing politics among youth.

GENERAL COMMENT ON MY FILE

There appears to be a lack of continuity of information in my file and I have concluded that much may have been removed to protect ASIO sources. It took ASIO nearly six months to respond to my application for the file, and their covering letter indicates that the organisation claims exemptions from full disclosure under various sections of the *Archives Act 1983*.

There is limited information on my union activity during the late 1960s and 1970s as State Secretary and Federal President of the PTTA, later to become the Australia Telecommunications Employees Association (ATEA) in 1976. For ASIO to become paranoid when they discovered I was a PMG telegram messenger, I find it difficult to accept that they took no interest during some of the union's major industrial disputes in the 1970s. I am not disappointed if ASIO lost interest in me, or if my membership of the ALP became a protective shroud, but I think it is highly unlikely.

My analysis of my father's file, and of my own, confirms that ASIO was an organisation serving the imperatives of conservative politics and not national security. ASIO's ability to influence people's lives without them even being aware of its actions should be a concern for all Australians. I particularly refer here to information supplied to employers, which happened in the case of both my father and myself. If you do not know what is being said about you, and to whom, how can you contest its accuracy? Of course, this assumes there is a practical and affordable process for people to challenge an ASIO report, and to my knowledge this does not exist.

Finally, I am not confident that any official history will represent supporters of the CPA in the favourable light I believe they deserve. I realise that there is every chance an objective account could start another chapter in Australia's history wars but I consider the activities of CPA members and ASIO's actions are an important part of Australia's social and cultural history.

CLIVE EVATT

Clive Raleigh Evatt was born in 1900 and educated at Fort Street Boys' High, which his brother 'Bert' also attended. Two older brothers were killed in World War I. He graduated with the King's Medal from the Royal Military College at Duntroon in 1921 but resigned from the Army and studied law at Sydney University, being admitted to the bar in 1926.

His law practice mainly involved workers' compensation, accident and criminal law, and he took silk in 1935. In 1939 he won a by-election for the seat of Hurstville for the Industrial Labor Party as part of a splinter group opposing Jack Lang. When Labor won government in 1941 under William McKell, Clive was elected to Cabinet and became Education Minister, later Housing Minister and then Chief Secretary. He continually clashed with McKell and on one occasion he successfully outlawed corporal punishment in public schools, only to have McKell overturn the decision.

Clive was ousted from Cabinet in 1954 but was successfully

re-elected to his seat in 1956. However, he was eventually expelled from the Labor Party in 1956 for voting against an increase in public transport fares. He stood as an independent but was defeated in the 1959 election.

He returned to the bar and developed an enormous practice appearing for impecunious plaintiffs in damages claims and for richer clients in defamation cases. He worked until well into his eighties and died in 1984.

Elizabeth Evatt is the daughter of Clive Raleigh Evatt and the sister of Clive Evatt Jnr and Penelope Seidler. She was the Foundation Chief Judge of the Family Court of Australia, President of the Australian Law Reform Commission, Deputy President of the Australian Conciliation and Arbitration Commission and Chair of the Royal Commission into Human Relationships.

She has chaired the UN Committee on the Elimination of Discrimination Against Women and was the first Australian elected to the UN Human Rights Committee. She is a commissioner on the International Commission of Jurists. In 2011 she was honoured by having her image on an Australian postage stamp.

CLIVE RALEIGH EVATT AND ASIO

by *Elizabeth Evatt*

THE STORY BEGINS: GETTING THE FILE

In 1990 an article in the *Good Weekend*, 'Seeing Reds' by David McKnight and Gregory Pemberton, revealed that during the 1950s, ASIO had kept files on many thousands of Australians. Of particular interest to ASIO were those who had signed a petition in 1952 against the re-armament of Japan. My father, Clive Evatt QC, was named in the article as one of this group.

Until then it had never occurred to me that my father could have been considered a threat to national security. It took more than two years, and an application to the Administrative Appeals Tribunal, to get the file of 115 pages. Even then, two pages were withheld and their contents summarised over the telephone.

The file had been opened in late 1950 at a time when the *Communist Party Dissolution Act 1950* was before the High

Court. That Act was found invalid and was rejected by the people at a referendum in September 1951. But its provisions continued to guide ASIO in its task of defending the Commonwealth against espionage, sabotage, or subversion. The Act defined as 'communist' and therefore subversive anyone who supported or advocated the policies, objectives or principles of Marx and Lenin.

WHY DID CLIVE HAVE A FILE?

Clive had been a minister in the New South Wales Labor Cabinet since 1941. In 1950 he held the portfolio of Chief Secretary, and from 1952 to 1954, that of Housing. Clive had never been a member of the Communist Party, but he was left leaning. He had been President of the Australia–Russia Friendship Society until he was forced by the Labor Party to end his connection with the Society in 1948.

In that year, Clive had complained publicly about the refusal by the Lord Mayor of Sydney, Ernie O'Dea, to allow the Town Hall to be used for meetings of the Australian Communist Party. This ban had also been applied to meetings held by the Australia–Russia Society, the Dean of Canterbury, Jessie Street, and others considered undesirable by the Sydney Council.

When Clive became Chief Secretary in 1950, he was responsible for the renewal of licences for town halls. He tried to get the Council to reverse its decision by drawing attention to the Universal Declaration of Human Rights and the right to freedom of speech and of assembly. This cut no ice with the Lord Mayor.

When Clive spoke at a United Nations Day event in

October 1950, he criticised the restrictions which had been imposed on freedom of speech and assembly, and denounced the police state which he foresaw if the anti-communist legislation came into force. His speech was reported in the *Daily Telegraph*, 24 October 1950:

> If we continue as we are going – denouncing a man because he has contrary opinion, denouncing the right of assembly and maintaining security police – we will be an example to the world not of democracy but of Fascism. We do not want people denied the right to stand up in public and express their views, however distasteful these views may be to the Commonwealth or State Governments. We want everybody to have the right to go into our public halls and say what he thinks of current problems. The right to go into certain halls is denied to people having contrary opinions to those who control the halls.

It is clear from his speech that he thought it highly likely that he was attracting the attention of the security police:

> One cannot attend a meeting today without somebody taking notes. Probably they are taking down what I am saying now, but I do not mind because I am standing up to defend human rights, the very corner stone of the UN.

Clive was right, for within a few days ASIO had opened a file on him. The first few pages are press reports about the ban on the use of the Town Hall.

WHAT IS IN THE FILE?

Most of the material in Clive's ASIO file is drawn from the media. It shows that Clive had spoken out not only against the ban on leasing town halls to alleged communists, but also about other threats to civil liberties, such as the arrest of Aboriginal activist Freddie Waters for organising a 'native strike' in February 1951.

The press reports collected by ASIO show that Clive supported a number of causes of varying popularity, such as repealing the ban on the sale of liquor to Aborigines; increasing war gratuities; and improving the living conditions of migrants. He made statements on many controversial issues. When these were reported in the media, they were also copied into the ASIO file.

Many of the issues reported faithfully in the file are quite remote from the mandate of ASIO. An example relates to Clive's attempt, when Chief Secretary of New South Wales, to overcome laws restricting Sunday entertainment. From a news-clipping in the file dated 22 November 1951 it is clear that he used an apparent loophole in the *Sunday Observance Act* to give permission to Hal Lashwood to hold a dance in Newcastle on a Sunday. The Dean of Newcastle dressed 'in mufti' to attend the dance 'to see for himself how it was conducted'. The Dean later had a summons issued against Hal Lashwood for holding a public entertainment in a public hall on a Sunday. The press reports about this event, about Clive's approval of Sunday film shows (August 1951), and about his involvement in an internal disputation in the RSPCA (September 1951) have been diligently copied into the ASIO file.

ASIO's efforts in retrieving and collating the material on

various topics with no obvious relevance to security confirm Clive's fears that Australia would become a police state. ASIO apparently took the view (no doubt reflecting that of the federal government) that anyone taking a stand against authority should be considered a security risk.

THE 'SECRET' FILES

Clive was not under direct surveillance, nor was he considered to be a member of the Communist Party. On 25 July 1952, a 'Political Note' in his file records:

> It is unlikely that either Clive Evatt or Senator Cameron are party members ... A member of the Communist Party recently stated that Senator Cameron is nearer to being a party member by the way he talks, and yet he 'hates their guts'.

Despite this, from 1952 onwards Clive's file included items marked 'secret' or 'top secret'. These 'secret' items generally relate to ASIO surveillance of other individuals or of meetings. When Clive had contact with someone under surveillance, or if his name was mentioned at a Communist Party meeting (despite the fact that he was never present), a copy of the report would be placed in his file.

One 'secret' entry reports that Clive, as the responsible minister, met with representatives of the New Theatre in September 1951 to discuss the banning of *How I Wonder* by the ABC. The file note says that Clive said 'they were all a lot of commos down at the theatre' and that he was not popular with them.

The activities of the Czech consul must have been under surveillance, as the file records that the consul had 'arranged to meet Clive' and, in May 1952, that he invited Clive to a function for the national day of Czechoslovakia. The ASIO report of the function solemnly records that Clive had talked to the guests. Nothing seemed to flow from this.

There are also three reports relating to Rex Chiplin, who wrote for *Tribune*, and who has an extensive file of his own. These reports record that Chiplin was trying to make contact with Clive Evatt. When Arthur Gietzelt, who was the subject of a 'top secret' ASIO file, made contact with Clive in April 1953, this led ASIO to make Evatt also the subject of a 'top secret' file. From 1953, most entries in Clive's file are marked 'secret'.

Another secret file has a rambling account of a meeting of the Eveleigh Carriageworks branch of the Communist Party, whose President was Ted Walsham. Those present appeared to be aware that they were being watched – as was indeed the case. Allegations were made by one of the speakers that Chiplin, Yuill and Evatt had supplied the Carriageworks branch with information on the security service. There were also allegations of 'shady deals' involving Gietzelt and Evatt. I know nothing that could possibly justify these assertions. But it seems that the accumulation of isolated incidents and unverified assertions was the way in which ASIO compiled its records.

More interesting than those rather remote contacts were Clive's ventures into international affairs. In 1951, he had been president of a large and diverse group opposing the Japanese Peace Treaty. Most of the group were not communists, but they were regarded as suspect by ASIO because Russia also opposed the peace treaty, and such opposition was contrary to the policies of the Australian Government.

Clive's alleged connection with the Council for Peace in the Pacific, which sent a delegation to Peking, and his later opposition to the re-armament of Japan in 1954, were noted in secret files (March to July 1952). When the New Theatre League was planning a protest against the re-armament of Japan in 1954, Clive is alleged to have suggested that they should pull a rickshaw down Martin Place and that he would defend them if they were arrested.

In the 1950s Greece was run by military dictators. The communist partisans who had fought the Nazis had been defeated in the civil war which followed the end of the world war. Many had been imprisoned, and some faced death sentences. Clive supported the League for Democracy in Greece (November 1951 to mid-1952) which sought amnesty for the prisoners and democratisation of the country. In addressing a meeting of the League in 1954, Clive attacked Australia's security service. He:

> ... said the Security Police in this country were here by the hundreds and they had pimps and spies who would go on to the ships and into the factories to spy and pimp and then are prepared to go to the Courts and perjure themselves and lie about you.

We know now that ASIO was doing just what Clive had alleged, observing and reporting on the meetings. The reports on these activities are all marked secret. A secret file on Jim Anastassiou, at about the same time, said that he worked for the Communist Party. He had said that 'the good Mr Evatt had saved the life of Tony from execution'. (This may be a reference to Tony Ambatielos, who had been reprieved from the death sentence.)

A few years later, in 1957, Clive was noted as being the Patron of the Executive Committee for Cyprian Self-Determination. Four secret pages in his ASIO file relate to meetings of the committee and to arrangements for an Austra-

Clive Raleigh Evatt with his wife Marjorie, son Clive and daughters Elizabeth and Penelope and Tim the dog, 1955.

lian Labor Party delegation to visit Archbishop Makarios, a leader of the independence movement.

When Clive addressed the Committee for Self-Determination, he said that some people had tried to destroy the Committee by suggesting that the committee was linked with communism: 'That is a falsehood. We have no political program.' He commented that their activities were being watched by the security service: 'We are proud of our work and they can come to all our meetings' (extract from Ken Buckley's ASIO file, quoting the *Sydney Morning Herald*, 29 October 1956).

The Cyprus campaign was supported by such anti-communists as the Greek Government, EOKA, Makarios and Grivas. But because the communists also supported Cypriot independence, the ALP delegation was considered suspect by ASIO. The Director-General thought that the Communist Party would welcome the actions of the ALP in setting up a delegation to go to Cyprus as a 'front' to conceal the communist interest. There is a kind of twisted logic here, which ignores the independent concern of the ALP about the issue. In the event, Clive did not go to Cyprus at that time. (Memo from the Director-General, 15 March 1957.)

EXCESSES OF ASIO

It is both absurd and anger-provoking that Clive was considered to be a risk to security, directly or indirectly. He certainly had a tendency to favour radical movements, and was often drawn to causes which were not popular with the government. He was considered somewhat controversial by his own party. The ALP had forced him to quit the Australia–Russia Society in 1948.

Nevertheless, most of the material in his file, even those marked 'top secret', had nothing to do with security. ASIO appears to have compiled files not only on those people who it believed to be either communists or sympathetic to communism, but also on those who it thought were sympathetic to causes which communists also supported. Much of Clive's file reveals criticism of, or dissent from, government action.

It is rather scary to realise that those who took different views from the government on issues of human rights, and on the independence and democracy of other countries or colonies, were regarded with suspicion as possibly subversive.

If Clive could have read his file, it would have confirmed his view that the government had spies everywhere, ready to denounce people whose views were unpopular with government. His concern, that our 'free country' was in real danger of becoming a police state as a result of the enactment of the anti-communist legislation, was well founded. ASIO thus aligned itself with those who were unduly alarmed by the free expression of ideas with which they disagreed.

Although ASIO cannot be compared with the Stasi in East Germany, central to its outlook was the credo of guilt by association. Even to support the human rights of communists against oppressive governments was to be labelled a sympathiser and a subversive.

No action of ASIO impinged on our family life at the time, though it is probable that Clive realised that some of the meetings he addressed were being monitored, as was in fact the case. This would not have affected him or changed his view in any way. The file, though of little relevance to security, is nevertheless a valuable resource for the family in assembling biographical material on Clive.

AN AMUSING STORY

The best story comes partly from the ASIO file and partly from a related file kept by the Prime Minister's Department.

Dad's support for Cypriot independence had put him at odds with the Commonwealth government. But it found favour with the Greek Government, which decided to confer on him the award of Commander of the Royal Order of the Phoenix in 1958.

The permission of Her Britannic Majesty was required for Clive to accept this award. The Greek Embassy in Canberra wrote the appropriate letter to the Australian Government. This should have been sent forward in the usual way with a recommendation for Her Majesty's approval. This appears to have been the preliminary view of the department. Prime Minister Menzies seems to have agreed; he endorsed the file in his own hand: 'I cannot find any good reason for saying "NO", therefore I say Yes. RGM.'

At this point the Secretary of the PM's Department, Mr EJ Bunting, was persuaded by the Assistant Secretary, WR Cumming, to intervene and to ensure the PM knew that Cypriot independence was contrary to British policy, which was supported by Australia. No doubt he told the PM that his preliminary decision was 'courageous', because it 'would seem to fly in the face of the British'.

No recommendation was made to Her Majesty, and there the matter languished. A few years later, Tom Uren intervened and persuaded Menzies to implement his earlier decision. The Royal Order of the Phoenix was duly conferred on Clive.

While this may amuse in one way, it reveals the willingness of the government to defer to the British. Cyprus had achieved its independence in 1960.

FINAL REFLECTION

In this age of fear of terrorism, restrictive security legislation and security services concentrating on the prevention and punishment of politically inspired violence, we would do well to remember that judgments about potential subversion and security risks are not always based on reliable grounds.

FRANCES LETTERS

Frances Letters was born in Armidale, New South Wales, in 1944. She was educated there at St Ursula's College and graduated with a BA from the University of New England in 1965. She worked as a journalist on the *Sydney Morning Herald* and the *Sun-Herald*, then spent a year hitchhiking around South-East Asia, including wartime South Vietnam, and another year travelling in India. She wrote and illustrated two books about these years: *The Surprising Asians*, which was a set text for NSW School Certificate English, and *People of Shiva*.

Having grown up in a conservative country town in old White Australia, Frances had never questioned the status quo until coming into contact with the effects of the Vietnam War. Despite a job offer from ASIO in 1968, with eyes newly opened she became intensely involved in three movements: the anti-war campaign, women's liberation and the anti-apartheid movement. In the end it was the third of these causes – the need to fight racism – that came to dominate her life. Of all injustices, race prejudice seemed the most intractable, and hardest for victims to escape. In 2013 she finished writing a memoir about her journey away from prejudice and racism.

During the intervening years Frances lived in Spain, and for shorter periods in England and Switzerland. From 1976 to 1980, with the aim of helping promote peace and unity, she taught Transcendental Meditation in Barcelona. She has done many other jobs: as freelance writer, editor, proof-reader, women's refuge worker, cook, cleaner, Portobello Road market stallholder and factory hand.

She has one son and now lives back in Armidale. She is involved with Australians for Native Title and Reconciliation (ANTaR), Armidale Rural Australians for Refugees, and Women in Black, a peace movement begun by Palestinian and Israeli women.

TWO CHEERS FOR ASIO!

by Frances Letters

'There is only one thing in the world worse than being talked about,' pronounced Oscar Wilde. 'And that is *not* being talked about.' Let me share a small deflating discovery with you. I've recently learned there is one thing worse than finding you've been spied on, secretly followed and photographed for years. It's being informed that, astonishingly, you have no ASIO file at all.

Granted, by nature I've always been more of a wary second-line supporter than brave front-rower – but to have registered nothing *at all*? Was I, alone among my friends, such a tame, pallid rabbit … so downright *uninteresting*?

Meredith Burgmann, an old friend with whom I'd once been arrested at an anti-apartheid demonstration, had suggested I apply for my ASIO file and write a chapter for this book. Even the slimmest folder would surely reveal a few tidbits of gossip to marvel at.

I protest! What about all my writing, arguing, cajoling about the Vietnam War, apartheid, racism and Aboriginal rights during those notoriously paranoid years? The conferences I spoke at; the meetings and lectures and demos ... all that leafleting and organising? The hours spent stuffing papers into envelopes to that background music of the revolution, the clatter of the Gestetner and the gurgle of flour-and-sugar glue boiling away on the stove, ready for the nightly paste-ups?

And what about being arrested, and spending umpteen days in court as witness to other arrests? All those anarchist and Communist Party friends and lovers? The handwritten numbers 4 and 8 over my head in declassified ASIO photos from Springboks demos, shown in the 2005 ABC TV program *Political Football*? My name appearing in friends' ASIO files? The South African Embassy's refusal to give me a visa? Anti-apartheid leader Peter McGregor's earnest little anarchist group that I later belonged to? And what about the Russian boyfriend in New Delhi, a journalist on *Pravda*? I know for a fact that the relationship was reported to the Australian Embassy there. But not even an official footnote? What, oh what, had I done *right*?

It is mystifying. Most of all because, in 1968, with the Vietnam War at its bleakest, 'a friend of a friend' brought me a job offer from ASIO. Very specific indeed – and bizarre and dangerous enough to chill the blood.

I'd spent the previous year hitch-hiking round South-East Asia, including South Vietnam, with my friend Judith Keene; afterwards I'd written a series of articles for the *Sydney Morning Herald*, my old newspaper, about the war's effect on people we'd met. Since at the time Australian passports were stamped 'Not valid for North Vietnam', my experiences had been entirely with people in the South. They'd been extraordinarily hospitable and kind. Naturally I'd come to see the war through their eyes. And like most South Vietnamese, their viewpoint – complex, fearful, and far from entirely pro-American – had nevertheless been pretty solidly anti-communist.

At twenty-three, like most of my friends, I was still unbelievably naïve about politics. At home in Armidale, an occasional word from my mother about the conservative virtues of 'country people' had been the closest we ever came to a political discussion: backbone of the nation ... droughts and flooding rains ... the sheep's back. So when an old family friend asked if he could interview me about my Vietnam experiences for ABC radio, I had no doubt that my duty lay with the status quo.

I'd known George Baker most of my life. Landed-gentry-born, ex-wartime RAF, ex-Oxford, he was a power behind the scenes in the Country Party with a boys' own glee for intrigue and a finger in every conservative pie in the land. He had encouraged me to write, and I was fond of him. I still have the reel-to-reel tape of the interview somewhere. I once tried to make myself listen to it – but it was too painful. It wasn't just the poncy accent – thousands of other nice Australian girls in the 1960s had managed to acquire one of those too. Much worse were the sentiments I poured into George's microphone.

'My friends in Vietnam will suffer terribly, perhaps die, if we Australians don't defend them from the red-in-tooth-and-claw Viet Cong!'

At some point in the interview I was puzzled to catch a glint of excitement in George's eye. A cat watching a mouse. It seemed odd; almost disturbing. It was only later that I understood. After the ABC broadcast, my emotional plea was to be a highlight of Coalition advertising for the upcoming Senate election. I was to be a wartime Whingeing Wendy for the Coalition.

But a guardian angel protected me. To George's fury,

behind the scenes someone pulled strings, and the broadcast was blocked … far too politically one-sided. George was sure my angel was his old foe Russel Ward, famous historian and commo. Later, when I'd come to know Russel quite well, I thanked him for having inadvertently saved my honour years before. How on earth had he managed it? He only smiled and uttered a slow, enigmatic 'Aaaah!'

So the broadcast came to nothing. But George was not so easily defeated. Soon afterwards I received a mysterious, commanding phone call from a friend of his with a proposition. I should wait on a corner in Martin Place. So I'd be recognised, what would I be wearing? Cute short black dress, black stock-

ASIO surveillance photo taken with a camera concealed inside a briefcase: Frances Letters (right) and Helen Randerson (left). From the file of Helen Randerson.

ings and a red beret. A big black car pulled up; I got in. All intriguingly cloak-and-dagger. The middle-aged driver and his younger companion drove me across Sydney Harbour Bridge to a sunny Kirribilli restaurant.

Nothing but chitchat and friendly questions about my travels and the book I was writing until the main course was finished. Then, pushing away his plate, the older man planted his elbows on the table, fixed me with a gaze of the utmost gravity, and got down to business.

They were from ASIO, he announced. Well now. Hmmm. Seems I'd had a good rapport with ordinary people in Vietnam, eh? Really seemed to get on with them. How would I like to put it all to good use? Would I consider going back there? To … umh … work? In a village in the Mekong Delta? How about it?

I was completely thrown off balance. Had the invitation come a couple of years earlier, I'd probably have felt compelled to leap to my feet, hand on heart, and, however terrified, pledge to take the oath then and there. George was not the only one whose fantasies leaned towards boys' own adventures. The Anzac legend; years of devotion to Biggles and Bulldog Drummond and Richard Hannay; countless books about British spies and war heroes: all had left me with earnest convictions about patriotism and duty. But by 1968 even in *my* country town political certainties were beginning to blur.

I remember the exact words of my answer – and the ASIO man's reply.

'To the Mekong Delta? To work? As a – a spy?' My voice shook. 'That's Viet Cong territory! I'd be dead within a week!'

The man leaned forward and looked me in the eye with a stern, steadfast gaze. 'For the sake of your country … would you mind?'

I coughed nervously at that. Then I frowned, drummed my fingers on the table, and took a quick gulp from my glass. What the hell did I really *think*? I did know one thing: that justice mattered. And that meant justice for those who weren't getting it ... the poor and the powerless.

A sudden thought occurred to me: a small lightbulb flash. Hey! Justice for the poor and powerless! Didn't that mean something sort of ... well ... left wingish? I took a deep breath.

'You know, I think I might say ...' I began haltingly. 'I'd probably think of myself as ...' Doubtfully I searched for a word. Then, out of the blue, one popped into my head. 'Well, as a – socialist.'

There was a long silence. My two hosts exchanged glances; the elder one flopped back in his chair, rolled his eyes, sighed heavily, and gave a rueful shrug. Bugger! A wasted day! Oh well, at least here comes dessert ...

The extraordinary thing is that the magic word that had come blundering out of my mouth to save me from the grand romantic folly of espionage in the Mekong Delta was one I knew next to nothing about. I was surprised and baffled by its potent effect on the two men.

Socialist! On hearing the word they'd instantly retreated. If they'd only known, at the time 'socialist' meant nothing more to me than some vague fair-go for all. But I've blessed the word ever since, and the fate that propelled it up from the depths of my unconscious mind just when it was needed. Without that lightbulb moment, like the good convent girl I used to be I might well have ended up – if still alive – doing my 'patriotic duty' in ways I'd now be ashamed of. I might even have been directed to 'befriend' suspected enemies of the state: perhaps some of the very people writing in this book. Who knows what pangs such betrayal might have caused now as declassified ASIO files revealed how crafty my smiles and protestations of comradeship had really been!

One small mystery. Were the ASIO men actually from ASIS, the Australian Security Intelligence Service? Until 1977 the existence of ASIS was kept completely secret, even from members of the government. Might that possibly explain my invisibility? Anyhow, I was never the same after that day. My entire life had turned on the pivot of a word.

After lobbing that small lunchtime bombshell, having labelled myself a socialist – however doubtful my conviction and wobbly my voice while saying it – it was obviously time to check out what it might mean. I started hovering round the Third World Bookshop, Bob Gould's little left-wing joint in Goulburn Street, hoping that someone might strike up a conversation. Warily I fingered the Marxist tomes there, and thumbed through copies of *The Peking Review* guaranteed to numb even the nimblest mind. But no one was interested in me. No diehard lefty reached out seductive hands to draw me into their murky world as I'd always been warned they would.

But seductive blandishments did come from other quarters. When my book *The Surprising Asians* was published, *Reader's Digest* laid out before me a future of fame and fortune: an American edition, speaking tours of the US, interviews, guest spots on all the best TV shows, and pots of money. There was only one proviso. I'd have to delete from the book the few mild criticisms I'd made of US behaviour in Vietnam. However politically naïve I still was, such a moral compromise was already out of the question. I declined.

Then, on 21 August 1968, crisis erupted in Czechoslovakia. When news of the invasion broke, the Communist Party of

Australia, so long denounced as a sinister Soviet tool, called a public meeting for 25 August in the Lower Sydney Town Hall to condemn it. I met a whole new group of friends that day – and my world opened up with a bang.

In the afternoons after work I began to join them in smoky pubs that fairly crackled with fiery politics. Wry-humoured old Aussie lefties and the new breed of ardent young ones drank and yarned and argued for hours on end about this theory and that for changing the world, about Lenin's gospel. Now, after a lifetime's loyalty to what they believed the Soviet Union had stood for, they suffered deep, life-changing grief.

Over the next few years many members of the CPA became deeply disillusioned and many left the party. In 1975 communist writer Frank Hardy published *But The Dead Are Many*, a novel about where he believed the Communist Party had got it wrong. I went to the book launch. It was held in the most unlikely place imaginable: the Sydney offices of the Communist Party of Australia. Such self-critical honesty was simply too much in a political world where backstabbing, ruthlessness and sheer hide are the rule. So it was hardly surprising that in 1991 most of Australia's communists got together and quietly and sadly voted the party out of existence.

I'm opting for an upbeat slant on my failure to hit the ASIO headlines: a wise, happy, commonsense scenario. Someone knew me, tried to recruit me, then must have been at least vaguely aware of my progress along an increasingly radical path. Yet that person saw the truth: that however defiantly I might kick against this or that government policy, I was no sinister threat, just a normal Australian with a heart in the right place, willing to invest a moderate amount of energy into making things better.

Exactly like so many who *did* star in ASIO files ... those who *did* get to experience a frisson of indignation, mirth, sorrow, and wry pride when their packages arrived in the mail. Those many good, normal Australians with hearts in the right place who *were* judged suspect – even traitorous ... those whose stories make up this book.

I don't mean to make light of ASIO's fundamental mission. Vigilance *is* vital: there *are* folk out there with bad intentions.

And I should add one heartening fact. I did meet the younger ASIO man a couple of times after that day in Kirribilli, and I remember him as open-minded and intelligent. Proof of this is a book he gave me: *Viet-Nam Witness*, by Bernard Fall. Far from being the right-wing polemic one might imagine an ASIO officer pressing on a prospective recruit in 1968, it is a thoughtful and far from dogmatic account of the war. I have it here beside me as I write; the donor's name, John McFarlane, is on the flyleaf. Google tells me he went on to become Director of Intelligence for the Australian Federal Police, and a high-profile advisor, researcher and lecturer on international security. I trust he continued to be open-minded and intelligent.

But an over-the-top zeal for surveillance can breed a strange, counter-productive blindness. I once ran into a South African on a Transcendental Meditation course in Switzerland. It turned out we'd had a previous encounter years before on Coogee Beach, where I'd been arrested trying to halt an all-white South African surf lifesaving team in mid marchpast. He and the rest of the team had been very frightened, he told me. Australian security officers had assured them we antiapartheid protesters would stop at nothing. Even murder.

Did they really believe it? Or were they simply wallowing in the thrill power gave them? We humans spring to life when the siren sounds. But this also leaves us prey to manipulation by the power-hungry. So it's crucial that those whose jobs carry particular clout – journalists, politicians, police, spooks – keep the wheels of reason cool and well-oiled.

In my case let's say that ASIO resisted any impulse to over-react, and did exactly the sensible job it was set up to do. May my well-deserved obscurity serve them as an example for the future. So here's two hearty cheers for ASIO! Hip … hip …

VERITY BURGMANN

1971 2013

Verity Burgmann is Honorary Professor in the School of Historical and Philosophical Studies at the University of Melbourne and a Fellow of the Academy of the Social Sciences in Australia.

She was born in Sydney and commenced an Arts degree at the University of Sydney in 1971. During the campaign against racially selected South African sporting tours, she became involved with the London-based anti-apartheid campaigner Peter Hain and moved to England in 1972, where she was awarded the University Medal in Political Science at the London School of Economics. She returned to Australia in 1977 and wrote her PhD on the Australian Wobblies at the Australian National University. She became a lecturer in the Political Science Department at the University of Melbourne in 1988. She subsequently became the first female professor there in 2003. She served as President of the Australasian Political Studies

Association in 2002 and as Deputy Dean of the Faculty of Arts at the University of Melbourne from 2004 to 2007. She retired in January 2013 and became the Ludwig Hirschfeld Mack Visiting Professor of Australian Studies at the Free University in Berlin in 2013.

Verity is the author of numerous publications on labour movement history and politics, protest movements, radical ideologies and environmental politics. Her twelve books include *'In Our Time': Socialism and the Rise of Labor; A People's History of Australia* (co-edited); *Power and Protest, Revolutionary Industrial Unionism; Green Bans, Red Union* (with Meredith Burgmann); *Power, Profit and Protest*; and *Climate Politics and the Climate Movement in Australia* (with Hans Baer). Her current research interests are utopianism, autonomist Marxism, and international labour movements' responses to globalisation.

She has remained an active supporter of progressive causes: some won, some lost, many drawn. Currently, she is President of the Public Education Group in Melbourne.

I WAS A TEENAGE TROTSKYIST

Verity Burgmann in conversation with Meredith Burgmann

Verity Burgmann was a member of a Trotskyist group, the International Socialists (IS) in Sydney and Canberra in the late 1970s.

MB: When did you get your file?

VB: I got the ASIO file recently. It's the Special Branch file that I got a long while ago that I have never been able to bring myself to look at. When I got my ASIO file I spent five or ten minutes leafing through it and was immediately horrified by the photographs.

MB: What, because they were all of you in a bikini?

VB: Yes [grimaces].

MB: Were you horrified by the detail of the meetings?

VB: Yes. I could see it was fairly obvious from the ASIO file that there was an agent reporting on me at the meetings held in Sydney. What I did realise, though, was that there did not seem to be any agent in Canberra.

MB: Is that the reason why you did not look at it in any more detail?

VB: I suppose I felt that it was too weird and spooky ... I was intrigued in a way to know that someone had kept a diary for me and that it could remind me about things that I had completely forgotten about. I found the ten minutes I spent on it intriguing ... reminding me about things and people I'd forgotten about, but I still felt it was all a bit yucky and it made me angry that so much precious taxpayers' money was wasted paying someone to keep a track of somebody as unimportant and as undangerous as me.

MB: Were you upset that the person might be someone you knew and liked or were you just upset that someone was spying on you?

VB: Both, and I would certainly like to find out, if I can, who it was in Sydney. I very much hope it was somebody who I have forgotten about or I didn't like very much. I would be very upset if it turned out to be someone that I felt close to.

MB: Here's a bit where the agent has a chat to Pam Townshend about you and Andrew and reports:

> ... she said they had married in England for immigration reasons. Agent comment: They both arrive together at meetings of the International Socialists and I had assumed that they were living together. Andrew is about 25 or 26 years old, fairly solid build, short black hair, gold rimmed glasses, English.

VB: He'd be horrified to know he had black hair. He always thought he was a blond.

MB: These are the ASIO reports of the IS meetings. Do you think they are an amalgam of the actual minutes of the meeting? Because they seem very detailed and some of it appears to be very ideologically correct. Are they the actual minutes with agent's comments?

VB: Yes, I'd be very surprised if any agent could report this well.

MB: And the wonderful bit about Janet Vaux being very upset about the unpunctuality of people arriving at the meetings.

VB: That's right, there's material in here that an agent wouldn't bother to report on.

MB: It reports, 'She stated that lateness was a matter of protocol.'

VB: Well, she was English.

MB: If they were taking notes that detailed …

VB: They'd be noticed!

MB: Now this is a report about a meeting in October 1978:

> The main topic for discussion was sexual discrimination against women in society, the role of women in IS and the objectives of the Rape Crisis Centres. Agent comment: There were 5 speakers on the various topics none of whom added anything new to matters previously reported about sexual discrimination against women in short the whole early part of the meeting was extremely boring and in my opinion of little intelligence value. There were no motions put to the meeting.

And so on. I'm inclined to think the informer is a woman because she was at the women's conference but she still found this discussion about women's issues very boring.

ASIO surveillance photo from Verity Burgmann's file, captioned *International Socialists' Beach Camp, NSW, 24 April 1978*. 2. BURGMANN, Verity Nancy; 3. Kerri (fnu); 4. HURST, Martin; 5. SHAW, David; 7. FREEMAN, Thomas Elliott; 8. ARMSTRONG, Michael Alan [HG 4835/2]. Number 1 is Mick Segreto, Number 3 is actually Pam Townshend and number 6 is Brad Bowden.

VB: I think it's extraordinary that she could think that reporting on a meeting on sexual discrimination in society could be potentially of any intelligence value.

MB: But later on they've got a copy of an article you wrote for *Battler* about abortion ... Here's a report about a court case where you are fined $100 and you refuse to pay the fine. It says 'that she would prefer to spend four days in Silverwater Gaol rather than pay the fine imposed'.

VB: That was because of the ridiculous nature of the reason for the fine. It was street theatre and I was playing the part of a prison warder with a paper truncheon and I hit on the head an extraordinarily nasty, large, plain-clothed detective who'd wandered into the street theatre and ground his boot into my very lightly clad foot. This caused me to have a pain reaction and I hit him on the head as hard as I could with my paper truncheon. I didn't know it was a policeman so then I got charged with assaulting police so I objected greatly to being fined $100 for that as he had been the first to cause assault.

MB: Then there's stuff about other members of IS, about Eric Petersen and later 'Martin Hirst is now employed in a Cahills Café in Sydney. Doug and Clare have recently had a baby daughter.' It's really very chatty.

VB: Well that's Doug and Clare McCarty who moved to Adelaide and became quite well known in Adelaide left circles.

MB: Now this is very interesting, this is the agent's comments yet again: 'Andrew is from South Africa, Zambia I think, and he has an extremely dark complexion.' Does that mean he was an African? And then ... 'Rodney is a taxi driver in Adelaide. I consider him to be one of the better types in the IS.' Can you remember Rodney?

VB: No. Nor that Southern African Andrew.

MB: How did you feel about stuff being written about you and your friends that you can't remember because it's so long ago?

VB: Well, I suppose it's a mixture of interest and astonishment. As I said, it's like someone kept a diary for me. But I'm also taken aback. It's so inconsequential I've forgotten it, so how could it possibly have been of any import?

MB: Your file is very interesting because it's much more about what was said and agreed to, whereas mine is very much them just following me around. There was a little bit of meeting stuff in my file about the Southern Africa Liberation Centre where they obviously had an informer.

VB: Those meetings were so long and boring, and that agent would have been on the payroll wasting precious money.

MB: Next meeting report is 1978 'International Socialists Women's Caucus' in Melbourne, which is the caucus the informant attended and makes me think it was a woman.

> This discussion concluded by being very fruitful in that without restrictions of a formal meeting it gave us the opportunity to discuss [she uses the term 'us', so she's identifying with the other IS people there which is interesting] those matters which had perhaps not been brought out earlier in the day. There is a very strong feeling amongst the IS women that we must assert ourselves far more than we have in the past and there was no doubt in my mind with people such as Janey Stone and Clare McCarty now in strong executive positions within the movement that this will most definitely occur.

Then the case officer comments on the informant's report,

> ... based on a review of intelligence from this source and other agents' sources over the last 18 months the following study of the personalities involved, comments made by the agent in this report would appear to be based on sound logic. The IS movement although termed a Trotskyist group does

> not fit squarely into this category and it is anticipated that
> the bias of activity within the next 12 to 18 months will most
> definitely be placed in the areas where involvement with
> workers will be a priority.

There's a bit of sophistication there that I didn't notice in mine. Maybe they used more interesting people to be the case officers.

VB: Yes, they're certainly right that Janey and Clare were the most forceful women in the organisation at that time.

MB: It says here (and I think this is still the case officer):

> The IS, probably more than any other radical Left Wing
> groups, have perceived the need to relate to the broad mass
> of the people by working at their level and not merely by
> shouting anti government slogans at demonstrations and
> public meetings.

So they actually approved of you!

VB: It's because we went on endlessly about the importance of talking to rank and file workers and being involved in our own workplaces.

MB: Which is still true.

VB: Absolutely correct. I still agree with all the analysis. It was all the methods of applying it which were so batty.

MB: And the methods of applying it were endless meetings?

VB: Endless meetings but also not getting ourselves into the perspective of realising that a bunch of 150 people spread across the country was not ever in any position to lead *anything*. That whole notion of leadership was absolutely loopy. When significant social changes occur, forms of organisation occur spontaneously out of the struggle itself and a bunch of people who have sat round in rooms discussing theory for decades are not going to be the people who will lead. They might be of some use in a subsidiary supporting role but they are not going to be the leadership of anything that's really important.

MB: This is interesting:

> March 1978 ... Agent's comment: Verity's father is a high ranking official with the CSIRO and she feels intimidated because of this. I believe that she wants to return to Canberra.

VB: Well, we'd just moved to Sydney and I would have been quite happy to go back to Canberra but not because I was intimidated by my father ... that is absurd.

MB: It says you were intimidated by the fact that he was high up in CSIRO. There was one occasion when Mum told me not to get arrested in the next few weeks because it was when he was going on the executive which I think was a Cabinet appointment.

VB: Well, Dad was about to retire at this point and he was Chair of CSIRO, and I felt no problems at all about his position at that stage.

MB: You will be pleased to know:

> Burgmann was reported as a sympathiser and member of Socialist Workers Party (British version of IS) ... girlfriend of Andrew John Milner SWP identity.

The sexism here is interesting. They also sent information

about Andrew over from England headed 'Scorpion', the same as in my file. So 'Scorpion' might be the code when they send information from Britain to the Melbourne office.

Here is another report:

> Verity Burgmann has been too busy recently to attend [Women's] Charter Meetings and similarly Janet Vaux has been heavily committed with her Battler responsibilities. As a result Bev Tierney suggested that she assist Burgmann and that the two women do what Vaux and Stone had previously, take the meetings in turn.

So you used to chair meetings of the Women's Charter?

VB: Yes, and I had completely forgotten about the existence of Bev Tierney but as soon as you said the name I can remember now what she looked like.

MB: The same for me. My file had reports of people talking to me and you remember them completely as soon as their name comes up.

On lists you are referred to as 'an ACT identity' so at least you were an identity. Here's another report:

> Rick Kuhn, Dave Shaw, Verity Burgmann and Andy Milner have all applied for full time membership with MAUM (Movement against Uranium Mining). They will be required to undertake office work and will be able to obtain all information on MAUM activities.

That makes you sound like undercover operatives in MAUM doesn't it?

VB: That's a very odd comment. The informer was probably thinking that ASIO might be able to get information about MAUM through us reporting back to IS meetings about MAUM activities. Perhaps that's the point of the comment. But Dave was an activist in MAUM before he joined up with IS.

MB: Yes, I would have thought they were co-existent.

VB: And Dave was always encouraging IS people to get involved more with MAUM.

MB: Then in reference to the expulsion of IS member Martin Hirst from Sydney University the agent comments:

> There is very little that can now be done to help these people and Hirst in particular was very dejected about the whole affair. It would not surprise me if due to his disillusionment with the IS, Hirst drops out of the scene within the next few months.

VB: Does the agent say what it was about?

MB: It's about him being expelled from the university and there's a bit later on where they talk about IS not doing anything to help him and Rick Kuhn saying more should have been done to help him.

VB: Again, I'd forgotten about Martin being kicked out of university but he ended up as an academic teaching journalism at Charles Sturt University so they must have let him back in to finish his degree at some point.

MB: Here's a piece about the expulsion of Mundey, Owens and Pringle from the Builders Labourers':

> Shaw was most adamant on the question of a fighting fund for the BLF: 'It is the International Socialists' duty to the worker

to give him all knowledge concerning worker control and assistance through the media.' Verity Burgmann and Andy Milner were nominated as co-ordinators to assist Dave Shaw in the fundraising question for rank and file builders labourers.

That was when they were trying to get their union tickets back.

VB: Yes.

MB: The informant comments on the split in the IS in America:

> The split is attributable to a difference in ideology between British and American viewpoints. There is at the present time a great deal of friction.

So she's obviously in there enough to know about the splits and things.

VB: The British IS or SWP as it had become known by then was called the 'Pomintern' and there were different degrees of objection to the right of the 'Pomintern' to tell us what to do. And what happened in the US was exactly the same, the local US IS people felt that the 'Pomintern' had no right to tell them what they should do, and so the split developed. One lot stayed loyal to the Pomintern and the other didn't.

MB: Now this part is very interesting, I think it's the sexism of the time because they talk more about what Andrew's motivations are than about yours:

> It was quite noticeable at this meeting that Andy Milner is striving for more officialdom. He was steadily cultivating Janey Stone by agreeing with most of her comments and it is quite obvious that he is pro the British IS line.

VB: Oh what a surprise.

MB: 'He is very well accepted by most members of the group and I have no doubt that he will progress due to this fact.'

VB: [laughs uproariously] We must read that to him.

MB: [reads]

> Verity Burgmann is presently residing with Andy Milner at 91 Strickland Crescent, Deakin. This address is Burgmann's mother's house and the IS are currently using it as their Canberra Headquarters.

VB: That is a load of rubbish. We were there for about one week to water the plants when Mum and Dad were away.

MB: Did IS people visit there?

VB: It is possible that David Lockwood might have dropped in because he lived in the vicinity but I very much doubt that we would have used it for a meeting.

MB: So poor old Mum and Dad had their house noted as the headquarters of IS.

VB: What if Dad was still Chairman then …

[On reflection, Verity remembered that they had given a large dinner there to farewell a comrade, Andrew Benjamin, who was leaving to do his doctorate in Paris.]

MB: Here's more judgmental agent gossip: 'Ric Petersen once again displayed his ever increasing hypochondria symptoms. This weekend it was headaches and stomach cramps.'

VB: So it's obviously someone who didn't like Ric.

MB: And it's not Phil Lee because they also report on him.

VB: Phil wouldn't have been the agent.

MB: Here's more: 'A fact not commonly known to IS is that Verity Burgmann and Andrew Milner are married and have been for the past three years.'

VB: It wouldn't have been three years because we got married in January 1977 when Australia House in London wouldn't give him a visa to come to Australia with me.

MB: Now this is a check up on your birth to check that Victoria Nancy Burgmann is in fact Verity Nancy Burgmann.

VB: Mmmm.

MB: 'From the forgoing there is no doubt that Verity Nancy Burgmann is identical with Victoria Nancy Burgmann and that the correct name is Verity Nancy Burgmann …' Mind you, they spell you wrong most of the time, including Borgmann.

VB: And at the age of six months in order to conceal my real identity from the forces of the state I decided to change my name.

MB: Here it is, 'to Scorpion Melbourne', which is obviously from MI6.

VB: But MI6 wouldn't know anything about me.

MB: I'm pretty sure it is because Scorpion Melbourne is the address my MI6 stuff went to and from.

VB: Andrew might have attracted an MI6 file but I wouldn't have … Wait a minute, unless it was because of my connection with Peter. [Verity's boyfriend in the early seventies was Peter Hain, the leader of the 'Stop the Tours' campaign in Britain and later a senior Blair government minister.]

MB: It is that connection because there's a newspaper clipping here about you and Peter.

VB: That is extraordinary. It never occurred to me that MI6 would have been watching me, but now that I think of it the fact that I was involved with Peter Hain and had my picture on the front page of the *Guardian* and *The Times* ... and the *Daily Telegraph* with him means that that is a possibility. Also I remember now the South African journalist who was the BOSS [South African Secret Police] agent talking to me a lot. We didn't know he was the BOSS agent at the time. Peter found that out subsequently. He chatted to me and kept on bothering me during Peter's conspiracy trial and trying to ask me about myself and so on and I remember feeling on my guard, and the Hains also felt that I should be on my guard. I think they had a sixth sense about the man, although he did end up actually helping out in Peter's conspiracy trial but that's all in Peter's autobiography. The prosecution felt that he would help them, they put him on the witness stand and he ended up helping Peter's defence. It transpired later that the reason for that was that he didn't want to blow his cover because BOSS wanted him to frame up Jeremy Thorpe and to remain a sleeper.

MB: Wheels within wheels.

MB: So it's quite clear that at this stage, when you arrived in Australia in 1977, ASIO had information on both you and Andrew. This is about Andrew again:

> In Canberra he has been associated with Verity Nancy Burgmann, previously recorded as an activist in Anti-Apartheid campaigns. Burgmann was resident in the United Kingdom during 1972.

Then ASIO would have contacted London and London would have sent information over. Hence the Scorpion reference.

Here's another quote:

> Unprocessed intelligence from New South Wales indicates that a leading member of the British Socialist Workers' Party Andy Milner is living in the ACT. The SWP is the British group affiliated to the International Socialists. Milner who has not yet been identified is a leading member of the SWP and is living in the same house as Verity Nancy Burgmann. He may have been a contributing factor in the recent IS expansion in Canberra.

What, from two to three?

VB: No, it expanded from four to six when we arrived.

MB: 'Milner arrived in Australia in February 1977. Could you please make arrangements to obtain a copy of his IPC.'

VB: Well, it's an exaggeration to describe him as a leading member of the Socialist Workers' Party. He was certainly a leading member in the London School of Economics branch of the Socialist Workers' Party and to some extent in Central London district, but certainly not a leading member nationally.

MB: This is a description of the Young Socialist Recruitment Rally in June 1977. It talks about Coranderrk Street as 'the residence of Verity Nancy Burgmann, sister of Meredith Burgmann' and her possible involvement with Young Socialists. Can you remember the Young Socialists? Because in my file it says that I applied for membership of the Young Socialists and I don't even know who they were.

VB: I was a member in Britain of the Labour Party Young Socialists but not of any organisation in Australia called Young Socialists.

MB: Well, I had that puzzling reference too. Here's your article in *The Battler* on abortion. Isn't it nice to have it and it's a really good article. It's completely correct and you've quoted Susan Ryan. But it's interesting that they seem to be interested in the abortion issue, I suppose because abortion was illegal, even though it was after the Levine and Menhennit rulings, it was still in the *Crimes Act*. And they were very interested in homosexuals and they do keep mentioning that Martin Hirst was homosexual.

VB: One thing I did notice when I went through the file briefly was the funny bit about following us back to Coranderrk Street to try and work out who lived there … which I found comforting. Because it reassured me that none of the people who lived in the house – who I was very close to – and none of the people in the Canberra branch in fact, were informants, because that house was the headquarters of Canberra IS, not Mum and Dad's house.

MB: Here's a page about you being arrested at the Sydney Cricket Ground in 1971. It's just a page with a list of those charged: 'Jim and Sekai Holland and Ralph Pearce.' They'd certainly made all that connection.

So finally let's talk about the photos. They are really interesting.

VB: They were taken at an IS Summer Camp held just outside Kempsey in January or February 1978.

MB: And who are the people in the photos?

VB: Dave Shaw and Graeme Grassie, both of whom died shortly afterwards. As you know, Dave – I still miss him – was killed on 20th December 1978, working as a rigger and scaffolder on the Northpoint shopping centre in Hornsby. He would have had a file for sure. Graeme died in a car accident in Turkey. He probably had a file too as he was the partner of Carole Ferrier and a leading figure in Brisbane IS. The other person in the picture is Mick Armstrong. I still see him around in Melbourne at meetings and demos.

MB: And that gives you a sense of horror … that someone was hiding in the bushes?

VB: Absolutely. They must have been sitting on the beach. It must have been somebody at the camp. And we wouldn't even have thought anything about a comrade taking photos of us.

MB: So does that give you any clue who it was? I still think it's a woman.

VB: No. I did actually look in my own photo albums to see if I had any photos that might have been taken in the other direction but I couldn't find any clues … I'll probably never know.

PETER MURPHY

1975   **2013**

Peter Murphy grew up in Brisbane's western suburb of Moorooka in the 1950s and '60s, part of a large Catholic family. He attended the local public school and convent school, then Christian Brothers College Gregory Terrace. He entered the Divine Word Seminary at Marburg, near Ipswich, to train to be a missionary priest. This took him to Sydney, where he also studied at Macquarie University.

After four years, Peter left the Divine Word, and in 1975 joined the Communist Party and became a student activist. He graduated with honours in anthropology and sociology and then worked for one year as an Australian Union of Students organiser. In 1978 he participated in the first Sydney Gay Mardi Gras, when he was severely battered by the Darlinghurst Police.

He moved to Adelaide, and in late 1981 obtained work as a marine steward, taking time out to stand for the CPA in the 1982

South Australian elections. In 1986 he started fulltime work for the CPA in Sydney, as an organiser or reporting for *Tribune*, until the CPA stopped operating in 1991. In 1989 he took part in the large anti-US base 'Peace Brigade' to the Philippines, and since then has volunteered in the solidarity organisation Philippines Australia Union Link.

He worked for the Rail Tram and Bus Union from 1993 through to 2007, and in 1995 he became the co-ordinator of the SEARCH Foundation, the only surviving component of the CPA. In 1999 SEARCH supported the foundation of the pro-democracy Zimbabwe Information Centre in Australia, and he was a special guest at the first congress of Zimbabwe's opposition party, the MDC, in January 2000. In May 2000, he was a guest at the first Fretilin conference in Dili. In 2002 and 2003 he worked in the huge Sydney campaign against the invasion of Iraq, and continues to work with the Iranian democratic movement.

THE NOT-SO-SECRET LIVES OF OTHERS

by Peter Murphy

In 1975, I was an idealistic young man, strongly influenced by my Catholic family upbringing and education. In fact, until the end of 1973, I had been training to be a missionary priest. I was encouraged by my priestly training to adopt a progressive and compassionate approach to people and issues, and had some important contact with anti-war and Aboriginal activists in the four years I was at the seminary near Ipswich, and later in Sydney. During this time I attended my first protest, the anti-Springbok tour demonstration in Brisbane in 1971, which was very dangerous; and I attended the protest in Canberra in 1972 when the Aboriginal Tent Embassy was dismantled by the McMahon Government. That was also very scary.

At the end of 1974, a year after I had stopped studying for the priesthood, I went with a group of friends, mainly students from Macquarie University, to attend a summer school in Alice Springs to learn elementary Pitjantjatjara language. I really enjoyed the classes and the experience. But I was shaken by the daily verbal abuse and threats which our Aboriginal hosts had to endure walking down the streets of Alice Springs. There I was accompanying black women and men who were my mentors in the class, and we were screamed at with foul language by people driving by in their cars. It was really raw racism which I had never witnessed before and it wasn't the police or the government, it was ordinary Australians who were behaving like this. It dawned on me that there was a deep problem in Australian society, which could not be addressed by 'normal' society because the racism was 'normal'.

On one occasion I had a very strange experience. A Department of Aboriginal Affairs officer offered me hand grenades and suggested I blow up the Kulgera Roadhouse, saying he was offended because the roadhouse only served Aboriginal people from the back door. But fortunately I had enough sense to change the subject and get away from him. Maybe he was my first contact with ASIO.

One of the people who was with me in Alice Springs was Helen Golding, a very engaging anarchist-feminist in her late twenties, studying law at the University of New South Wales. She encouraged me to go with her to the Australian Union of Students (AUS) conference in January 1975, and introduced me to a circle of friends who were in the CPA student group at Sydney University. Again, I had never attended any event like this before, with ardent debate, intrigue, and lots of fun.

Soon after, I went with some friends to a Liberal Party rally at Randwick Racecourse, where the Opposition Leader, Billy Sneddon, was trying to mobilise an anti-Whitlam movement, but was in turn upstaged by Malcolm Fraser, who was working the crowd in an effort to destabilise Sneddon and take over himself. Even Ross May, known as 'the Skull', was happily strutting around in his Nazi uniform, having no problems with the event organisers or the crowd.

Totally surprisingly there was a sudden rush into the crowd by about twenty young men and women carrying a huge National Liberation Front flag – the flag of the Viet Cong. The whole crowd gasped and then a few seconds later a wild melee broke out, with the group of leftists being attacked on all sides and the Viet Cong flag being torn to pieces by the Skull. The police then moved in and arrested all the leftists. I recognised many of them from the CPA student group.

Pondering both the Alice Springs experience, and the venomous atmosphere at Randwick, and drawing on my positive feelings about the CPA activists I had met, I decided to take a very big plunge and join the CPA. I knew that its members were pushing the issues I cared about and shared the concern that I was already feeling. I knew its members were in the trade unions as well as the student movement. I put in my application form at Dixon Street (Sydney CPA headquarters), had a testy discussion with a rather suspicious Judy Mundey, then the District Secretary, and then travelled home to West Lindfield feeling physically dizzy at what I had done.

After all, my father and my older brothers in Brisbane were militant anti-communists, and the church had always taught me that communism was evil. I had stepped off solid ground and didn't really know where this decision would lead me. But I hoped that it would help me learn how to change our society to one that did not rest on foundations of violence, abuse, intolerance and exploitation.

My ASIO file covers the years 1975–79, because I joined the Communist Party in February 1975, at the age of twenty-one. The most interesting thing is the blanket access ASIO had to documents at the CPA's Dixon Street office. The file actually begins with a photocopy of my membership application form, and this is followed by many reports on meetings of the Sydney District Committee and the Sydney District Conferences in those years.

Who was that person who supplied all those documents? From seeing much older ASIO files, it is clear that ASIO had had similar access from the 1940s, so it wasn't just one person. It had to be someone with access to the filing cabinets, who worked in the office. But many people worked in the national and Sydney offices of the CPA, so it is a mystery.

It is strange that my file has a strong focus on certain areas of my political activity, and complete silence on others.

For instance, the file shows an interest in Palestine and East Timor and about internal CPA dynamics, but no interest in the gay liberation movement, or even major political events such as the Dismissal in November 1975. The file contains lists of people seen attending Timor protests in December 1975, but no mention of attendance at much larger and wilder protests about the Whitlam Government's sacking in the very same few weeks.

I was arrested several times at political protests, in 1975, 1977 and 1978, but none of these is mentioned, even when I knew that police had pointed me out to be arrested. The protest issues were apartheid, uranium exports, and homosexual rights. My role in the Printers' Union picket line at Fairfax, or in student protest marches about university issues or Medibank, also don't rate a mention.

I was stopped by Federal Police outside the Indonesian Consulate in Bridge Street late at night on 9 December 1975, two days after the Indonesian invasion of East Timor. The consulate had been heavily painted up with protest slogans. This incident did not find its way into the ASIO file, nor did my participation in a lightning occupation of the consulate on 16 October 1976, the first anniversary of the murder of Australian journalists at Balibo.

So the file shows ASIO as erratic and not engaged with the subjects of its surveillance. It is preoccupied with some issues and not others. I suspect this is because higher level authorities, such as US and British intelligence, to some extent dictated the priorities. Consequently domestic issues were less interesting to ASIO than were international issues, particularly those of concern to the US.

The heavy use of phone taps is a strong feature in the file, confirming what we were told at the time – that your phone is tapped and you have to be careful what you say.

As I read different parts of my file, my mood changed. I was shocked by the obvious ASIO penetration of the CPA. I was angry that ASIO had investigated my father, who was a public servant in Brisbane, and an enthusiastic member of the Army Reserve. I was angry that ASIO had recommended to the Commonwealth Public Service Board that I be banned from taking up a job offer as a graduate clerk in the Department of Capital Territories in Canberra in 1977. Fortunately, I was elected as an AUS regional organiser in New South Wales, and so ignored the job offer.

I laughed when I found that ASIO had investigated who had organised a telephone connection in my name at the house I lived at in Erskineville in 1979, only to find out that it was me! There was the copy of the PMG form in the file!

I didn't know much about ASIO then, but I was aware of it, and I was taught by the CPA that ASIO was anathema to any genuine democracy, a right-wing political police force there to defend a global establishment, which should be abolished. This view only deepened as I saw ASIO in action.

One day in 1978 I had an extraordinary experience. I was confronted by an intelligence agent while I was alone in the office of the Trans National Co-operative (TNC) in the old Boilermakers Union building in Castlereagh Street. He tried to interrogate me for forty-five minutes, and I tried to be evasive. He was an Australian with an American accent, perhaps in his mid-thirties, fit and with a moustache. He did not identify himself directly as an intelligence officer but made it clear from his conversation that this was the case. He told me he was just back from Nicaragua. 'How is Judy Mundey going?' was one question. 'What is Laurie Aarons up to now?' was another. That was harrowing. I just had to wait until he decided he'd had enough fun and left. I pondered how that had happened, and presumed someone was keeping a close enough eye on me to engineer that kind of meeting. It was after the Hilton Bombing in February that year and just before the Fraser Government passed a new *ASIO Act*.

Once that year, while at the TNC, I telephoned the CPA office in Dixon Street, only to have the call answered by a police officer saying 'police intelligence unit'. He quickly hung up when he realised what he had done.

I was involved in some aspects of the clandestine radio link between Darwin and East Timor in 1976–79, and I had to be secretive about this. I found it hard to follow the telephone and meeting procedures I was instructed to use at the time, but realise now how important they were. I was surprised that my file had no record of this activity, whereas the overall secret operation was recorded in detail in ASIO files described

ASIO surveillance photo from Peter Murphy's file, captioned *May Day March, NSW, 6 May 1979 – 1. Peter MURPHY 2. Unidentified 3. Aileen BEAVER 4. Robert DURBRIDGE* [HG/5175/41].

by Mark Aarons in his book *The Family File*. I think the reason is that I was careful enough on the telephone and that the main ASIO informant simply protected me. He was a lover at that time. When I eventually found out that he was an informant, it was a wrenching realisation.

There is another odd point in the file. Whereas the names of all the ASIO contacts are deleted, the name of an Arabic language speaker used to interpret phone taps on the Iraqi

Consulate, Mr G Khouzam, was not blacked out. The name means nothing to me but it could to others.

The file seems to be devoid of any real knowledge of me, so it isn't accurate at all about important things. But it contains many documents I recognise as genuine.

There was one glaring mistake when they clearly mixed me up with another Peter Murphy, who lived in Melbourne and was also a student activist in another left party, and was recorded as being elected to the AUS executive. This mistake shows how mechanical the system was that was used to create my file.

Some of the phone tap transcripts gave me a laugh. There are the ones where I get criticised as unreliable by other people, like the Iraqis, or a Timorese activist called Chris Santos, now deceased. There's another where I get a mention, but most of that transcript consists of two comrades talking about how an anti-uranium protest is being organised and many people get a mention for how helpful or unhelpful they are.

There is one transcript where a national CPA leader, Mavis Robertson, was really hot under the collar that we had held a meeting of CPA students in Melbourne and she clearly wasn't in control of it. 'Who is this person, who is that person,' she was asking; 'make sure they only make decisions by consensus,' she instructed.

The file also contained a set of documents outlining the strong efforts by the CPA office in Sydney to stop me being elected as an AUS organiser in New South Wales in 1977. That didn't work! I'd forgotten about these unpleasant things, and looking at them now I have to laugh. Some of the CPA's history and dynamics, of which I was largely unaware, did impinge on me, and here was ASIO recording it. You can never tell how this sort of information will be used.

Today there are some voices on the left who argue that, with the end of the Cold War, ASIO is different, it is not focused on the left, and that it has an important role in protecting society against terrorism. But ASIO has acquired more powers and a hugely expanded budget to enable it to put more people under surveillance. The brutality of its absolute power is apparent in the non-reviewable adverse findings against asylum seekers, and it continues to be a sub-branch of British and American intelligence, delivering political and commercial information for the Western world's corporate elite.

TONY REEVES

1975   2013

Tony Reeves was a long-time Sydney and Brisbane journalist who, in the early 1970s, began investigating and exposing organised crime and police, political and judicial corruption – a passion which he continued to the end.

Tony's family migrated to Australia from the UK in 1954 and a year later he took a job as copy boy at the Sydney *Daily Mirror*, where he stayed for nine years. He did a stint in public relations before settling into journalism in 1969, working at the ABC, the *Sunday Australian* and as Sydney correspondent for interstate media outlets.

In 1972 he spent months probing the activities of the US mafia in Australia. His subsequent story contributed to the establishment of the Moffitt Royal Commission in the early 1970s. He became a feature writer for the *Sunday Telegraph* and in 1975 he and colleague

Barry Ward started a three-year probe into the murder of Sydney heiress Juanita Nielsen. He lectured briefly at the NSW Institute of Technology and became editor of the inner-suburban weekly paper *The Guardian*. He edited other publications in Sydney and Melbourne before moving to Brisbane in 1992.

He was an active member of the left of the Labor Party from 1971. In 1977 he was elected to the City of Sydney Council and became a vocal opponent of inappropriate development, chairing the council's Planning and Development Committee. In the late 1980s he was expelled from the ALP on factional grounds. He rejoined the ALP in 1987 but resigned in 2011.

Tony's book *Mr Big: Lennie McPherson and his life of crime* was joint winner of the 2005 Ned Kelly Award for true-crime writing. His latest books are *Mr Sin: The Abe Saffron Dossier* and *The Real George Freeman*. Recently he was working on the 1973 Whiskey Au Go Go firebombing, and on a biographical work detailing the fight against corruption by former New South Wales Attorney-General Frank Walker. Tony died while on holiday in Indonesia in late 2013.

MY LACKLUSTRE LIFE ACCORDING TO ASIO

by Tony Reeves

When I met Detective Frederick Francis Longbottom socially in the mid-1970s and asked if I could get a look at any dossier on me compiled by the notorious NSW Police Special Branch, of which he was commander, he smiled and said: 'All those files have been destroyed, Tony. You should know that. If we had a file on you, it's gone up in smoke with the rest of them.' He then added: 'That is, except the ones we sent down to ASIO.'

It took me more than a quarter of a century to establish that I had indeed qualified for a Special Branch file, and that it had indeed been destroyed, as Fred had assured me; it had not gone 'down to ASIO'.

I was reminded during 2011 by a friend and fellow journalist from the '70s that Australians could now access their ASIO dossiers. Having done the form-filling and waited patiently, I finally acquired a copy of my ASIO file in September 2012. It was, for me, a disappointingly slender volume.

Apart from the National Archives explanatory pages, my entire history according to ASIO came down to a mere nine pages, one of which was a photograph of me taken as I left the Communist Party office in Day Street, near Sydney's Chinatown, in 1971. That left eight pages with words.

In a chapter such as this, focused mainly on the *contents* of the ASIO file, it is difficult to overlook the major omissions from the document. There were a few.

On 13 April 1971, I was sacked as a reporter from the ABC News, having written stories which, the remarkably-titled Controller of News had told me, were 'embarrassing for the government and damaging for the [Immigration] Department.' My axing for being a good reporter was raised in the Federal Parliament by Senator Lionel Murphy, who condemned my dismissal and accused the ABC of political cowardice and fear of upsetting the conservative federal government. Murphy's speech was given extensive coverage in a story in that weekend's edition of the *Sunday Review*. These events did not trigger an entry in my ASIO file. Indeed, it appears that my file did not exist at the time.

However, ASIO did show an interest in me ten days after my ABC crisis, but it was triggered by another unrelated event, a phone call I made to a journalistic acquaintance.

An ASIO agent in Sydney, identified only as EW 372, wrote his report at 3.15 p.m. on 23 April 1971, shortly after listening in to my phone call. With some code-type references deleted, the report started:

> On Friday 23.4.71 Tony REEVES contacted Malcolm (Malcolm Frederick) SALMON at the Communist Party of Australia premises and after exchanging greetings Salmon remarked that Reeves had been in the news – Reeves commented that it was a 'good stir'.

The report said that I went on to tell Salmon, who wrote for the Communist Party weekly paper, *Tribune*, that I was doing some casual work at the *Sunday Australian* and had been caught up in a battle with my union (the AJA) over the ABC sacking. The report goes on:

> Reeves then told Salmon 'we' were working on a story 'here' … He [Reeves] said the ABC were trying to send John Penlington to Peking and McMahon (Rt. Hon. William McMahon, PM, MP,) stood up in the House the other day and spoke about it – Edward (Edward Fowler) Hill and what-have-you.

ASIO surveillance photo from Tony Reeves' file, captioned *CPA Headquarters, Sydney, 14 July 1971, Anthony Reeves [HG2058/931/6]*.

Ted Hill was a Melbourne-based barrister and pro-China communist who, I had learned, had quietly given some advice to the ABC on how to best deal with the Chinese on the issue of the proposed Beijing news bureau. My file continues:

> Reeves said 'we' had done some checking 'rather carefully', and have reached a deduction that 'we' will probably be prepared to say on Sunday that the only way McMahon got the information was through one of two sources – (a) (Talbot) Duckmanton (General Manager, ABC) told him, which 'we' feel is quite improbable at this stage or (b) the office of Edward Hill is bugged and/or his telephone is tapped.
>
> Reeves commented that for 'us' to reach the stage where 'we' could say this is rather an interesting development ... Salmon agreed. Reeves said quite a lot of work had been done on the story and he had received considerable help from guys within the ABC – 'there's a number there that are interested in the story being used, sympathetic for my cause, combination of a lot of things ...'
>
> Reeves then obtained some information on Ted Hill from Salmon, purely for 'our' own background; as Reeves explained 'they' had been unable to contact Hill.
>
> Reeves then invited Salmon to a party 'we' are holding on Saturday at 164 Liverpool Street, East Sydney. He added that Mr (David) Halpin (Press Secretary to Senator L.K. Murphy) would be there. Salmon accepted the invitation, saying he would bring a friend.

This then was my first entry into the filing system of our security organisation. Four hundred-odd words, seven lengthy paragraphs, about a story that maybe I (or the more suspicious-sounding 'we') *may* get to write. I cannot recall ever writing the story. Interestingly, in 1972, Penlington was sent to Hong Kong, not Beijing, to set up an ABC office.

It took eleven days for the Sydney agent codenamed EW 372 to file his report on my phone chat with Salmon on the CPA's bugged phone line. The agent dated his report 4 May 1971 and, for reasons we will never learn, headed it 'Communist Party of Australia Interest [obliterated word/s] In Visitors from China' and gave it a 'B.2' evaluation. What we had discussed was actually the possibility of somebody *going to* China.

The report seems to have caused a minor problem at ASIO headquarters: they didn't know who this Tony Reeves was. On 2 July, an internal ASIO minute sent to Sydney (not provided to me, but referred to in another document) requested identification of the Tony Reeves mentioned in EW 372's missive. The Sydney office got busy and sent back an extensive 500-word report in less than three weeks. Possibly in their haste, or in a more recent oversight by ASIO, the names of two of their informants were revealed to me.

Dated 20 July, and headed with the correct spelling of my name: Antony (without the 'h') Reeves, it opened with:

> Please refer to P.S.O. 'F' minute dated the 2nd July 1971 headed Tony REEVES, which requested identification of a Tony REEVES referred to in New South Wales Intercept Report No. New South Wales/W.851/18 EW.372 dated 4th May 1971 ...
>
> On the 12th July, 1971, our ABC *official contact* [my emphasis] Mr P.A. Dorrian, orally advised details of a former ABC employee named Antony Reeves who had been the

subject of some considerable publicity in about April 1971, and who had resigned.

I have been unable to trace any PA Dorrian and former ABC colleagues could not recall any person by that name in the news department or elsewhere in the organisation. That may explain why Mr Dorrian got the details of my departure from the broadcaster wrong: I was *sacked* by the ABC, I did not *resign*.

'Mr Dorrian commented that this person would have been sacked if he had not resigned and that he had a knack of causing trouble in the ABC and would not be re-employed,' it continued.

The report then tabulated background information provided by Dorrian: the place and date of my birth, present and previous addresses, and my previous employment history (as apparently provided by me to the ABC), which started with my first job at the Sydney *Daily Mirror* newspaper in 1955 as a fifteen-year-old copy boy.

One source used in the report was not identified:

> [Obliterated], Sydney, Mr. [obliterated] who is also [obliterated], on 15th July 1971, orally advised that Reeves had been employed from 29th August 1966 – 30th August, 1968 with TAA, and that TAA would not re-employ him. He provided a number of problems for TAA and was inclined to 'hit the grog'.

Another informant was named:

> The staff manager for the Sydney office of BP Australia Ltd, Mr Noel Harris [Poss TS 32116] (who is also Key Point Security Liaison Officer), orally advised on 13th July 1971 that Antony Reeves, born 6th May 1940, and educated at

Queen Elizabeth Grammar School at Carmarthenshire, United Kingdom, had been employed by the company from 16th July 1964 to 26th August, 1966, when he had resigned of his own accord ...

Mr Harris commented that Reeves' services would have been dispensed with if he had not resigned, i.e.: he would have been sacked. Mr Harris stated that Reeves joined the company as a probationary assistant in the public relations section. It was subsequently ascertained that he did not have his Leaving Certificate (as stated), but only the Intermediate Certificate. Mr Harris was aware that Reeves had subsequently received some considerable publicity in the Press as a result of his services with the ABC, and suggested that inquiries with TAA should be made by this office. Mr Harris was formerly employed by the Sydney office of the Broken Hill Company Pty Ltd.

This one-sided history naturally failed to mention the major issues I had with these employers. BP decided to move me from weekly to fortnightly pay, in arrears, and I simply could not afford the three-week break in income that meant. The firm's absolute refusal to listen led to some angry scenes. At TAA (Trans Australia Airlines) during strikes by baggage handlers, office staff donned overalls and went to the airport to load and unload passenger baggage. I considered this basically to be 'scabbing' against the striking unionists, and resisted. During one stoppage I flatly refused. I took my case to the airline chairman, Sir Frederick Scherger, who endorsed my actions. It marked the end of an otherwise successful period promoting the publicly owned carrier. But none of that, of course, made it to my ASIO file.

The lengthy report was sent from Sydney to ASIO headquarters in Melbourne on 5 August 1971, with the notation: 'Forwarded for completion of unidentified trace procedure.'

I was unknowingly able to provide a little more action for the Sydney agents as the job of checking on who I actually was kept them busy.

On the day that informant Noel Harris was telling them about my sad career path at BP Australia, I made another phone call to Malcolm Salmon at the CPA headquarters. The call was bugged by ASIO, as no doubt was all phone contact with the CPA in those days. The intercept report read:

> 1. On Tuesday 13.7.71 Tony REEVES who said he was a friend of Malcolm (Malcolm Frederick) SALMON contacted Alec ROBERTSON at the Communist Party of Australia premises. Reeves was informed that Salmon was ill.
>
> 2. Reeves said he understood that Salmon had a good dossier on members of the Nazi Party in Australia and Robertson said 'we' did have some material on them. Reeves said he had a photo of a Nazi who was at the demonstration at the Cricket Ground on Saturday and who was pointing out demonstrators who were throwing things to the coppers. Reeves said he wanted to identify this Nazi if possible. It was agreed that Reeves would come in to Day Street the following morning and see Denis Freney who was the 'expert' on Nazis in an attempt to identify the person.

So it was that on 14 July 1971, as mentioned earlier, I was photographed leaving the CPA headquarters, a copy of a folded newspaper (undoubtedly that week's *Tribune*) in my hand. I can't recall whether Freney helped me identify the cop-collaborating Nazi, but I can assure ASIO that it was me they photographed that day in Day Street.

And then, ASIO left me alone for about five years, ignoring my gathering of evidence about the US mafia making moves to set up shop in Australia; my public appearance at the Moffitt Royal Commission which my earlier research had helped to establish; and my three years investigating the 1975 murder of Kings Cross identity Juanita Nielsen, which resulted in frequent media mentions of my colleague Barry Ward and myself.

ASIO also ignored – or never became aware of – the appointment of my then partner and me to the position of joint convenors of the Australia–Cuba Friendship Society, which we had done at the suggestion of CPA personality Mavis Robertson. Mavis had suggested it would be better for 'the public image' if the organisers of this putative pro-Castro organisation were members of the ALP (which we were) rather than CPA heavyweights. An association with communist-run Cuba surely should have interested our security service at the time. Also ignored by ASIO were my foot-in-the-door media stories about the split in the CPA with the formation of the pro-Moscow Socialist Party of Australia.

One event in 1976 again drew the attention of the security organisation back to me. An unnamed ASIO informant reported seeing me drinking at the Evening Star Hotel in Elizabeth Street, Surry Hills.

I was a regular at that venue as it was the social hub for the editorial staff of the News Limited papers just up the road, and I did work with them around that time and maintained good friendships and contacts with a number of them. Other journalists and people who thought they 'had a good story to tell' also came and went. Only one visitor, however, got me a further page in the ASIO file: it was written in August 1976, at least three months after the event had allegedly taken place.

> Vladimir (Vladimir Viktorovich) BOLSHAKOV (B/42/60), Pravda representative, Sydney, was observed drinking at the Evening Star hotel, 370 Elizabeth St, Surry Hills, in May 1976, with Tony (Antony) REEVES (T71/390), a Freelance journalist.

The ASIO contact's added comment was extraordinary in its vagueness and inaccuracy, but ASIO never bothered checking the facts before adding it to their slender dossier tagged T71/390 which had my name on the front cover.

'I don't recall the exact date in May,' the contact wrote:

> Reeves is an *avowed Communist* [my emphasis], and is presently a candidate for election to the Committee of the New South Wales Branch of the Australian Journalist Association.

I vaguely recall once meeting the Russian reporter casually. Maybe he was a spy, but I had no further contact with him. Despite my alleged political allegiance, I did, however, win a spot on the New South Wales branch committee of my union (of which I have more recently been granted life membership).

A few more years were to pass before the agency honed in on me again.

A fellow housemate and journalist colleague of mine, Chris, was a member of the CPA. He had been profoundly influenced by the devastation and poverty he personally witnessed in Vietnam immediately after the final withdrawal and defeat of the United States forces. In Australia he worked at trying to repair the damaged relationships. In early 1980 he began to organise an event which was quickly reported by telex from one ASIO office to another on 14 May 1980:

It was headed 'Indo-China Solidarity Conference':

1. U/P T/1 revealed that Chris [surname withheld] [R/41/76] is seeking assistance from the 'Peace Committee' for 'credentials, just sort of geeing up the guests … and making sure they are comfortable'. Joyce CLARKE agreed to request.

2. Chris stated that their guests included 'two Vietnamese' and one from the Embassy, the Laotian Charge-D'Affaires from the Laos Embassy and his interpreter and then 'Whitlam, Bowen and poss Cairns at the reception but possibly not at the conference.'

3. He told Clarke about the violence in Melbourne and Adelaide and said that it hadn't been given much publicity in the Sydney papers '… so we're expecting considerable trouble at the conference'. He has spoken to the Seamen, the Wharfies, the Painters and Dockers, about security arrangements and has arranged a preliminary meeting on Wednesday night. He then asked if Clarke saw anyone 'You could ask them to come along on Saturday … say an hour before one o'clock'. He said he would also contact the BWIU for assistance.

4. It was arranged that Clarke would invite people from the consulates and 'the TASS people' Vailiev and Oleg Skalkin. Tony Reeves will be handling the press statements and the Ambassador has requested 'not to have open press conference, just selected interviews.'

And then there were more paragraphs about who should be told about these arrangements, including the NSW Police and their federal counterparts. Agreeing with Chris that I would be happy to handle media statements for the Solidarity Conference had been enough to earn me another ASIO report.

The death of controversial journalist Wilfred Burchett on 27 September 1983 triggered another page in my ASIO file. I had met Burchett in Sydney in late 1973 when he came to Australia to mount a court case. I joined a small group to help raise funds internationally for his legal action.

A fortnight after he died, ASIO learned of plans to hold a remembrance gathering. A report written on 10 October headed 'Socialist Party of Australia, Contact with Communist Party of Australia' used Harry Bradford Black as its main source of information.

Black was a long-time waterfront union activist (he died in May 2011), and the report does not make it clear whether he volunteered the information or if it was gathered by phone call intercepts. A reference in the header of the report to 'Spool 580' supports the latter option.

It said that Black contacted Raymond George Clarke '… and told him about the remembrance gathering for Wilfred Burchett that the CPA are organising.'

The event was to be held at the Graphic Arts Club on 14 October at 5.30 p.m., the report noted.

> Black said [to Clarke] people who will contribute will be Malcolm Salmon, Mavis Robertson, Tony Reeves and Alan Ashbolt, who is expected to be chairman but is overseas at the moment …
>
> Clarke said he had worked with Burchett when he first came out for the Democratic Rights Council …

Black then read to Clarke the circular he had received from the CPA which: '... invites all who knew "Burchett" to attend. Clarke thanked Black for letting him know.'

This simple interaction triggered further entries in the files of all who were mentioned, with their ASIO file reference noted against each name. The notation at my name merely said 'NSW File Destroyed', just as Fred Longbottom had told me it had been all those years earlier ... that little bit of my personal history lost in the authorised arson carried out by Longbottom's snooping officers, the unofficial state branch of the national spy network.

One of the major omissions from my ASIO dossier was my earlier friendship with Wilfred Burchett, who was considered by conservative governments in the US, UK, and certainly Australia, to be a communist sympathiser and supporter of the supposed 'yellow peril'. Indeed the Menzies Government had refused to issue Burchett with an Australian passport – to which he was legally entitled – after he lost his UK passport. Burchett was clearly high on ASIO's list of 'persons of interest', but my close and very public association with him didn't rate a mention.

And so in late 1983, not only did we lay Wilfred Burchett to rest, but ASIO also laid Tony Reeves (or at least his dossier) to rest. Maybe. If there is more, I would hope they get it right, make it relevant to something important, or stop wasting their time studying the life of a person who has been just a bit of an activist, but on the left ... where ASIO spent most of its time snooping since 6 July 1950, the day that extreme anti-communist, Brigadier Sir Charles Chambers Fowell Spry took control of the organisation.

Writing this has made irrelevant a thought that has been buzzing in my head since I first saw my ASIO file: that I should write to them to correct their errors and tell them of the significant events they had missed. I've no longer a yen to do so.

I am reminded in closing of a true story, of a Canberra man, very senior on the staff of a minister in the Whitlam Government, who, 'high' after a long lunch, went to the ASIO office and demanded to see his file. He waited for a while in the foyer. The officer returned to report that they had no file in his name. Some time later, after relating this story to friends at another long lunch, he decided to have another try; after all, he was controversial, worked for a controversial minister: there *must* be an ASIO dossier on him. This time, after a brief wait in the foyer, the man came out and handed him a file, marked with his name. It had one page: stating that on the earlier date, this person had come to ASIO and demanded to see his file.

So if any reader feels they have missed out by not having attracted the dubious accolade of an ASIO dossier, they may well be able to start one by demanding to see their file.

TIM ANDERSON

Tim Anderson is a social justice activist, writer and academic. He lectures in political economy at the University of Sydney. He has published in a wide range of journals and books on topics including Latin American and Pacific development, trade agreements, agriculture and food security, health systems, rights and self-advocacy. His next book will be *Land and Livelihoods in Papua New Guinea*.

In the late 1970s he was arrested and jailed for supposed involvement in a terrorist act in Sydney. After seven years in jail, where he undertook most of his university studies, he was exonerated and paid compensation. In the late 1980s New South Wales police tried to resurrect the case, without success. His account of these court cases and prison can be read in *Take Two* (1992; available at <http://lorikeet.and.com.au/t2/t2.htm>). He describes this book as:

> ... both a catharsis and an opportunity to set down a substantial personal history. To have written about this experience is, in some ways, to have personally dealt with it and to have cleared my life for other things ... I've never cherished the idea of repeating jail or courtroom stories in my old age, like an old digger telling war stories.

As an activist he has campaigned for prisoners' rights and civil liberties. As Secretary of the NSW Council for Civil Liberties between 1997 and 1999, he was appointed to a government committee set up to recommend what to do with the old NSW Special Branch records.

In recent times he has returned to internationalism, focusing on solidarity with independent peoples, including the Cuban and Venezuelan peoples, and on autonomous development and self-determination in the Pacific region and Timor Leste.

POSTCARDS FROM THE SECRET POLICE

by Tim Anderson

I was probably less enthused than others over the release of old ASIO files, as I had seen many of them before. Throughout thirteen years and ten court cases (1978–1991), my lawyers had extracted large numbers of police Special Branch and ASIO files from a reluctant state bureaucracy. The two spy agencies often exchanged files.

Boxes of these documents appeared during a 1984–85 Special Inquiry in which I was involved. I had been arrested and jailed on two politically related charges, brought by New South Wales police in 1978, then again in 1989. The first was a supposed conspiracy to bomb a tiny group of right-wing extremists; the closely related second case was an attempt to link me to an actual bombing outside a 1978 political conference at the Hilton Hotel in Sydney. I was then a member of the Ananda Marga group, which was campaigning for the release of political prisoners in India. At the end of the first case a judge heading the Special Inquiry recommended that I and my two friends be exonerated. We were pardoned, released and eventually paid a sum of money in compensation. At the end of the second case I was acquitted. Details of these long trials can be found in my book *Take Two* (1992, Bantam or at <http://lorikeet.and.com.au/t2/t2.htm>).

Abolition of the NSW Special Branch in 1997 led to the release of more files, under a liberal interpretation of the state's Freedom of Information rules. This was one consequence of the systematic corruption exposed by a Royal Commission into the NSW Police (1995–1997). I was at that time Secretary of the NSW Council for Civil Liberties and was appointed to a committee set up to recommend what to do with the secret police files. That the new organisation created to replace the Special Branch – the Protective Security Group – wanted hardly any of these files tells us something about their forensic value. The Police Minister at that time, Paul Whelan, had more than a passing interest in the Special Branch. He had acquired a Special Branch file of his own after attending a public meeting in support of me, back in 1991. After allowing individual access to some of the files, the rest were archived.

As a result of this history, many of the ASIO documents released in more recent years under thirty year archive rules were not news to me. They just added a few more examples to patterns I had already observed. These documents were mostly collections of surveillance and trivia, including news clips, and cold trails of the many attempts to gain compromising material on mostly left-wing activists. They were riddled with errors, but that did not prevent many expressions of great confidence in their false conclusions. After all, who would contradict these secret files?

However, since those documents were created, there have been swings and roundabouts in systems of scrutiny. On the one hand, Australian public servants subject to adverse ASIO findings have gained the right to have these findings reviewed by a tribunal. On the other hand, asylum seekers subject to similar adverse findings are denied rights of review. That is alarming, considering the poor quality of much of the information contained in these old 'postcards' from the secret police.

FALSE IDENTIFICATIONS

Some errors in both the ASIO and Special Branch files were surprising. On more than one occasion, my address was wrongly recorded. The NSW Special Branch had also repeated a false Commonwealth Police claim that I had acquired a 'criminal record' after I'd been acquitted of a 1976 'obstruction' charge at a demonstration in Canberra. Several false identifications were included. These were both errors from police and from independent witnesses, who were at times manipulated by police.

In the ASIO files released to me in 2010 it emerged that the Victorian Special Branch had produced a series of documents in October 1977 which claimed I had assumed a false identity, was living in Melbourne and working at the Victorian Railways. At this time I was actually living in Newtown (Sydney), and had spoken publicly to both police and journalists. Nevertheless, the Victorian Special Branch gave chapter and verse of my supposed whereabouts and movements in Melbourne, based on surveillance in mid-October. After ten days of this surveillance ASIO concluded:

> Victorian Police Special Branch enquiries have established that Tim Anderson ... is currently employed by Victorian Railways as a sorter ... [he] is employed under the name Glen

Anderson and has supplied his employers with a fictitious Broadmeadows address. It is suggested he is currently residing at 1225 Hoddle Street East Melbourne.

Later that same day someone noted the error: 'Victorian Police Special Branch have advised error made in identifications of Tim Anderson ... Anderson is still resident in Sydney.' Nevertheless, two weeks later, the NSW Police repeated the error, saying I lived at East Melbourne and had given a false name to Victorian Police. Of course such secret files are rarely, if ever, subject to correction.

In a more serious example, on the day of the February 1978 Hilton Hotel bombing in Sydney, a man called Manfred Von Gries told police he had seen a man acting suspiciously outside the hotel at around the time of the blast. He made a tentative identification of this person, from NSW Special Branch photos, as a person who was 5 feet 6 inches tall and thin with shoulder-length, blond curly hair and no beard. I am 5 feet 11 inches, of medium build and at the time I had collar length straight brown hair and a dark beard. Almost five years later, at the 1982 inquest into that bombing, Von Gries would claim I was that man. Several years later, New South Wales detectives claimed they used this identification, along with a story from a prison informer, for my 1989 arrest. This story was discredited and ultimately not used at trial.

There were other mis-identifications, for example, one which had me visiting Canada – I wouldn't have that privilege until 2002.

A more frightening mis-identification was of another person, also at the time of the February 1978 Hilton Hotel bombing. It relied on a witness called Malcolm, presumably an independent person, who reported to police seeing a man in a cafe near the hotel, and overhearing him say that a person could 'make a name for himself' at a conference like this.

The usual Special Branch suspect photos were shown to Malcolm, who at first identified a man called Brent, a member of Ananda Marga, one of the suspect groups which had held demonstrations outside the hotel prior to the bomb blast. However, police soon discovered that Brent was in Melbourne at the time in question. They called Malcolm back and asked him to reconsider, and in a second statement, he picked another man, also an Ananda Marga member, named Andrew. This statement made no reference to the earlier 'identification', and on its face appears to be an original identification. It's only by comparing the dates that one knows the Brent identification occurred before the Andrew identification. However, police discovered that Andrew had also been in Melbourne at the relevant time.

Special Branch surveillance photo of Tim Anderson with a friend, Queen Street, Newtown, 1978.

They called Malcolm in a third time, and this time he obligingly identified a third person, Carl, not an Ananda Marga member but someone with a Special Branch 'record' because of his arrest at an anti-apartheid demonstration. Again, Malcolm's third statement made no reference to either of the earlier two 'identifications'. If there had been a prosecution against Carl, and if Malcolm had chosen not to mention those earlier statements, there would have been no hint of a discrepancy, and he may have appeared to have made a positive identification in unbiased circumstances. Carl's denials of being the man in the cafe could then be portrayed as lies indicating a 'consciousness of guilt'.

This is not a fanciful scenario. Carl was an anarchist who'd also attended the demonstration outside the Hilton Hotel and had become a police suspect for the bombing. He'd carried an original placard at the demonstration, which read, 'Politicians are the pus of a suppurating society.' The placard was mounted on a seven-foot-long wooden stake and, when Carl became tired of carrying it, he drove it into the garbage bin that exploded some hours later, killing three people. Twelve years later a court saw video evidence of Carl's sign in the bin before the explosion, evidence which caused Chief Justice Murray Gleeson to refer uncomfortably to 'that offensive sign'.

Police took a nine-page, signed record of interview from Carl, in which they obtained a denial of any knowledge of the bombing, but also an admission that he had some knowledge of electronics. The stage had been set for a powerful circumstantial case: an anarchist who despised politicians apparently identified and overheard planning a provocative act, with all the skills to make a bomb and probably the only person who could be identified as actually planting an object in the fateful garbage bin. Add a 'police verbal' (a fabricated 'confession') and he'd quite likely be convicted. But police decided to go after some other people.

TELLING THEM WHAT THEY WANT TO HEAR

Low-grade spies are well known for reporting only what their masters want to hear. So it was with Special Branch agent Richard Seary, who infiltrated the Ananda Marga group in 1978 and helped Special Branch fabricate a conspiracy case against me and two friends, Ross and Paul. This conspiracy case was eventually discredited at the Special Inquiry in 1984–85.

Seary reported to his Special Branch handler, John Krawczyk, in taped interviews, usually conducted in a dark-curtained kombi-van, or at the back of an inner-city pub. He told Krawczyk that Ross wanted information on lock picking, as he wanted to pick a 'large chrome lock' in Canberra. In fact, Ross wanted to pull down the Australian flag on Capital Hill and put up another flag in protest at the cost of the new parliament house (in 1978 this was reported as $150 million; the cost eventually came in at more than $1 billion). This publicity stunt would involve opening a small locked door to an electrical pulley system on the flagpole. Yet by the time Seary told the story, a relatively harmless publicity stunt had become a paramilitary plot. Special Branch tapes, when they finally emerged, would include these conversations:

> Seary: The lock they want picked is on a government building in Canberra … [security] will cover us and they'll be with their weapons and all our job would be to do would be

> to open the door to let another team in ... they have to go to an electrical control box. That was one thing he did say, and mentioned ventilators ... there was a lot of avenues leading up to it [the building] and it was in plain view ... near the site of the new Government [sic] House ... the first thing they're doing is they're going to the electrical box to cut the lighting.

The flagpole was right in the middle of Capital Hill, the site of the new parliament house, with avenues leading up to it. NSW Special Branch passed on Seary's story to the ACT Special Branch, who concluded that the 'target' must be the Qantas building, as this was the only one with round chrome locks visible from Capital Hill; and it also housed the Deputy Crown Solicitor's offices, which held exhibits in an unrelated court case involving another Ananda Marga member. Seary's plot seemed to be confirmed.

Three days later, on the day of our arrests in June 1978, Ross had another conversation with Seary and repeated the rather more mundane purpose of the exercise. Seary reported this to Krawczyk; but it was so at odds with what he had first reported that they refused to believe what they were being told. They fell into a confusion based on their mutual desire to find paramilitary conspiracies, the problem of Seary's original twisted story, and his desire to impress Krawczyk:

> Seary: ... he said they were going to do a political act and it involved the flag pole on Capital Hill in Canberra ... he spoke about the type of lock. He said it was chromed; the door was made of steel.
>
> Krawczyk: Now earlier you mentioned that they said they had to go to the power and then to the ventilators ... they

didn't elaborate on that at all?

Seary: No, I mean you don't have ventilators in flag poles!

Krawczyk: Right, now do you think they'll just go down there and raise a flag?

Seary: That's possible.

Krawczyk: Do you think they would do just that?

Seary: But I mean, they pride themselves on intelligence and if they were going to simply raise a flag ... it would implicate them for a start and unless it's some very, very strange ideological thing – I, I really can't see the sense in making any attack or whatever on a flag pole ... now either they're giving me a bum steer ...

Krawczyk: Now, earlier you mentioned that um, the [security] would look after it, they'll have weapons.

Seary: Oh yes, they'll be on guard duty ... [but] if you're just going to raise a flag, why would you want to keep it such a secret?

Krawczyk: No point is there ... Alright then, so we don't know why they're going to Canberra really?

Seary: Well it's ... it's a political act ... their idea is to challenge the government wholeheartedly.

Krawczyk: Now?

Seary: Oh yes.

It could have been a great story, but was very soon overtaken by the 'conspiracy case', and their attempts to link us to a supposed attack on a right-wing group and to blame us for the unsolved Hilton Hotel bombing. But that's another story.

SUPPRESSED FILES UNDERMINE A CRIMINAL TRIAL

Information held on me in ASIO and Special Branch files was mostly useless and often inaccurate. Of all the notations in my fairly extensive dossier, from 1976 to 1984, nothing collected by the Special Branch was ever of value to any criminal prosecution. However, material that ultimately compromised a police prosecution was actively suppressed. This example shows the 'one way street' these secret files represent: they are there to help the state, but only hurt the targeted citizen.

I and my two friends spent seven years in jail (1978–1985) until an inquiry led to our exoneration and release. That inquiry was initiated because of suppressed tapes of the Seary–Krawczyk interviews which only came to light some years down the track, at a High Court appeal. These tapes had been produced on subpoena at our first trial in early 1979, where the jury failed to agree on a verdict. However, trial judge Justice John Nagle upheld a claim by a crown solicitor (who hadn't himself heard the tapes) to have them suppressed. Nagle said:

> I have formed a clear view myself that [transcripts of the tapes] would come within a proper claim of privilege ... I have read the documents in the lunch hour and I can assure counsel in the absence of the jury that I do not think they can gain any assistance from any of them. [27 February 1979].

How Nagle could possibly have read and understood the 160 pages of transcripts in his lunch hour was a question that deserved more attention. In 1984 the then Solicitor-General, Mary Gaudron, and Crown Prosecutor Malcolm McGregor told the state government that as regards the conspiracy case, this material:

> ... was of such cruciality as weakening the Crown case and tending to support, at least by strong implication, the defence case ... [that] the failure to grant the defence access to this material must be viewed as a very serious failure of the legal processes.

One of the main reasons Justice James Wood (the judge at the Special Inquiry) found in our favour was the significance of material contained in these tapes. The suppression of the tapes was a process involving: Special Branch police wanting the same secrecy privileges as ASIO; a legal bureaucrat mindlessly supporting the police claim; and a judge mindlessly supporting the tradition of state secrecy. In the end, no one was held responsible for this debacle because, following Nagle's assurance, our lawyers had not subpoenaed the tape at a second trial in 1979, at which we were convicted. Based on this technical distinction Justice Wood, while finding that the tapes were very important, also found that there had not been a miscarriage at trial. No-one was to blame.

INFORMERS AND DOUBLE AGENTS

ASIO has its euphemisms for sources of information. Of course, there is surveillance and 'camera observation'. 'Intercept reports' signified phone taps. Then there was 'unprocessed bugle (intercept) info', which might have been a nicer way of saying third-hand information from paid informers. 'Unprocessed bugle info' sounds slightly better than 'gossip', anyway. Nevertheless, this gossip remains an important source of 'intelligence', even in the digital age. It is quite cheap, after all, to pay someone $50 or $100 to attend a meeting and report back on who the main 'troublemakers' might have been. Wading through hundreds of phone calls or emails might not necessarily produce such neat conclusions.

There are always informers, and they are usually eager to please. With greater financial resources, ASIO was able to sustain an even greater network than the Special Branches. 'Ron', for example, was a middle-aged businessman who attended some Ananda Marga meetings in the late 1970s and boasted about owning some rifles. Ten years later he approached a prosecutor and claimed, amongst other things, that while he had no specific information about the 1978 Hilton Hotel bombing, he had undertaken 'terrorist training' overseas and had overheard some incriminating conversations. He was unable to explain why he hadn't come forward much earlier.

With the proliferation of informers in the Ananda Marga group in the late 1970s and early 1980s, it was inevitable that some would make more creative use of the ASIO bankroll. ASIO's powers and budget had skyrocketed in this period, largely because of the political fallout from the 1978 Hilton Hotel bombing. 'Peter' was a young man who had been approached by ASIO in the early 1980s. He spoke to an Ananda Marga monk about this and the monk told him to go ahead: take the money, report to them but then tell him (the monk) what ASIO wanted to know. Peter gave the payments to Ananda Marga. In this way ASIO funded one of its targets for a year or so.

While the ASIO 'handlers' were fairly careful about not passing information back to Peter, they did let him know what they were interested in at particular times. For instance, when an event of some sort was about to happen they'd ask many questions about certain people, travel plans and so on. In this way some in the group would be kept informed of ASIO's interests. The information Peter passed on to ASIO was common knowledge stuff, and it seems he was sensitive enough not to exchange potentially embarrassing or intrusive gossip. As innocent as it is in reality, this spectre of a double agent was a great fear for Justice Wood in his 1985 inquiry. His concern about Special Branch's handling of Seary seemed more to do with a fear that the informer may have turned on the police, than of the damage that deranged informer actually did to us.

No doubt phone tapping and digital surveillance has increased greatly since the 1970s. But when targeting community groups the old-fashioned informer is still the simplest, easiest and cheapest form of 'intelligence' gathering. The body of gossip, slander and half-truth obtained in this way is often used to confirm what those with privileged access to the secret files already know. Anyway, who is going to check?

PENNY LOCKWOOD

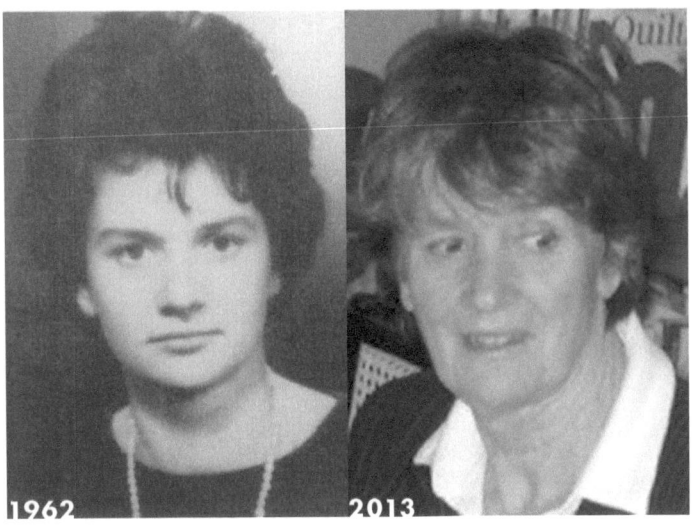

1962   2013

Penny Lockwood was born in 1943 and grew up in Sydney with her communist parents Rupert Lockwood and Betty Searle. Her father was a well-known journalist and prominent in the communist movement. He was a key witness in the Petrov Royal Commission in 1954. Penny was educated at Moscow University, the Australian National University (ANU), and briefly at the University of New England before the birth of her son Loren. She studied languages, history and politics at university, and worked in Canberra at the ANU, the Commonwealth Parliamentary Library Research Service and then for a Labor politician for almost a decade from 1983.

In 1991 Penny was preselected to be the Labor candidate for the New South Wales seat of Monaro. She did not win the seat, but subsequently was elected to the Yarrowlumla Shire Council in the same year with overwhelming voter support. Penny moved to the

Office of the Status of Women in 1992 and worked for a period in Minister Wendy Fatin's office on status of women issues. She took up a position in the Australian Quarantine and Inspection Service in 1996, representing Australia on several occasions at the UN International Maritime Organisation on ballast water management. Penny's last job before retirement was in the ACT Chief Minister's Department working on social inclusion issues.

She has been a keen horse rider since the age of ten, when her parents bought her a horse to compensate for the cruel attention she received at school during the Petrov Royal Commission – at the time her father was front page news for weeks on end. Penny has been obsessed by her horses since then and in the mid-1990s she converted a large woolshed into a house on her property at Burra Creek, where she now lives.

LACK OF EVIDENCE PROVES NOTHING

by Penny Lockwood

I met him at an anti-war demo in 1967. He was attractive and it had been an exciting few months together – almost a year – when he stopped the car and leant over. He looked serious. 'Ah, perhaps this is the proposal,' I thought. He moved closer and whispered, as if someone else might be listening, 'I can't do it any more. I don't love you. I'm working for ASIO.'

I have to concede that ASIO might have had some cause to get excited about whether I was a 'subversive'. In the 1960s I travelled to Eastern European countries and lived with my communist parents in Moscow in 1965–66 – an opportunistic adventure allowing me to study Russian for two years at Moscow University. My father, Rupert Lockwood, was *Tribune*'s correspondent in Moscow for three years from 1965. He was under constant surveillance as a person of interest to ASIO, British and European security agencies, and finally the KGB.

ASIO continued to hound my father for years after he resigned from the Communist Party of Australia in 1969 on his

ASIO surveillance photo from Penny Lockwood's file, showing Penny Lockwood at the front of an anti-Vietnam War demonstration, Canberra, late 1960s. The woman in the white beret is Ann Kent.

return from Moscow, despite the considerable national publicity this attracted. His ASIO files are voluminous.

My files can't compare, but, along with the files of thousands of others under surveillance, reflect an ASIO mentality of the 1960s and '70s that was obsessed by perfectly legal democratic 'left' movements and alliances.

Exposed to talk of social justice as a child, I joined various anti-war, Aboriginal and women's rights movements as an adult, and consequently ensured ASIO's continuing interest in me as a 'subversive' for years beyond the Moscow adventure. This is despite never having been a member of a communist party, and reports on ASIO's files indicating my aversion to non-democratic regimes.

Concerns I felt about the non-democratic nature of the Soviet Union were already emerging in my ASIO records by the late 1960s. In a debriefing in 1968 to the Department of External Affairs on his return from studying in Moscow, Robert Jones (now Robert Dessaix) reported meeting me in my parents' Moscow apartment. An ASIO officer was present during the debriefing and recorded the conversation for the file:

> Lockwood's daughter Penny did not clearly indicate her political views and ... it was by no means clear to Jones what her political views were. Penny Lockwood left the USSR soon after and Jones gathered that she was glad to leave.

(Robert later became my Russian lecturer at ANU.)

My relationship with ASIO started in the early 1960s, several years before Moscow, when I attracted some attention from security agencies overseas. Participating in London in the Campaign for Nuclear Disarmament, a potentially 'subversive' activity, earned me a note on file. There is also a reference on family files around that time about my visits to some Eastern Bloc countries, and to the Netherlands.

Then I was almost certainly watched by the KGB when I lived in Moscow. My father was beginning to fall out of favour with the Russians for being too critical, and I was friendly with a 'hero' of the Bay of Pigs (which sadly led to him being sent back to Cuba before completing his Moscow studies). A report on my ASIO file from the Australian ambassador in Moscow at the time notes that the Soviet authorities were concerned 'that his [Rupert Lockwood's] reporting of events in the Soviet Union has not been sufficiently "objective"'.

As soon as I returned to Australia in 1967, ASIO intensified their surveillance. During intercepts of my mother's telephone calls they were able to determine my movements. These intercepts allowed ASIO to note that 'one of the twin daughters [although I was not one of the twins] has attempted to obtain an appointment as secretary to the Russian Language School of the Australian National University'. It goes on to say, 'It is not likely that Miss Lockwood's application will be considered favourably.' This memo was dated two weeks before I returned to Australia and before I had even had an interview. It must have been a surprise to ASIO when I was appointed at the conclusion of the interview a couple of weeks later. Knowing what we now know about ASIO's interference with people's jobs in those days, and comments made to me at the time about pressure around my appointment, it is possible that they tried to influence my recruitment with university authorities.

In June 1967, just a few months after my return from Moscow, and during a visit to Melbourne, ASIO knew of and recorded my movements. This included a visit to author Alan Marshall and to the head of Melbourne University's Russian Department, Nina Christesen. Now, as I sit and read my files, I wonder about my acquaintances from those days, and who might have been providing information to ASIO.

ASIO's surveillance of my time working in the Russian Department and studying at the Australian National University in the late 1960s and early 1970s was not only based on telephone intercepts and surveillance, but clearly involved asking fellow students for character assessments. One was Tony Kevin, a young Department of External Affairs diplomat sent to the ANU to learn Russian. He told me recently that he was asked to provide comment on me to an ASIO officer. He recalls that he did so once, and it now appears as a flattering comment on file – not much comfort to ASIO.

I was also to discover in my ASIO files that my employer, the Professor of Russian at the ANU, was under surveillance. Merely attending a linguistics lecture she chaired was enough to get several pages from her ASIO records copied onto my file indicating a list of potentially subversive attendees, including me.

Other surveillance reports in the late 1960s reveal a desire by ASIO to dig into the thoughts and personalities of student activists. One report on my file is headed 'The Australian National University ... information relates to persons of ... interest associated with the A.N.U.' In it, a now well-known Canberra identity is accused of 'Taking freedom of thought to its extreme'. The report's assessment of me is concerned with what I might be concealing:

> It would appear that Miss Lockwood strives to project an apolitical image, and while she will comment on general issues (academic freedom, rights for Aborigines, the need for a hurried peaceful solution to the Vietnam conflict etc) she parries questions which would tend to commit her to a political doctrine.

It goes on to say: 'Personally, Miss Lockwood is attractive, blonde, and very quiet in company. It is difficult to gauge whether this apparent timidity is a result of deliberate circumspection.'

These reports indicate a distressing closeness of ASIO operatives to their subjects – although I was never a true blonde.

ASIO also felt itself duty bound to monitor friendships and warn people away from me. Director-General Charles Spry wrote to Sir James Plimsoll, Secretary of the Department of External Affairs, in December 1967:

> ... [name deleted] stated she was also on friendly terms with David Brennan, who is believed to be the son of Mr Keith Brennan of your Department. You may consider it desirable to bring this to the attention of Mr Brennan or alternatively, that an ASIO officer advises him informally.

In the same letter the Director-General discusses my relationship with the ASIO boyfriend mentioned earlier:

> I was greatly concerned to learn recently that a close association had been formed between Miss Lockwood and one [name deleted.] He has since [blacked out] Miss Lockwood.

There is a note in the margin adjacent to this text to 'see staff file ... ACT office'.

To this day I cannot say whether the boyfriend was directed to befriend me or whether we met by accident. However, it is clear that he was supplying information about me to ASIO, mainly about my political views. There are notes in the file to this effect. It is also clear that the agency was concerned that he was becoming increasingly close to me. Soon after his confession to me, he left the agency, telling me 'I'm sick of doing this'.

It is difficult to continue writing about my ASIO files without mentioning the historical context and the issues facing my family in the 1950s. The fear campaign led by the government in those days, and supported by the Australian media, deeply affected many of the children of left-wing parents. The right to engage in democratic movements became a personal crusade for us.

ASIO's 1950s mentality survived well into the 1960s and '70s, and is apparent in the files of many people who were engaged in democratic movements. This is alarmingly apparent in my own file when an internal struggle takes place in ASIO in 1973 over my security clearance for a job in the public service (the Australian Parliamentary Library Research Service, Social Welfare Section).

ASIO was very concerned about giving me clearance for any classified information. They were not even happy that I had already been employed temporarily pending security clearance: amusing, because my first task was to provide research justifying the retention of the sales tax on the contraceptive pill proposed for abolition by the Whitlam Government. I behaved in the best traditions of a truly apolitical and unbiased public servant and wrote a persuasive research paper, a difficult task admittedly, since I was a committed activist in women's groups advocating the removal of the tax. But it wasn't enough.

Instead, the memos between officers dealing with my security assessment demonstrate a rogue culture still existed in ASIO in 1973. Despite the fact that there was 'no evidence that she is a member of any subversive organisation or group', ASIO was nevertheless reluctant to give me clearance. They found my parents' background distasteful (although neither was in the Communist Party at the time) and the fact that I 'dabbled in what can be reasonably described as left wing affairs'. ASIO intercepts and surveillance had shown that I had 'taken part in various anti-war, anti-apartheid and civil liberties activities over the last few years'. Yes, civil liberties.

The discussion goes on in ASIO, with one officer arguing that lack of evidence was not relevant to the case for an adverse assessment: 'Lack of evidence proves nothing … we have here a case of a person who … is intelligent enough to hide her political affiliations …'

The same officer goes on to remind his colleagues that ASIO did not work for the government of the day or its policies:

> In this case I am of the opinion that the doubt should be decided in favour of the Commonwealth, which means in favour of Australia, not in favour of some presently existing government policy, vague though this may be and subject to change as are all Government policies. The security of the country … can hardly change with the seasons.

This law-unto-itself culture and political sentiments expressed by ASIO officers at the time were too close to the rationale used by security systems of non-democratic regimes for comfort. It makes for chilling reading.

As the memos worked their way up the system, the question of an appeals process for adverse ASIO assessments was being discussed by the ASIO officers dealing with my case. A senior ASIO officer was concerned and wrote:

> The views expressed by Mr [name blacked out] at para 5 of his minute are laudable but in the climate of moves towards an appeals tribunal we have to try to conclude how such a tribunal is going to view our recommendations and the

supporting information. I think it would hold that our case rests mainly on presumption …

Another ASIO officer suggested that a way to resolve the issue would be to interview me:

> There is a conflict of opinion in this case between Mr [name blacked out], the assessing officer, and Mr [name blacked out] of 'B' Branch. I consider that Penelope Dalgarno's [Lockwood's] background is such that she should not be permitted access to classified matter without at least an attempt to explore her attitudes …

However, this also created a problem. Another officer responded:

> As to the proposal to interview, I agree that an interview could be of assistance, in cases such as this, but not for Penelope Dalgarno [Lockwood]. She is too well known, too active in political affairs to justify the risk.

In fighting the undemocratic nature of the Soviet Government and its security arm, it seems Australia was happy to waste time and money on a security service bent on pursuing people who were simply active in legal human-rights movements and nothing more. Commentators, including Justice Hope, have argued that ASIO was too politically motivated, aligning its focus with the right of Australian politics. Perhaps it is time to be reminded that many human-rights issues were not supported by conservative governments of the time. The 'left', including unionists, church activists and left Labor Party members as well as communists, were demonstrating on a large number of human rights issues. An examination of ASIO files shows that all these causes were treated by them as subversive.

As is the case for most people who were ASIO targets, I was largely unaware at the time of how pervasive the surveillance was. So during my time at the Parliamentary Library in 1973, the most remarkable thing that happened was that from my first day I was placed at a desk outside Michael Thwaites' office. Thwaites had been ASIO's Director of Counter Espionage. He had played a leading role in the defection of the Soviet diplomat Petrov in 1954, which led to the Petrov Royal Commission and the involvement of my father for over a year as a 'key witness'.

Thwaites was a name spoken with fear and hostility in our house – it had been a terrible time for the family. My father had a nervous breakdown at the conclusion of the 'Petrov Affair', and my mother suffered ASIO agents walking into our kitchen without invitation and front windows being broken by stones. I remember being followed to school at the time by men in dark coats declaring that my parents were evil, and being bullied and teased at school. At the age of ten I also had a breakdown and was kept out of school for some months. But it was not long before my hackles were calmed and I grew to like Michael Thwaites, albeit reservedly.

His son Richard Thwaites told me that shortly after the Petrov Affair his father was transferred to a new branch called Counter Subversion. Richard said Michael Thwaites resigned from ASIO in 1971 'because he was disillusioned with ASIO's approach to subversion' and 'left, alienated from senior ASIO management, and not happy about the way it operated'. Michael Thwaites resigned without a job to go to and it was some six months before he secured the position of Assistant Commonwealth Parliamentary Librarian. When his son Richard told me that his father was liberal on civil rights matters and would probably have voted against the referendum to ban the communist party in 1954, I warmed to him a little more than I had in 1973. Indeed, in a transcript held by the Department of Veterans' Affairs, Michael Thwaites says: 'I, personally looking back am glad that Menzies' attempt to declare the communist party illegal was defeated.' Sadly, at the time we were colleagues in the Parliamentary Library, Michael Thwaites wouldn't talk about his ASIO days, or his role in our family's surveillance, to a person hungry for explanations.

Recently, Richard Thwaites sat with me in the National Archives examining my father's ASIO files and identifying his father's handwritten notes in the margins. It was a very strange feeling indeed.

I saved ASIO and the Parliamentary Library from the difficulty confronting them over my security clearance by resigning in late 1973 and going overseas. The surveillance did not end with the Parliamentary Library though – they kept on my tail.

A 1974 ASIO telegram from Canberra to ASIO headquarters in Melbourne, announced:

> She is in the U.K. at present and whilst there met a member
> of the British High Commission staff and has promised
> to renew their acquaintance when she (Penny Lockwood)
> returns to Australia later this month. The FADG [First
> Assistant Director-General] will like advice on the decision in
> your memo of … 1973.'

Of course I don't recall the meeting. It was probably just another person to whom one chats. Clearly it was dangerous to chat in those days.

One of the last notes on my ASIO file from the 'open period' – currently up to 1983 – has me chauffeuring the renowned Professor Stuart Hall and his luggage in my car in April that year. Professor Hall, born in Jamaica, a Rhodes scholar, and a well-respected academic at Oxford and Cambridge universities, came to Canberra for a day. He is described in my ASIO file as being 'coloured'. Hall was to dine at Parliament House with those subversives Arthur Gietzelt, Tom Uren, Gordon Scholes and NSW Deputy Premier Jack Ferguson, and the Minister for Finance whose name the ASIO agent did 'not remember'.

In a way it is flattering to be pursued, and much of it does feed one's ego, but at the same time it creates a certain paranoia.

It is now somewhat painful reading ASIO reports and learning about the efforts they made trying to get a fix on where I lived, worked and studied, what I thought, what meetings and demonstrations I went to, and who my friends were. If only they'd asked, I could have made their lives a lot easier. It would at least have prevented the errors.

There were two particular errors on file that point to ASIO's gender blindness in the 1960s – both highly amusing, and I would have thought a potential security threat in themselves. One gender oversight involved friends I stayed with when I first arrived in Canberra to take up work at the ANU. I had known the woman of the house since childhood because her parents were also communists. ASIO recorded on my file how diligently they had researched her husband's politics and background, including his birth details and work, but were unable to find anything. However, they missed the real connection – the woman – and also missed things that, given their focus, they might have wanted for the file.

One such omission was that I had attended Junior Eureka League meetings when I was about twelve and was made Treasurer. However I was sacked at the next meeting because I'd spent the meagre funds on ice cream. They have, however, noted my sisters' membership of the Eureka Youth League. Another sister was initially refused a US visa in the early 1970s on the basis of her membership years earlier. She was shocked to discover recently from her file that ASIO had followed her to a job in the US, and were preparing to recommend against her appointment.

Although I have to wait to get access to them, there is still fodder for my ASIO files in the 1980s and 1990s, and so plenty to look forward to. In 1991 I ran for the ALP for the New South Wales state seat of Monaro, and the communist bogey was pulled out numerous times, including by a few members of my own party. This time I thought the ASIO plant was pretty obvious – but perhaps that's my paranoia.

Later that year when I applied for another public service job, this time in the Office of the Status of Women, Department of Prime Minister and Cabinet (PM&C), it took over six months to get a 'security clearance'. Once again the arguments must have flown around ASIO and I look forward to reading them if I live long enough. Although the Cold War was all but over, on this occasion security did interview me before issuing a clearance.

The interview was in a windowless basement room with one desk and three chairs. Two men grilled me for what seemed like some considerable time on my political philosophy, time in Eastern Europe and Russia, and then suddenly said 'and do you believe in PMV?' I have to admit that stumped me. Keen to get the job, I eagerly tried to help, suggesting several possibilities, and finally tried Pre Menstrual Vomiting, but that didn't hit home. They left me hanging for a while, just repeating 'you know what we mean'. Finally, they succumbed and said it was Politically Motivated Violence. 'Of course,' I thought, but until then I had never given it a thought or heard the abbreviation. And then I was a bit angry, because it wasn't the left that had been violent in Australia, it was the right. ASIO intelligence had missed the Hilton and Croatian Embassy bombings and Ustaši training camps because it was too preoccupied with people on the left, including Labor politicians, as we now know.

About a year later, around late 1992, a plain unmarked brown envelope appeared on my desk at PM&C. It was not addressed to anyone, and had no sender's address. It was strange that it found its way to my desk without an address in an obsessively secure government building – Prime Minister and Cabinet. Another daughter of communist parents, working in a government building nowhere near mine, but just as secure, received the same envelope. Inside was material on the Petrov Affair, which of course mentioned my father and hers. It was a disturbing incident for both of us.

Overall, however, I have had an exciting life as an ASIO target, and wouldn't swap it for another. That would have meant not having my wonderful parents, not having the intellectual stimulation growing up, and perhaps not being interested in pursuing human rights issues, which have made life fulfilling and interesting and are still important to me.

To access some of the ASIO reports on my activities, I had to look at family files as well as my own. ASIO doesn't always file relevant personal notes on one's own file. Trawling through all these files has been, on the whole, an enjoyable exercise, particularly reading my own file – although I had to control my occasional guffaws and cries of surprise in the National Archives reading room.

The only emotionally distressing experience for me was reading my father's many files. A man of immense intellect, entertaining, personable, and passionate about human rights to his death, he was hounded by ASIO all his life, by the KGB in Moscow, and branded a 'bastard' and a 'traitor' to the cause by leading members of the CPA when he resigned in 1969 in protest at the Soviet Union's methods. He remained a true advocate for human rights, reflected in all his writings, from his earliest reports for the Melbourne *Herald* from Singapore, to fascist Germany and Franco's Spain during the civil war, to his last articles in *The Bulletin* and *Annals*.

Each year, more ASIO files are released. For me it will be like an exciting sojourn into my past, but I have no doubt my father's file will continue to sadden me.

PETER CUNDALL

Peter Cundall was born and raised in Manchester, England, where he grew up during the Depression years. His first gardening experience was sowing some peas his mother gave him at the age of four. One of six children in the family, he left school at the age of twelve.

He was conscripted into the British Army during World War II and witnessed the aftermath of war in both Europe and Japan. At the age of nineteen he spent six months in solitary confinement in a military prison in Yugoslavia. After answering an advertisement calling for volunteers for the Australian Army, Peter came to Australia hoping to obtain work as a military librarian, but found himself posted almost immediately to the Korean War. He returned to Australia from Korea with a total hatred of war.

At the end of his military service he began a new life in Tasmania. There he raised a family and took up gardening, providing pruning and clearing services. While pruning roses for the manager of a local radio station, he was asked to provide a service on talkback radio answering listeners' questions on gardening. Television quickly followed radio and a new career was born. Always interested in current affairs and the bigger picture, Peter continued to develop his interests in improving and protecting the environment, promoting organic gardening and sustainability, and fighting inappropriate developments.

In 2007 Peter became a Member of the Order of Australia for his services to the environment, particularly the protection of wilderness areas in Tasmania; and to horticulture as a presenter of gardening programs on television and radio.

In 2009 Peter was arrested for refusing to move from the steps of the Tasmanian Parliament during a peaceful protest against a pulp mill in the Tamar Valley.

THE RED WITH THE GREEN THUMB

by Helen Randerson

The distinctive northern English accent and friendly round face of Peter Cundall AM are well known to Australians from over forty years of broadcasting on radio and television, particularly as the long-term presenter of the popular ABC TV show *Gardening Australia*. He has been a resident of northern Tasmania around Launceston since the 1950s. Before taking up life in Tasmania, Cundall had been a soldier who had experienced the horrors of both World War II and the Korean War. He had also spent six months in a military prison in Yugoslavia.

There are three volumes of ASIO files on Peter Joseph Cundall held by the National Archives of Australia. Volume 1 (1960–67) contains 114 folios, Volume 2 (1966–69) contains 128 folios and Volume 3 (1969–1976) contains 63 folios – altogether 305 pages.

It's refreshing to see a couple of corny jokes in his file and to be reminded that in the 1960s Tasmania was still known as the 'Apple Isle': Peter's 1967 YMCA newsletter was called *Apple Juice*, and ASIO reproduced a copy in his file, including the jokes. There's even a reference in it to the successful catchline of the 1960s TV commercial for Peck's anchovette paste — *'A little Peck's goes a long way'*. But there's nothing else in Peter Cundall's multi-volume ASIO file to make you feel nostalgic for 1950s and 1960s Cold War Australia.

Why was Cundall's editorship of the YMCA newsletter *Apple Juice* considered subversive in 1967?

Could it have been because it contained an advertisement for a film about the 'rugged south-west of Tasmania' and a discussion on the 'Lake Pedder controversy'? Should we be interpreting Cundall's ASIO file as a prediction by ASIO analysts of the development of a future environmental movement in northern Tasmania, seeded by a man with a green thumb?

One entry reads: 'Cundall is regarded as an expert landscape gardener in the Launceston area.' Another states: 'Cundall occasionally addresses various Launceston clubs on the subject of Landscape Gardening. During these lectures he makes no mention of politics.'

Throughout the 1960s and '70s, ASIO agents recorded Cundall's various gardening and landscaping activities, but what did they think when they recorded that he'd won a Winston Churchill Fellowship in 1973?

Cundall commented later, 'The agents must have died of boredom because they were reporting on just about everything. God knows what it must have cost, but the madness of it was that they never caught any spies … because nobody was ever doing anything wrong.'

Cundall's brief but very up-front participation in the Launceston branch of the Communist Party probably triggered the creation of his ASIO file, and his comments at meetings, together with the predictable stoushes, personality clashes and various disagreements within the party, are recorded in infinite and boring detail. His involvement with cultural and community organisations such as the Australia–China Society, the Northern Council of the Parents and Friends Association, the Launceston Film Society, and his editorship of *Apple Juice* all receive similar detailed attention. Cundall later observed:

'The sad part was that they were people in the local community who were going to the meetings, taking notes and doing the recording for the files. I'm anti-war like every other soldier that's been to war, but that, of course, horrified them ... I even briefly joined the Communist Party in an effort to get the things that I believed in, which is racial equality, education for everyone, an end to poverty, an end to war, all these things, but of course I left when I found out it was getting nowhere. That sent them into a frenzy of excitement.'

ASIO surveillance photo from Peter Cundall's file showing Peter Cundall (left) and Ernest Honey (right) attending the 1964 ALP State Conference in Hobart.

ASIO surveillance and reporting of Cundall's involvement and attendance at Launceston branch meetings of the Australia–China Society extends at least until December 1976, three years after the Australian Government had recognised the People's Republic of China and established an embassy there.

Cundall was interested in all of the political issues of the time and some of those issues are still relevant fifty years later. In the early 1960s, ASIO reported he expressed the view that Cold War relations (including trade) between Australia and Russia and China should be improved, as it would be better for Tasmanian primary industry and world peace.

ASIO extensively documented his areas of interest, including: Tasmanian primary industry, poverty in parts of Launceston, the need for more parks, improvement of working conditions, support for funding of state schools, the situation of the Cape Barren Island Aboriginal people, ending the Vietnam conflict, the need for links with and recognition of China, the need for more Asian languages in Australian schools, concern with Australian involvement in the Omega navigation system (the Stop Omega campaign), concern with Soviet testing of nuclear missiles, wariness about U2 planes flying over Tasmania, support for the 1967 referendum to approve rights for Indigenous Australians, and concerns about apartheid in South Africa.

In 1963, correspondence between Cundall and famous South African anti-apartheid activist Helen Joseph was somehow intercepted by ASIO. This report reads:

> Attached hereto is a lumoprint copy of a letter written by Helen JOSEPH of 35 Fanny Avenue, Norwood, Johannesburg, dated 30th May 1963, and addressed Dear Mr & Mrs Cundall ... together with various attachments

as under:

(a) Pamphlet headed 'Mrs Helen JOSEPH'
(b) Letter to Mr & Mrs Cundall from Helen Joseph
(c) Pamphlet headed Helen Joseph
(d) Pamphlet headed 'A Visit to the Living Dead'
(e) Pamphlet headed 'An Appeal by Albert LUTHULI'
(f) Pamphlet headed 'Apartheid in Action'

According to ASIO, Cundall always assumed there would be 'security snoopers' reporting on political activities critical of government policy. ASIO reported him saying, 'Don't worry, ASIO always have plants on all tours and in all groups.'

Possibly the extent of the surveillance over such a long period and the detail provided is the biggest surprise in the files. Some entries appear fairly straightforward, such as this 1961 description of Cundall:

> Age 34, b 1/4/1927, Height 5'10", Hair Dark, slightly wavy, Build Medium/Heavy, Eyebrows dark, Other Distinguishing Peculiarities Round face, square jaw, clean-shaven. Usually dressed in neat, dark suit – no hat, Speaks with strong Northern English accent.

The funniest entry that jumps out at you from the file is from 1973. Here is a man who is regarded as subversive enough to have been followed by ASIO over the previous twelve years, and who wins a Winston Churchill Fellowship (for further study of developments in landscaping) while still being under security surveillance. A newspaper clipping in the ASIO file reports that after learning he'd won the Fellowship, Peter immediately went out to weed his own garden, which is delightfully Voltaire.

When Cundall was asked to comment about his ASIO file for this book, he said:

'As for the South African connection – especially with Helen Joseph – it may be of interest that my Churchill Fellowship actually took me there in 1974 – into the awful horror of the apartheid system. That's when I became aware of sinister links between ASIO and the South African security people and the way they were exchanging information about each other's citizens. I didn't want to go to the place – but the Churchill selection committee actually insisted that I include a visit and even added an extra three weeks to my study tour so that I could do so. Obviously someone on the committee hoped I'd come back raving with enthusiasm about the place.

'I was given a sealed letter by this committee member (who happened to be a strong supporter of the regime) to be handed over to a leading South African government official. Naturally I carefully steamed it open. All it contained was a request that "Peter Cundall be given full support in his Fellowship studies etc. etc." However, when I arrived in South Africa I was immediately separated from all other airline passengers by plain-clothes security people who opened my luggage for no other reason than to carefully read every document I possessed, especially my travel diary notes.

'However, it turned out that the official to whom the letter was addressed also happened to be a leading figure in the South African security system. When I turned up at his (heavily-concealed and guarded) office, I couldn't help but notice a thick file sitting on his desk with my name printed clearly on the front. Despite this – or perhaps because of it – they provided an escort and driver to take me wherever I went. But they still searched my hotel room regularly.

'I had a camera with a powerful telescopic lens. On one occasion I was talking to a group of Africans (about politics, of course) when I noticed something briefly glittering on a roof a few hundred metres away. So I clipped the lens on to my camera (which can operate like a powerful telescope) and quickly pointed it at the roof. And there were two men, one with field glasses watching me. So I stuck up my arm and waved. And the bloke with the glasses waved back! Perhaps he too had a sense of humour …'

Other humour in his ASIO file is provided by Cundall's observations on the quality of the Soviet and Chinese communist literature of the 1960s. ASIO records that Peter regarded the Russian and Chinese propaganda material as fit for the rubbish tip (1967). Soviet literature he considered 'dull and second rate' and Chinese literature evinced the response 'I'm sick of the stuff – it's just too corny'. Unfortunately, none of this propaganda material has been reproduced in the file, perhaps because it had already been composted in Cundall's garden.

The most straightforward humour in the file is a Cundall joke from *Apple Juice*:

> Q. Did you hear the one about the man who crossed the homing pigeon with a woodpecker?
> A. He produced a bird which knocks before delivering the message.

There are a number of comments attributed to a 'friend' of Peter's wife (who was obviously unaware that she was speaking to an informant), which are just normal friendly conversations and comments about Peter's car and his landscape gardening activities. This type of reporting is particularly scary.

The different descriptions or quasi-psychological character assessments of Cundall made by the agents are of similar concern. It seems that some of the ASIO agents liked him and some were cynical and suspicious of him. Nonetheless, it all went into the files to be recorded forever in the National Archives. One such description reads:

> Up until a short time ago, Cundall used to attempt to put over 'the working man's' image, however he has recently changed and is now on the committee of the Children's Film Society, he had his name in the social pages of the papers recently attending a 'first night' film and has become quite a society man.

Another agent's colloquial comment in relation to Peter's interest in an Adult Education Board seminar on China and South-East Asia demonstrates that this ASIO agent found Peter a rather interesting character. He reports, 'All small beer except Peter Cundall ...'

Cundall is reported as arguing for more democracy and honesty in the CPA and as feeling 'removed from the Chinese–Soviet disagreements'. ASIO documents that he got himself into trouble within the party when he publicly condemned the resumption of nuclear testing by the USSR and called for demonstrations against it.

In September 1960, ASIO recorded that in response to their request to some unnamed overseas security agency for a check on him, there was 'no trace of Cundall in their records'.

Throughout these files, Cundall comes across as an independent spirit, someone vocal who can't quite be pigeonholed, or made to conform. Perhaps this is the real reason ASIO followed him for so long. An independent spirit is what all organisations fear as a potential threat. ASIO notes an article written by Cundall in May 1967 where he is very outspoken about the leadership of the Communist Party in Tasmania and which he concluded with the sentence, 'STALIN is dead – but let's face it – his ghost still walks.' Anyone reading his ASIO file would probably agree.

However, the major lesson to be learnt from reading Cundall's file was that if you're a law abiding citizen who values privacy and the freedom to express yourself freely, the freedom to be critical of government policy, the freedom to attend a 'first night' film without surveillance, and even the freedom to *think* subversive thoughts now and again, then the very worst thing you can do is join a small organisation in a small northern city in the smallest state in Australia.

Also, it is quite disappointing that in spite of all the detail, there is a complete lack of any good gardening tips. We're left wondering if ASIO tuned in to watch *Gardening Australia* to keep tabs on Peter Cundall long after the Cold War ended.

Perhaps Cundall himself should have the final word about his surveillance:

'Actually I almost felt sorry for the ASIO people who – fifty years ago – were obliged to keep an eye on me (poor buggers are probably still trudging around gardens following my footsteps), and report my boring activities. A couple of years ago I had to go to Canberra to speak on the subject of this infantile surveillance to a large audience – and expressed my pity. I also said – rather jokingly – that there were a couple of ASIO blokes present, somewhere at the back, furiously taking notes. As the forum closed I was astonished to be approached by a couple of shifty-eyed blokes who sheepishly admitted they were from ASIO and were there to find out what I had to say about their organisation. In fact one of them even ventured a kind of embarrassed apology for previous, time-wasting snooping – "Long before our time," he said. "We have different policies and targets now."

'Seemed like a nice bloke really.'

MEREDITH BURGMANN

Meredith Burgmann was born in Beecroft, but in the mid-sixties escaped to inner-city Glebe and to Sydney University. Although coming from a humanitarian Christian background, it was student activity against the Vietnam War that completed her radicalisation. Anti-Vietnam War involvement was soon followed by anti-apartheid action, particularly against the 1971 Springbok tour. She was a founder and co-convenor of the 'Stop the Tours' campaign. Then followed Aboriginal rights, green ban actions, 'women's lib', prison reform and gay rights (she marched in the first Gay Mardi Gras in 1978). She was arrested many times but was only found guilty on ten occasions.

Meredith was an academic at Macquarie University for eighteen years and wrote her PhD on the Builders Labourers' Federation and the green bans. She became active in her union and was elected as the first woman President of the New South Wales branch of what is now the National Tertiary education Union (NTEU). In 1991 she became a Labor member of the New South Wales Legislative Council and was elected President in 1999, a position she retained until her retirement in 2007.

In her spare time Meredith was active in the women's movement and was a founder of the National Pay Equity Coalition in 1988 and the originator of the long-running Ernie Awards for Sexist Remarks in 1993. She has continued her solidarity activity and is particularly involved with the democracy struggles or independence movements in Zimbabwe, South Africa, Timor Leste, Myanmar, Iran, West Papua and Western Sahara.

Since leaving Parliament, Meredith has done work for the United Nations Development Program and until recently was the President of the Australian Council for International Development. Meredith has co-authored two books, *Green Bans, Red Union* and *The Ermies Book: 1000 Terrible Things Australian Men Have Said About Women*.

She is a cricket tragic but her proudest boast is that she is an ambassador for and foundation member of the Sydney Swans.

THE SECRET LIFE OF B/77/26 (AND FRIENDS)

by Meredith Burgmann

When I received my ASIO file in 2005, I was intrigued and quite excited, but reading it was confronting as I realised that I had probably destroyed the career of one friend and seriously compromised the working life of a mere acquaintance.

It had been a remarkably easy task, ordering my ASIO file. The most peculiar aspect was that when I asked the man on the phone, 'Who should I make the cheque out to?' he said, 'Oh just make it out to ASIO.' The idea of making a cheque out to ASIO still thrills me. (Unfortunately in later years this practice has changed, so that payment now is made to the more prosaic-sounding National Archives.)

When the huge box of papers (342 pages) and photos arrived on my desk, it was an extraordinary experience – my life of forty years ago suddenly laid out before me. I felt like Faust seeing his youth in the bowl of time. All the conspiracy theories, all the stories we had told each other, turned out to be true. Our phones really *were* tapped. There really *was* an ASIO cameraman on the third floor of Woolworths overlooking the Sydney Town Hall steps during the Vietnam demonstrations. There it was, the perfect picture of me as a fresh-faced student standing on the Town Hall steps speaking at the September 1970 moratorium, the angle just right for the third-floor shot.

There were photos of friends I hardly remembered, photos of people whose faces were familiar but whose names now escape me. There was a chilling picture of my housemate, Helen Randerson, and me walking through an unidentified door. Whose place was it that was being photographed in this mysterious way?

While the photographs were nostalgic and evocative, my actual file was extremely disturbing.

My ASIO file turned out to be very different to my NSW Police Special Branch file, which I had applied for in 1997 when the Carr Government abolished the increasingly incompetent state Special Branch and released the files to a delighted bunch of ageing chardonnay socialists.

My Special Branch file had been a detailed account of my political activity from 1968 to 1994, cataloguing in minute and boring detail where I was from morning to night, even on one occasion noting that my car was outside 26 Darghan Street, Glebe at 5.45 in the morning. The fact that I lived there and it was bleeding obvious that my car would be parked outside, I found quite funny. These details of my life I did not find disturbing, more amusing and informative. As I joked, I didn't need to keep a diary, I always had the Special Branch to keep a record of my life.

But my ASIO file is very different. There's obviously some division of labour between the two spy branches. The Special Branch follows, photographs and records everything they see and hear, whereas ASIO pokes, pries and interferes.

ASIO's tentacles appear much longer than those of the NSW Special Branch, and one extraordinary episode in my file occurs when I go overseas at the end of 1968. I had only come to ASIO's attention six months earlier, so I presume I was not high on their list of radical troublemakers.

I met up with my boyfriend and two other friends in London and together we planned to travel through Wales to Ireland. It is at this stage that we seem to have attracted attention, and there in my file is a request from a British agency (presumably MI5) wanting further information on our records. I remember our car being stopped in Wales and my boyfriend being questioned as we approached the ferry, but until now had never put two and two together.

A heavily blacked-out letter from Director-General Spry himself requests further details of my boyfriend, a totally apolitical New Zealand veterinarian, and more extraordinarily, asks for fingerprint checks on our two travelling companions, even though one was a sixteen-year-old boy!

Colonel Spry's letter to MI5 actually alerts them to my suspicious activities, such as protesting against the Russian invasion of Czechoslovakia. Presumably they believed we were headed for Ireland in order to liberate the Fenians from British oppression. One of these extraordinary 'agent' cables is sent to 'Scorpion' in Melbourne, a code name straight out of *The Bourne Conspiracy*. Another refers to Operation 'Whip', which I have recently discovered refers to anti-Vietnam activity. These cables were also stamped 'ENCRYPTED' in huge capitals.

However, much more disturbing is the story of my friend in the Navy. In 1969, at a meeting in the MacCallum Room at Sydney University, a spy in our midst had obviously sat beside me and had noted down a number of names that were in my diary. One of the names and phone numbers so obtained was that of Petty Officer Peter Andrews (name changed to protect the extremely innocent). He was in my address book as an old family friend and presumably had no radical political leanings and may well have been a conservative. However, ASIO went to town. There are pages and pages of discussion about my poor Naval friend.

The main problem for both ASIO and the Navy seems to have been that Peter was employed in the cryptography section of *HMAS Kuttabul*:

> Lieutenant Commander Evans also advised that Andrews had been cleared to the intermediate level on 22/1/62 and also for crypto access. Lieutenant Commander Evans has simply been asked to play this rather 'close' but has not been told the reason for the enquiry.

Later there is a postscript:

> Understand that you will be reporting the incident to Headquarters. Would you please include a suggestion that the implications be considered by C Branch in relation to this case of PO Andrews.

Imagine what these enquiries from Australia's intelligence organisation had on Peter's future career in the Defence Forces. Poor Peter, he was just an ordinary guy in the Navy who was really good at cryptography and may never have been trusted again – at this stage of intelligence paranoia, if you had friends who thought the war in Vietnam was wrong, you probably *were* sending encrypted messages to enemy agents.

To this day, I have never told Peter what I think might have happened to his career. I feel like a coward but I can't bring myself to talk to him about it.

Another name in my book which received a lot of attention from the ASIO agents was that of Ralph Goldstein, whom I hardly knew. I was Secretary of the Sydney University Dramatic Society (SUDS) and I think he was the President, so I would have been in contact with him about SUDS stuff. ASIO was very excited by the fact that he was in my book, because he had some sort of Commonwealth public service job for which he'd had to have a security clearance. There are over twenty pages in my file relating to his background and his security checks and many tiny details of his life that I probably do not wish to know. This was a surprising aspect of my ASIO file — I almost had more access into the lives of my friends than ASIO had to me. I felt quite grubby. I was obviously fair game, but ASIO delved into the lives of my innocent friends and probably had effects on their lives in ways they will never know.

Later the peek that the ASIO agent had had of my notebook was compounded when I was arrested in Canberra on my way to give evidence at a friend's court case. Because I thought that I was simply giving evidence in court proceedings I had my handbag with me. At a normal demonstration or political event I would never have carried anything at all revealing. However, because I was arrested in my good court outfit and in fact flown down to Sydney and incarcerated in what was then Silverwater Gaol, they got access to my address book and had plenty of time to note its contents. This report is fascinating because it not only lists everyone in my address book of May 1970, but it also indicates who had ASIO files at the time.

Handwritten ASIO file numbers appear against almost every name in the book including Michael Kirby, David Kirby, Jim Spigelman, Peter Mason, Bob Connell, Aidan Foy, Paul Brennan, Dennis Harley, Rodney Henderson, Bruce Miles, Murray Sime, Peter Simpson, Nadia Wheatley and even my father, who was the Chairman of CSIRO. However, Geoffrey Robertson and Alan Cameron did not (at least at that stage) have numbers.

The world of the ASIO agent is quite remarkable. There seem to be two sorts, semi-amateurs who supply information from inside meetings and rallies, and professional officers whose reports are quite different, almost public service-like. One report from a 1971 anti-apartheid meeting in the MacCallum Room at Sydney University is unintentionally hilarious. The po-faced agent reports that, 'Peter McGregor said that we had been warned from South Africa about the possible presence of police spies.' It was decided that 'any suspicious person will be asked to leave. Anyone who is dressed in a suit and tie will be suspect.'

Their reports vary from detailed in the extreme, to slightly careless and inaccurate. Surprisingly enough there is no analysis of any pattern of activity, or of the differing political beliefs amongst the demonstrating fraternity. For instance I am continually reported (inaccurately) as having applied for membership of the Young Socialist League, which was a Communist Party youth organisation, and yet they recorded me at the same time appearing at a May Day rally holding a banner headed 'Anarchists and Miscellaneous'.

The mundanity of their reporting is also quite extraordinary. They followed me from meeting to meeting and from rally to rally. They had spies reporting on my activity in protests about nuclear tests in French Polynesia; against the South African Economic Affairs Minister (I remember that one – his name was Jan Haak and we had a ready-made cry as we roamed through the streets of Sydney calling 'Faak Haak'); protests involving Bougainville, the South African Tourist Bureau, the visit of US Vice President Spiro Agnew, women's lib, the *Police Offences Act*, Rhodesia, a Teachers Federation strike, the Gurindji, the Mataungans, a strike of metalworkers at Commonwealth Engineering, Black Power, land rights, Free Angela Davis, Newcastle Women's Day, the Greek Junta, the rent strike at Woodenbong, the Jack Mundey Defence Campaign, Recognise Guinea Bissau, Free Kevin Gilbert, Prisoners Action Group, Women's Abortion Action, and meetings of the Builders Labourers' about the green bans. I was obviously pretty busy. But so were they!

No issue was too trivial or parochial for ASIO. There are also detailed reports about my opposition to corruption on Leichhardt Council and the famous 1969 Glebe Old Men's Home Affair where some of the old right-wing Labor councillors were accused of stealing washing machines from the old men's home. There were agents inside Leichhardt Town Hall reporting on council meetings on at least three occasions. They describe in great detail my arrest for calling the Mayor a 'silly old twit'. I'm glad their crack agents were on the case.

Some of these issues I can hardly remember, but most of the protests were peaceful, if not totally laid back. One demonstration in support of gaoled anti-conscription activist Geoff Mullen is described as 'protesters singing folk songs and distributing anti-conscription leaflets to passers-by'.

ASIO agents continually noted down vehicle number plates and then did a check on the registered owners of these vehicles, which of course led to a bunch of North Shore housewives being considered highly dangerous urban terrorists because of the activities of their privileged young.

The agents' descriptions are surprisingly non-judgmental. They have obviously been trained only to describe and not to analyse. They rarely attempt to describe our philosophy, only our appearance. It is in describing our appearance, though, that their distaste for us is shown. I am described variously as 'thin and untidy' and 'smokes heavily'. Later an agent remarks disdainfully that my hair is 'obviously dyed'. These comments about appearance mesh with recent revelations that Paddy McGuinness's file contained numerous references to his unkempt appearance and personal hygiene. At one stage my eyes are noted as 'blue' and this is later corrected to 'green'. Which agent got close enough to make this important discovery? Probably the one who peeked into my address book.

However, a fellow meeting attendee, 'Bob', gets much crueller attention. He has 'eyes which are beady looking and close together … and has buck teeth. He dresses in a way out of fashion and speaks with a high pitched nasal voice.'

The one time that comment about our political direction takes place is when an agent lets fly at my provocative Aboriginal activist friend, Gary Foley. The agent, who is sitting in a meeting with us, reports, 'Gary is a pest and appears to be a member of the Black Power movement.'

Another agent who had sat through an obviously long and dreary meeting of the Socialist Workers League reported:

> Bob Pringle talked of the current dispute in the Builders Labourers Federation and said that Norm Gallagher (Victorian personality) had told lies concerning alleged

malpractices in the New South Wales Branch. Agent comment: The talk was very boring and nothing was raised that hasn't already been printed in the papers.

The description of me as untidy reminded me of a funny section in my Special Branch report. My share-house in Darghan Street, Glebe, which was operating as the headquarters of the Stop the Springboks campaign, had been broken into and when the police arrived, one Detective Gartrell had noted that, 'the premises in question were untidy and littered with boxes of protest buttons, literature and posters'. This obsession with tidiness probably indicates a vast chasm between the neat suited men of ASIO and the time-poor, politically obsessed students of the seventies.

There are other interesting insights into ASIO practices. For instance, they used the excellent press cutting service of the *Sydney Morning Herald* to supplement their own activities. They have an almost chatty style in their presentation of reports, most reports concluding with, 'Perhaps this can now be filed and referenced.' They also obviously had a spy inside Communist Party headquarters, because one extraordinary entry is headed 'Two Canberra identities who subscribe to ALR' (*Australian Left Review*, a communist publication) and then the informant describes my handwritten letter asking to renew my subscription. I could well have been expelled from the Labor Party for this action but it certainly wasn't illegal.

We do know that ASIO tried to recruit people to spy on the student movement at the time. A friend of mine, Kerry Watson, who was involved with Students for a Democratic Society, had a father who was an executive in the Bank of New South Wales. He was approached by ASIO and asked whether he would talk to his daughter about being an ASIO informant. He of course said that ASIO would need to talk to her directly, but if they did, her likely reaction would be to notify *Honi Soit*. Nothing more was heard from that approach.

There is also much evidence that ASIO were willing agents of their political masters rather than an apolitical intelligence-gathering organisation. For instance, on 29 May 1970 the Director-General of ASIO sends the Secretary of the Prime Minister's Department a report on my interjections at an Australia–Rhodesia Association meeting addressed by a Liberal Party member of parliament, EJ McLeay. This right-wing white supremacist organisation was an international pariah and the meeting had been the subject of Labor Party questions in the House, yet the Director-General's report paints us as the villains in the case.

I could make serious points about the totally ineffective nature of ASIO's interventions but others have already done this. They needlessly blighted some careers with their endless inquiries yet they remained incapable of protecting their own interests. For instance, during the anti-Springbok campaign, a red wig and a false South African accent gained me entrance to the Sydney Cricket Ground at a time when known demonstrators were being excluded. This weak disguise allowed us to dash across the pitch and resulted in the only game stoppage in Sydney.

Another interesting issue was the way that some of the secret police, particularly those in the Special Branch, seemed to become quite close to those they were following. In particular, the head of the NSW Special Branch, Sergeant Longbottom (later Chief Inspector) was well known to the students and had an easy familiarity with them.

ASIO surveillance photo from Meredith Burgmann's file, showing the Third Moratorium, June 1971, Sydney Town Hall steps, taken from the third floor of (then) Woolworths. Meredith Burgmann at microphone (numbered 1 with arrow). Left to right behind are Laurie Carmichael (far left, in suit and tie), Jim Percy (with beard and long hair), Professor Peter Mason (in suit and tie), Professor Tony Blackshield (bald with goatee), Ralph Pearce (in jumper and sunglasses), Tom Uren (tall, side on) and John Ducker (in horn-rimmed glasses, side on).

One incident demonstrates this. In 1975 I attended a protest against the pro-apartheid golfer Gary Player. I had called out 'Go home racist' as he was making a putt and had been leapt upon by three angry golf fans. Sergeant Longbottom appeared from nowhere, as did my fellow demonstrator Robert Tickner, who saved me from these angry and agitated men.

ASIO surveillance photo from Meredith Burgmann's file, showing May Day, Sydney, 1972. Left to right are Graeme Watson (ASIO number 1), Ralph Pearce (number 3), Diana Talty (number 4), Peter O'Reilly (number 5, behind Di Talty), John Berwick (number 6, partly obscured behind flag), Debesh Bhattacharya (number 7), Meredith Burgmann (number 8) and Verity Burgmann (number 9).

Longbottom then escorted Robert and me away from the fracas. Two uniformed police arrived and dragged us off, arresting us both. In court, the uniformed men claimed that Longbottom was not at the demonstration. We produced a *Sydney Morning Herald* photograph of Longbottom, resplendent in a polkadot short-sleeved shirt, escorting us away with Robert and me draped over either arm, as if we were off to the Policemen's Ball.

That was the last I saw of the photograph. Longbottom was called into court and did eventually admit that he was there on his day off and he had come to my aid to stop me being injured by the spectators. I lost the case, of course, and never saw the photograph again until twenty years later, academic Andrew Moore was interviewing Longbottom for a piece on his work as a police officer and Longbottom delved into a chest full of memorabilia and produced the photograph. The copper had nicked 'Exhibit A'.

When I was talking about this incident with Anna Funder, author of *Stasiland*, the excellent book about the East German secret police, I said that Longbottom had reported to Andrew that he felt he was helping me. She observed that many Stasi agents said exactly that; that they were actually helping those that they were in fact surveilling.

I often wonder what they were thinking as they sat through our endless meetings and listened intently to our speeches at demonstrations. Did they read our literature? In my file there is an article by the London *Times* correspondent in Australia, Stewart Harris, about how he became converted from being an onlooker during the anti-Springbok campaign to a devout believer in the anti-apartheid cause. It was a delightful piece by an intelligent man about the horrors of racist sport and a tyrannical regime, and how a conservative with ethical values could change his position. Did the agents read this material? Did they ever doubt their own position?

On another occasion the agent describes anti-apartheid South African Bishop Crowther as 'a very forceful speaker'. What if the agent was a Christian? Might he have been troubled by Crowther's words?

In the early seventies anti-racism campaigners were continually harassed and occasionally assaulted by Australia's own Nazi Party led by Ross (the Skull) May. Of our many clashes with the Nazis, the agents take no side. They report our presence at demonstrations without identifying who were anti-racism demonstrators and who were Nazis. I read in my file a list of those present at a particular demonstration and realised I didn't recognise some names. Only later did I realise that these unfamiliar names belonged to demonstrators who were there dressed in their Nazi uniforms as agitators against us. The agent's report made no distinction.

In fact the agents obviously had the Nazis under surveillance too, and on one occasion, late at night in March 1971, they watched as the Nazis threw a brick through my window, daubed swastikas on my front fence and wrote 'Red Rat' on the footpath outside the house (which we later changed to Fred Rat because it sounded nicer). Yet they did not intervene to stop these activities.

Another one of the stories we always told ourselves was that our phones were being tapped. This does not seem to have been completely true for us young student radicals, although my file contains many intercepted phone conversations when I rang other places that *were* tapped. As we all suspected, Communist Party headquarters was subject to interception, as was the Third World Bookshop and, more surprisingly, the Association for International Co-operation and Disarmament (AICD), a reasonably mainstream left-wing organisation which helped coordinate the moratoriums.

My phone conversations with my fellow convenor of the 'Stop the Tours' campaign, Denis Freney, who worked out of Communist Party headquarters, are well documented. It's a bit creepy to have your conversations of forty years ago come back to haunt you. However what I found even weirder were the intercepted conversations between others when they were talking about me. You suddenly realise that the opinions of others are noted down in your file as if they are fact. Thank goodness Denis Freney always thought 'Meredith is reliable'.

We also believed that the listening agents could hear what was going on in the room through the telephone. This was an urban myth at the time, but we believed it implicitly. Whenever we had meetings in our sitting room, which happened every second night, we would pile cushions and telephone books on top of the telephone to try to muffle our important organisational secrets.

Another aspect of our files is that the blacking-out process which is meant to conceal the identity of informers has been neither effective nor consistent. For instance, on 9 October 1975 my dossier reports that: 'Meredith Anne Burgmann and Russell Herman and Caroline Vernon Weate were seen at 9.30pm on 3/10/75 entering the Bottle Dept. of the Burdekin Hotel, Oxford St, City.' This entry is frighteningly banal, but when I discussed this with Russ Herman he reported that the copy of this entry in his file had my name and Caroline Weate's blacked out. Presumably I was allowed to know who was with me, but Russ wasn't.

The process of protecting the identity of informants by suitable 'blacking out' was also not efficient, as on reading my Special Branch file it soon became obvious that there was informant activity happening inside a very small organisation I was involved with in the mid-seventies called the Southern Africa Liberation Centre (SALC). It becomes quite clear from these reports who the informant was and when I voiced my suspicions to others who had been involved with SALC, they all agreed with my analysis. Strangely I did not feel outraged by this betrayal as I had never liked the man to start with. As the person involved was still involved with radical politics, we decided that those around him should be told that he did have a past history of informing for ASIO.

On the whole, the blacking out process seems totally arbitrary and for the reader terribly frustrating, like reading a detective novel with the last page torn out.

My ASIO file only covers the period 1968–1975 because of the then 'thirty-year rule'. However, my Special Branch file covers the period of 1968–1997, when Special Branch was closed down. It is salutary to realise that the last entry in my Special Branch file was 1994. These secret operatives were still following me and reporting on my activities after I had been a member of parliament for three years.

My 'clandestine' activities recorded while a member of parliament included being involved in the launching of the *Broadside Weekly* in 1992, which took place in the Parliament House press conference room. Which of the bored journalists or underpaid cameramen filed an informer's report? Later in 1992 I was recorded as participating in a protest rally against killings in the Ciskei in South Africa, and the final report was in February 1994 about my attendance at a meeting held between the Consul General of Mexico and Amnesty International to protest against human rights abuses in Mexico. What utterly mundane and appropriate parliamentary activity!

There is a huge irony in this 'parliamentary spy' situation. As President of the New South Wales Legislative Council, one of my departmental responsibilities was the security of Parliament House. One day in 2005 shortly after I had received my

ASIO photos, I had twenty or thirty of them scattered over my desk. In walked two officers who introduced themselves as 'from ASIO' to talk about a difficult security issue. Taken by surprise I offered them the chance to look at my photos. With great embarrassment, they declined.

During all my time as a political activist I have never advocated violence or subversion. I believed in and practised 'direct action' tactics when appropriate. I may well have been a threat to public order but never a threat to life or limb and certainly never a threat to the state. My friends and I should never have been under surveillance.

ACKNOWLEDGMENTS

I would like to thank all the contributors who strip-mined their lives and revealed themselves to the reader with remarkable honesty and humour. They have been generous in their self-reflection about their early beliefs. I especially thank Michael Kirby for coming up with the title *Dirty Secrets*. We hope that the irony is appreciated.

I thank Linda Funnell, Uthpala Gunethilake and the NewSouth publishing team, especially Phillipa McGuinness, who uged me to undertake the project in the first place. I am also grateful to Haydn Keenan and David McKnight, who shared their specialist knowledge with me, and to the National Archives of Australia.

I also thank my family and friends, especially Helen Randerson, Heather Goodall, Nadia Wheatley and Beverley Firth for helping me complete the project, and the Duchess and the rest of the Primates who did their best to stop me finishing by providing me with other distractions.

INDEX

Note: page numbers in italics refer to photographs or captions.

Aarons, Laurie
ASIO file on 27, 208, 273, 274
and the Communist Party 54, 154, 229, 231, 273, 275, 277; and Frank Hardy 223, 226
Aarons, Mark 271-2
ASIO file on 14, 271, 273; as broadcaster with ABC 286, 287-9; as member of CPA 274, 276-81, *282*, 283-5, 289-90
books, 271, 272, 289; *Family File* 154, 271, 371
interests/causes 286-9
political activism 271; CPA 273-4, 275, 282, 285
Aarons family 273, 275; and ASIO 274, 279
ABC (Australian Broadcasting Commission/Corporation) 272
and ASIO 191, 223, 226; informants for 381-2

see also media
Aboriginal Australians
Council for Aboriginal Affairs (government body) 103, 105
education 296-7
government policies 97, 296-7
and land rights 224, 231, 249, 258, 259, 293, 295-6, 333
and racism 366, 367
see also ASIO
Aboriginal Tent Embassy 91, 94, 99-100, 102, 104, 106, 301
dismantled by government 365
ACT (Australian Capital Territory)
police Special Branch 203, 206, 345, 400
Adams, Phillip 14, 171-2, *179*
and ASIO 173, 174
ASIO file on 175-80
political allegiances 172, 173, 176, 178
Altman, Dennis 14, 147-8, *152*
ASIO file of 149, 156; anti-Vietnam war

activity 150, 154-5; gay liberation 150, 153-4
books of 147-8, 151; *Homosexual* 147, 151, 153
travel 150, 156; study overseas 155, 156
Ananda Marga 400-1
and Hilton Hotel bombing 268, 393, 397, 399, 401; and informers 268, 399-401, 404-5
Anastassiou, Jim 325-6
Anderson, Tim 391-2
ASIO file on 18, 393; errors 395-6
books 391; *Take Two* 391-2, 394
court cases and imprisonment 393, 394, 402; and Hilton Hotel bombing 396, 399; Special Inquiry 393-4, 399, 402-3
as member of Ananda Marga 268, 393
police Special Branch file on 393, 397, 402
anti-racism movements/

457

activists 202, *230*, 276, 285, 332, 333, 366, 452, 452
anti-apartheid activism 204-6, 258, 333, 334, 341, 430, 447, 448
anti-Semitism 150
see also ASIO
anti-Vietnam war protests 33, 276
see also ASIO
Armstrong, Mick *348*, 361
ASIO (Australian Security Intelligence Organisation)
employees of 13, 341, 418-19; behaviour of 19, 22, 409, 414; and competence 18, 19, 20, 35, 107-8, 116, 132, 173, 178, 187, 299; as public servants 26
ethos and political stance 24, 25, 26, 67, 96, 105, 142, 145, 151, 163, 170, 233, 263, 274, 323, 325, 328, 373, 410, 415-16, 417-18, 422, 448, 451
files of: acronyms and terms used 44-5, 403; content 165-6, 422, 444, 453, 454; errors in 18, 40, 85, 117, 140, 166, 184, 185, 189, 240, 262-3, 308, 312, 356, 372, 386, 390, 394, 395-6, 420-1, 444; as internal working documents 25; management of 34, 35-6, 67; number of 38, 319; and preservation 15; release of 20, 22, 37-9, 40, 84, 108-9, 164-5, 251, 316, 394
formation and early years 20, 22-3, 29, 132, 275, 276
methods: accumulation of detail 18-19, 22, 27, 30, 83, 105, 157, 165, 267, 324, 445-6; agents/informants 17, 32, 79, 82-3, 84, 94, 105, 108, 117-18, 125, 139, 143, 150, 164, 168, 175, 180, 184, 185, 189-90, 220, 229, 234, 239, 245, 251, 253, 258, 262, 287, 294-5, 315, 347, 349-50, 371, 381, 388, 403-4, 412-13, 433, 444, 447, 453-4; break-ins 134, 136, 164, 261; harassment 17; illegal and extra-legal activities 30; opening mail 189, 192; operations 41-2, 151, 164, 165, 261, 441; personality profiles 124-5; surveillance 13, 16, 22, 28, 40, 42, 64, 73, 79, 94, 100, 104, 106, *120*, 134, 137, *141*, 143, 162, 165, 166, 177, 179, 184, 190, *230*, 265, 267, 268-9, *282*, 307, 323, 325, 334, *348*, 350, *379*, 403, 417-18, 431, 435-6, 444-5, (observe criminal acts), 452; telephone intercepts 19, 22, 30-1, 79, 109, 118, 123, 185, 192, 193, 207, 208, 211, 222, 223, 226, 227, 231, 260, 262, 263, 277, 278, 280-1, 282-3, 288, 294, 301, 312-13, 369, 378, 412, 439, 452-3, (and mobile phones), 267; use of press cutting service 447
persons of interest 12, 13, 14-15, 20, 25, 27, 31, 77, 80, 98, 107, 133-4, 137, 142, 165, 167, 215, 278, 287, 306, 370, 389, 409, 411, 423, 431, 444-5; and children 16, 17, 56;
unwelcome discoveries 16
resources and powers 12, 20, 164, 373, 404
after royal commissions 35, 36, 275
structure of 27-30, 33, 83, 164, 168, 266, 273
as target of protests 267-8
targets' views on 14-15, 20, 22, 88, 118, 132, 146, 154, 156, 157, 170, 263, 341, 370, 394, 455; anger 75, 118, 369; effect on friends/family 14, 15-16, 18, 118, 181, 232, 240, 276, 277-80, 283, 418, 439, 441-3; incompetence, 82, 85, 105, 111, 394, 395; personal comments 79, 81, 189, 196, 239, 265-6, 295, 420, 446; waste of resources 116, 145, 185, 194, 309, 346, 349, 389, 417, 428, 445; wrecking careers 274, 448
tasks of: counter espionage 28, 29, 87-8, 275, 276, 285, 320, 417, 418; keeping tabs on 'subversion' 18, 20, 24, 26, 28, 29-30, 84, 99, 104, 168, 275-6, 289, 320, 413, 428, 431; monitoring politically motivated violence 20; preparing briefings for government 40-1; security checks (vetting) 29, 62, 71-2, 86-7, 278, 415-17, 421
and terrorism 289, 422
and threats to 'national security' 20, 260, 278, 281, 281, 284, 289, 309, 319, 327-8
used for party political objectives 19-20, 41,

458   DIRTY SECRETS

198, 276, 316
  see also intelligence services in Australia; legislation
ASIO: target groups and movements
  Aboriginal political and rights groups 12, 14, 20, 93, 94, 96-7, 98-101, 102-7, 109, 202, *230*, 231, 297, 298-9
  anti-apartheid movement in Australia 15, 19, 107, 151, 155, 202, 350, 451, 452, 453-4
  anti-Vietnam war (and conscription) movement 12, 20, 24, 42, 71-2, *73*, 74-5, 76, 107, 150, 151, 154-5, 161, 162, 164, 177, 182, 184, *188*, *190*, 191-2, 195, 198, 201, *205*, 208-11, 260, 276, 439-40, 441, 449
  civil liberties groups/ supporters 64, 67, 68, 265, 268, 321-2
  communism 23, 28, 82, 96-7, 106, 126-7, 154, 288-9, 320, 418; Eastern European embassies/consulates 118, 119-20, 324
  Communist Party of Australia (CPA) 13, 14, 16, 23-4, 26, 27, 30-1, 33, 40, 79, 97, 104, 169, 183, 189, 193-4, 196, 218, 224, 226, 227, 231, 234, 240, 254, 259, 262, 263, 269, 274, 276-87, 323, 324, 367-8, 378-9, 384, 388, 421, 428, 447, 447; change in 163; and disaffected members 42; and (alleged) influence of 24, 25, 28-9, 40, 67, 75, 94-6, 97, 98-9, 102, 110, 154-5, 161-2, 163, 176, 183-4, 191, 327

gay rights activists 14, 20, 244, 245-7, 265, 360
Labor MPs 16, 19, 154, 192, 265, 267, 320-8, 422
left-wing groups 17, 40, 76, 84, 163, 177, 251-2, 253, 255, 257-8, 263, 267, 294-5, 296, 334, 417, 422, 452; the New Left 23, 163, 252, 253; Trotskyists (International Socialists) 12, 16, 17, 111, 163, 263, 297, 298, 301, 345, 347-57, 359
student unions and activists 14, 18, 23, 65, 67, 68, 73, 149, 150, 164, 186, 201, 258-9, 262-3, 447
Third World Bookshop 40, 118, 123, 253, 339, 452
trade unions 40, 254, 261, 268-9, 295, 417
women's liberation movement 14, 17, 23, 75, 77-8, 79-80, 143, 194-5, 196, 210, 263-4, 266, 347-8
Askin, Robin 144, 252
Australia-China Society 267, 429, 430
Australia-Cuba Friendship Society 385
Australian Federal Police 23, 203-4, 341, 395
Australia-Russia Friendship Society 320, 327

Bacon, Jim 14, 195, 250
  ASIO file on 254, 262; student/political activism 255, 258-9, 260, 266, 267-8; as union official 261, 268-9
  as a politician 250, 269-70
  as student activist 250, 254, 258-9
Bacon, Ted 228
Bacon, Wendy 14, 249-50
  ASIO file on 80, 251-2, 253, 254-5, 258, 261, 262-5, 268, 269, 270; as resource 261, 262
  civil liberties and student activism 249, 258, 261-2, 268; arrested 249, 259, 262; prison reform 249, 259, 261-2
  journalism, 250, 268
Bacon family 259-61, 267
  and ASIO 255-8, 261, 267, 270
Baker, George 335-6, 337
Baker, Suzanne 80
Bandler, Faith 96, 97
Bandler, Hans 119
Bannon, John 73
Barbalet, Jack 76
Barnett, Harvey 174
Bedford, Ian 253
Bialoguski, Michael 138
Bielski, Jerzy (George) 129, 137, 138-40
  and ASIO 139-40, *141*
Bielski, Joan (nee Ward) 129-30
  ASIO file on 14, 16, 132, 139-140, 141, 142-5; teaching at Soviet Embassy 133-6, 145-6
  activism on women's issues 130, 143
  and Resident Action Movement 144
  Women Engineers 18
Bijedic affair 207
Bjelke-Petersen, Joh 297
Black, Harry 388
Boas, Gloria 54, 55, 63, 67
Boland, Lynda *282*
Bonner, Neville 101
Breaking the Codes (Ball and Horner) 42
Brennan, Gerard 65
Britain
  intelligence agencies 19, 27-8, 33, 289, 353, 373, 409; MI5 441; MI6 357-8
  Wolfenden Committee report 241
Brown, Bill 226, 228

INDEX 459

Buckley, Ken 167, 168, 327
  and Committee for the
    Rights of Servicemen
    168
Burchett, Wilfred 217, 388,
  389
Burgmann, Meredith
  activism of 437, 438, 441,
    448-9, 455
  ASIO file on 13, 15-16,
    19, 118, 126, 350,
    351, 359; activism
    439-47, 448, 449,
    450, 452-5; as aid
    to memory 353;
    travelling 441
  books, 438
  interest in ASIO 12, 333
  as Labor member 447;
    MLC 438, 454-5
  police Special Branch file
    on 440, 447; as Labor
    MLC 454
Burgmann, Verity 12, 16,
  343-4, 348, 450
  ASIO file on 345-51,
    352-60; as aid to
    memory 353
  books 344
  as Trotskyist 345, 351-2,
    356-7, 359, 360
Burgmann family 352
Burns, Creighton, 81
Burroughs, William 156

Cahill, Rowan 17, 159-60,
  168, 169-70
  anti-Vietnam war and
    -conscription activism
    162, 167-8
  ASIO file on 162; errors
    166; student and
    political activism 164-
    5, 166-7, 168-70
  books 160
Cairns, Cice 188
Cairns, Jim 19, 190, 192, 267
Callinan, Ian 61
Calwell, Arthur 12
Capp, Fiona
  Writers Defiled 165-6
Carr Government 14, 246,
  440
cases

Communist Party Case
  61, 67
Thomas v. Mowbray 61
Chandler, Bert 218
Chifley, Ben 132, 275
Chifley Government 138
  and ASIO, 276
Childs, Bruce 154
China 267, 430
Chiplin, Rex 324
civil liberties groups/supporters
  249, 268, 321-3, 416
  Council for Civil Liberties
    168, 241, 394
  Humanist Society 142, 176
  prison reform movement
    249, 259, 261-2, 263
  see also ASIO
Coe, Paul 104, 231
Cold War 22, 94, 132, 173,
  243, 257, 263, 267, 274,
  289, 430
Coleman, Peter 153
Student Power (booklet)
  164
Combe, David 88, 89
Combe-Ivanov affair 35, 88,
  89, 207
Communist Party of Australia
  (CPA) 51, 53, 66-7, 79,
  131, 219-20, 237, 254,
  271, 316
  change in direction 275,
    285
  dissatisfaction with 174,
    184, 253, 340, 429,
    434, 435; dissolved
    340, 364; split in 385
  during WWII 54
  Eureka Youth League (EYL)
    184, 187, 192, 239,
    305, 307, 315, 421,
    421
  and Menzies Government,
    26, 57-8, 161
  and Soviet Union 60, 174,
    228, 229, 275, 286,
    339-40, 423
  students 366, 367
  see also ASIO
Cook, Kevin 14, 18, 291-2
  ASIO file on 293, 295,
    296-301
  and land rights campaigns

295, 296
Cooper, Alan 305, 306, 313
Cooper, Colin 303-4
  ASIO file on 13, 16-17,
    309-10, 315-16; and
    the CPA, 305, 306-7,
    308, 313, 315; as union
    official 311-12
  with the PMG 305-8; as
    unionist and official
    308, 309, 310, 311-12
  as member of ALP 309
Cooper family 305, 313
  and ASIO 305, 307
Counihan, Noel 222
Cox, Eva 80
Coxsedge, Joan 267
Cundall, Peter 19, 425-6,
  427, 429
  ASIO file on 427, 429,
    430-2, 433-5; as
    member of CPA
    428-9, 434
  environmental issues 426
  political and social views
    429, 430
Curthoys, Ann 12, 161

Dalziel, Alan 42
Davies, Dave 189
Davis, Angela 100, 262
Dedman, Jack 12
Dessaix, Robert 411
Dexter, Barrie 101, 102-3
Diment, Mark 244
Duguid, Charles 99
Duncan, Peter 73
Dunstan, Don, 246
Dunstan, Graeme 82, 263
Durack, Peter 65

East Timor (Timor Leste) 182,
  286-7, 368-9, 370, 392
environment and conservation
  426, 428
Evatt, Clive R 14, 317-18, 326
  ASIO file on 324;
    defending civil liberties
    321-3; international
    issues 319, 324-7,
    329; as resource 328
  as Labor Cabinet minister
    320, 322
  supporting civil liberties

320-1, 328
Evatt, Elizabeth 14, 318, *326*
Evatt, HV 19, 42, 58, 228
Evatt family *326*, 328

Fall, Bernard
   Viet-Nam Witness 341
films/documentaries 43
   *The Chant of Jimmie
   Blacksmith* 235
   I Spry 42
   Legal Resident 43
   Mad Dog Morgan 235
   In the Year of the Pig (de
   Antonio) 123
Fisher, Elizabeth 78
Fitzpatrick, Brian 178
Flick, Barbara *296*
Foley, Gary 91–92, 446
   ASIO file on 14, 95–6,
   100, 104, 105, 107,
   110–11; information
   in 108
Foucault, Michel 156
France 156
Fraser, Malcolm 185, 366
Fraser Government 286
   and ASIO 370
Freney, Denis 384, 385,
   452, 452
Funder, Anna 451
   Stasiland 451

gay liberation/rights movement
   147, 151, *152*, 153, 156,
   241–2, 243, *244*, 245–6,
   265, 368
   and homophobia 153, 242,
   246
Germany (GDR)
   Stasi and files 175, 328,
   451; informers 175
Gietzelt, Arthur 154, 324,
   420
Gillard, Julia 156
Golding, Helen 366
Goldstein, Ralph 443
Gould, Bob 79, 151, 339
Grassie, Graeme 361
Great Depression 51, 52

Hain, Peter 357–8
Hall, Stuart 420
Hardy, Alan 14, 16, 223, 229,
   235, *238*, 239
   anger at FH's ASIO file
   232
   ASIO file on 237–8; as
   supposed member of
   CPA 239; as son of
   FH 237; as member
   of New Theatre; *238*,
   239
Hardy, Frank 213–14, 233
   ASIO file on 13–14, 215,
   219, 221, 226, *230*,
   237; and the CPA,
   216, 219–20, 222,
   223, 224–5, 226,
   227–9, 232; and the
   Gurindji 224, 225,
   226, 231; information
   in 16, 216, 218, 233;
   and *Power Without
   Glory* (criminal
   defamation trial) 16,
   215, 216–17, 218
   books 213, 220, 222, 232;
   But the Dead Are Many
   340; *Power Without
   Glory* 16, 214, 233;
   The Unlucky Australians
   224, 225
   and Campion Society 223
   financial difficulties 218,
   219, 220, 221, 222,
   223, 224, 225, 233
   and Gurindji people 214,
   215, 224–5, 233
   as member of CPA 216,
   217–18, 231, 253;
   relations with party
   219–20, 221–2, 223,
   224–5, 227
   and Soviet Union 218, 221,
   222, 227, 231, 232,
   233
   travel 217–18, 232–3, 237
Hardy, Rosslyn 216, 217–18,
   220, 227, 237
Hardy, Shirley 232, 237
Harris, Stewart 451
Hartley, Bill 150
Hasluck, Paul 191
Hawke Government 88, 156
   and ASIO 38, 89
Hazard, Noel 104
Heym, Stefan 175

Hill, Ted 160, 380
Hirst, Martin *348*, 354, 360
Hocquenghem, Guy 156
Holding, Clyde *190*
Holt, Harold 219
Hoover, J Edgar 153
Hope, Justice Robert
   royal commissions 18; first
   33–5, 36, 245; second
   35–8, 89, 207, 275
Howard, John 172
Hyde, Michael 259

immigration to Australia
   post-war 131–2, 138, 139
intelligence services in
   Australia 14, 23, 82, 330
   and accountability/oversight
   67, 194, 197–8
   before ASIO 22–3
   ASIS 339
   Attorney-General's
   Department 135
   and intelligence/information
   sharing 20, 27–8, 33,
   37, 76, 77, 84–5, 162,
   164, 189, 196, 217,
   218, 247, 255, 268,
   297, 310–11, 358, 359,
   377, 389, 400, 411,
   434, 441
   Joint Intelligence Agency
   82
   need for such bodies 67
   Office of National
   Assessments (ONA)
   37, 67
   royal commissions into 18,
   20; first, 33–5, 36,
   245; second 35–8,
   89, 207, 275
   and surveillance role
   108–9, 157, 167, 341;
   and communications
   technology, 267
   see also ASIO; legislation;
   states
International Socialists
   (Trotskyist) 355
   see also ASIO

James, Francis 31
Jockel, Gordon 82
Johnson, Betty, 277

Johnson, Brian, 277-8
Johnson, Pauline, 277
Johnson, Steve 64
Jones, Barry 171
Joseph, Helen 430, 432

Kevin, Tony 413
Kirby, Corrine 191
Kirby, David 52, 54, 57, 64, 444
Kirby, Diana 52
Kirby, Donald jnr 54, 56, 57
Kirby, Donald snr 51, 53, 56, 59, 60
  and the Communist Party 54
Kirby, Michael 49-50, 52, 64, 65
  ASIO file on 13, 14, 62, 63-7, 444; at age twelve 16, 51, 56; errors, 64, 67
  on communism 56, 57
  and the Communist Party 51, 55, 59
  police Special Branch file on 68
  serves on High Court 61-2
Kirby, Norma (Gray) 51, 52
  and the Communist Party 52-3
  marriage to Jack Simpson 54, 55, 56, 59
Kirby, Victor 51, 53
Koshlyakov, LS 88

Lane, Terry 192
Langer, Albert 151, *254*, 260
Latham, Sir John 67
Layton, Robyn 73
legislation
  Archives Act 1983 37-8, 39, 108, 287, 316
  ASIO Act 1978 370
  Communist Party Dissolution Act 1950 57-8, 61, 62, 319-20, 321, 328; and ASIO 320
  Crimes Act (ACT, NSW) 241, 360
  Freedom of Information Act 203
  Land Rights Act 1983 296
  Police Offences Act (NSW)

445
  Sunday Observance Act (NSW) 322
  Telephonic Communications (Interception) Act 30, 313
Letters, Frances 331-2
  activism of 333-4
  and ASIO 336, 342;
  approached to work 337-9, 340
  books 331; *The Surprising Asians* 331, 339
  and the CPA 340
Leyden, Elsie 222
Lockwood, Penny 14, 16, 407-8
  as activist 410, 415-16, 421, 422
  and ASIO 409, 421, 422; file on 410, 411-17, 419-20, 423
Lockwood, Rupert 134, 135, 408
  ASIO files on 409-10, 419, 423
  as communist and journalist 407, 409, 411-12, 418
Lockwood family 412, 415, 418, 419, 421, 422
Longbottom, Frederick 244-5, 377, 389, 448-51

McCarthy, Eugene 243
McFarlane, John 341
McGahan, Andrew
  Last Drinks 157
McGuinness, Bruce 101, 107
McGuinness, Paddy 266, 446
Macintyre, Stuart 56
  The Reds 53, 56
McKell Government 317
McKnight, David 12, 319
  books on ASIO 13;
  Australian Spies and Their Secrets 42, 163, 289
McLean, Eric 185, 186
McLean, Jean 181-2
  ASIO file on 14, 16, 177, 186-7, 197; and CPA 183-4, 185, 187, 191; Vietnam war 184, *188*, 189, *190*, 191-3, 194

  as ALP member and MP 185
  travel to North Vietnam and elsewhere 182, 184
McLean, Neil 186-7
McMahon Government 101, 107
McQueen, Humphrey 197
  mafia in Australia 385
  and Moffitt Royal Commission 385
Manne, Robert 172
Marshall, Alan 226
May, Ross 'the Skull' 366-7, 452
media
  radio: ABC 335-6; *AM* 227
  television: ABC: *Gardening Australia* 427, 435; *Monday Conference* 153, 242; *News* 378, 382; *This Day Tonight* 226, *244*; Channel Nine: 268; *A Current Affair* 262
  see also newspapers and magazines
Melrose, Robin 278-9, 280
Menzies, Robert 58, 137, 329
Menzies Government 162, 329, 389
  attempt to ban CPA 26, 57-8, 62, 173, 419
Middleton, Hannah 294
Miles, JB 54
Millis, Roger 124, 222
Millis, Susë 222-3
Milner, Andrew 346, 353, 355-6, 358, 359
Mitta, Alexander 126
Moore, Andrew 451
Moorhouse, Frank 253
'Movement', the
  information sharing with ASIO 30
Movement against Uranium Mining (MAUM) 353-4
Mundey, Jack 144, 354
Murphy, Lionel 155, 174, 207, 287, 378
Murphy, Peter 14, 17, 18, 363-4

462   DIRTY SECRETS

as gay rights activist 363, 368
ASIO file on: as member of CPA 367–8, 369, 371, 372; omissions 368–9, 372
as (student) activist/CPA member 363, 364, 365, 367, 368

Nagle, Justice John 402–3
National Archives of Australia (NAA) 175
ASIO file holdings 22, 29, 38–43, 62, 108, 164, 175, 251, 419
National Civic Council 162
Nazi Party in Australia 40, 367, 384, 452
Nazi war criminals and ASIO 287–9
New Left 23, 159, 163, 169, 252, 253, 269
New South Wales
green bans in 144, 291, 445
illegal telephone intercepts 313
police corruption 268; Royal Commission 394
New South Wales Police Special Branch 16, 68, 99, 167, 244–5, 255, 273, 310, 389, 396–9, 400–1, 448
closed down 14, 394, 440, 454
files 17, 83, 246, 377, 395, 402, 440, 453, 454, 396, *397*, 440, 454
and Hilton Hotel bombing 268, 370, 396–400, 402, 422
informants/agents 268, 396, 399–401
newspapers and magazines
Age 98
Apple Juice (newsletter) 427, 428, 433
Arena 79
Australian 174, 178, 224
Australian Financial Review 83, 143, 185

Australian Left Review 169, 447
Battler 348, 360
Canberra Times 207
Communist Review 218
Courier-Mail 101
Daily Mirror (Sydney) 252
Daily Telegraph (Sydney) 321
Guardian (Melbourne communist paper) 217, 256, 257
Honi Soit 159, 166
Living Daylights 81
National Times 83, 250
Nation Review 81, 149
New Matilda 250
News Weekly 144, 177
Oz 162
Refractory Girl 79
Soviet Union 55
Sunday Australian 379
Sunday Review 378
Sunday Times 227, 232
Sydney Morning Herald 227, 309, 319, 334, 450
Tharunka 249, 252, 259
Thor 249
Tribune 30, 104, 196, 379
New Theatre 239
and ASIO files 124, 125, 217, 219, 234, 238, 323, 325
Nicholls, Pastor Doug 98, 99

O'Dea, Ernie 320
Onus, Bill 96
O'Sullivan, Fergan 136
Owens, Joe 105, 144, 295, 354

Palmada, Joe 83
Pavlov, Demetri 133, 146
Peckham, Ray 96, 97, 226
Pemberton, Gregory 319
Perkins, Charles 98
Petersen, George 265
Petrov, Vladimir 16, 133, 137–8, 145–6
Petrov Affair 29, 138, 140, 422
Royal Commission on Espionage (Petrov Inquiry) 41, 58–9,
136, 138, 140, 207–8, 257, 407, 408, 418
Pile, Marcel 64
Prichard, Katharine Susannah 23, 82
Pringle, Bob 105, 354

Queensland
demonstrations 297–8, 301
police force 157, 175, 297
racism 333, 365–6
Randerson, Helen 336, 440
Reeve, David 279, 280–1
Reeves, Tony 14
ASIO file on 377–8, *379*, 380–9; omissions 378, 383, 389
books 376; *Mr Big* 376
as journalist 375, 378, 382, 385
Reid, Elizabeth 80
Ridley, John 150
Rivett, Sir David 12
Robertson, Belinda 282–3, 284
and family 283–5
Robertson, Mavis 254, 262, 264, 372, 385
Roxon, Nicola 19
Russia. *See* Soviet Union

Salmon, Malcolm 189, 378–9, 384
Santamaria, BA 30, 144, 162, 177, 223
Seary, Richard 268, 399–401, 405
Sharkey, Lance 54, 59
Shaw, Dave *348*, 353, 355, 361
Simpson, Jack (Maurice Flynn) 52, 56, 60
ASIO file on 56
and the Communist Party 52, 53–4, 55, 57, 58–9, 60
war service 53, 61
Skipper, Matcham 192
Skripov, Ivan 29, 43
Snedden, Billy 201, 366
Socialist Forum 156
South Africa

INDEX 463

apartheid 84
Bureau of State Security
 (BOSS) 85, 358,
 432-3
South Australia
 police Special Branch 75,
 76, 246
Soviet Union 127, 275, 411
 and anti-Vietnam war
 movement 161
 Embassy in Canberra 16,
 29, 43, 88, 106, 117,
 122, 133, 134, 137, 227
 espionage 275, 276, 285-6
 invasion of Czechoslovakia
 126, 127, 229, 232,
 339
 and KGB (officers) 28,
 42, 43, 86, 88, 409,
 411, 423
Spann, Dick 79
Spock, Benjamin 193
Spry, Sir Charles 19-20, 42,
 94-5, 96, 97, 211, 281,
 307, 389, 414, 441
Staples, Jim 64
Stout, Prof. 119
Stratton, David
 ASIO file on 14, 16, 118,
 119, *120*; activities of
 Sydney Film Festival
 115-16, 121, 122-3,
 125-6
 at SBS 118
 travel in Eastern Europe
 (and elsewhere) 116,
 122-3, 127-8
Summers, Anne 69-70
 ASIO file on 17, 20, 74,
 75-8; anti-Vietnam
 war activities, 71-2, *73*,
 74-5, 77, 87; ASIO's
 lack of knowledge
 86; as a journalist
 83; random interest
 80-1, 83; and women's
 liberation movement
 77-8, 80, 86
 appointment as head of
 Office of the Status of
 Women 86-8
Summers, John 71, 82-3
Sweeney, Jack 64

Sydney Film Festival
 and ASIO files 115-16,
 117, 119

Taft, Bernie 183, 191, 194
Taylor, Frank 244
Teichmann, Max 177, 194
Theodorakis, Mikos 193-4
Throssell, Ric 81
Thwaites, Michael 418-19
Thwaites, Richard 418, 419
Tickner, Robert 449-50
Tierney, Bev 353
Tomasetti, Glen 177, 192
Torsh, Dany 80
Townshend, Pam 346, *348*
trade unions/union officials
 57, 58
 as ASIO targets 40, 136
 Builders Labourers'
 Federation 103, 105,
 144, 250, 354-5
 information sharing with
 ASIO 32
 Australian Workers Union
 138
Trotsky, Leon 169

United States
 intelligence agencies 33,
 373; CIA 268, 289;
 FBI 153, 234, 289
 McCarthyism in 243, 257
Uren, Tom 15, *190*, 329, 420,
 449

van Moorst, Harry 192
van Vloten, Johan 50
Vaux, Janet 347
Victoria
 police Special Branch 189,
 193, 195-6, 197, 395
 Royal Commission into
 the Communist Party
 215, 216
Von Gries, Manfred 396

Walker, Denis 104, 107, 110,
 230
Walker, Kath (later Oodgeroo
 Noonuccal) 98
war
 Korean War 427

Vietnam War 334-5, 337;
 aftermath 386
World War I 53, 198
World War II 54, 129, 138,
 427
Ward, Barry 376, 385
Ward, Russel 336
Waten, Judah 222, 226, 228
Waterford, Jack 14, 199-200
 ASIO file on 208-10;
 anti-Vietnam activism
 205; anti-apartheid
 activities 207;
 information in 208,
 212
 as journalist 207-8, 212
 as student activist 201-3
 police Special Branch on
 203, 204, 206-7
Watson, Kerry 447-8
Watson, Lex 14, 153, 241-2
 ASIO file on, 246-7
 gay rights activism 241-3,
 244, 245
Wheatley, Nadia 12, 444
Wheelwright, Ted 81
Weinberg, Jack 269
Whelan, Paul 394
Whitlam, Gough 33, 80, 154,
 178, 194, 214
 and reform of ALP 150
Whitlam Government 266,
 267, 286
 and ASIO 85, 174, 207,
 287; raids 207
 Dismissal 368
WikiLeaks 12
Wilde, Oscar 333
Wills, Sue, 241
Wolfe, Tom
 Radical Chic ... 151
women's liberation movement
 79, 144-5, 360
Women's Electoral Lobby
 (WEL) 143
 see also ASIO
Woodcock, Lucy 14
Wran Government 293

Yates, Alan 125
Yeend, Sir Geoffrey 86
Yuill, Bruce 136, 137, 146

www.ingramcontent.com/pod-product-compliance
Ingram Content Group UK Ltd.
Pitfield, Milton Keynes, MK11 3LW, UK
UKHW041302180426
11947UKWH00009B/620